Johansen

Collective Security
in a Changing World

Emerging Global Issues
Thomas G. Weiss, Series Editor

Published in association with the
Thomas J. Watson Jr. Institute for International Studies,
Brown University

Collective Security in a Changing World

A World Peace Foundation Study

edited by
Thomas G. Weiss

Lynne Rienner Publishers ■ Boulder & London

Figures 4.1, 4.2, 4.3, 4.4, 4.5, and 4.6 are reprinted from
International Organization, Vol. 37:2, Ernst B. Haas,
"Regime Decay: Conflict Management and International
Organization 1945–1981." Reprinted by permission of MIT Press,
Cambridge, Massachusetts, and the World Peace Foundation © 1983 by the
World Peace Foundation and the Massachusetts Institute of Technology.

Published in the United States of America in 1993 by
Lynne Rienner Publishers, Inc.
1800 30th Street, Boulder, Colorado 80301

and in the United Kingdom by
Lynne Rienner Publishers, Inc.
3 Henrietta Street, Covent Garden, London WC2E 8LU

Library of Congress Cataloging-in-Publication Data
Collective security in a changing world / edited by Thomas G. Weiss.
    p. cm.—(A World Peace Foundation study) (Emerging global
issues)
  Includes bibliographical references and index.
  ISBN 1-55587-338-3 (cloth) (alk. paper)
  1. Security, International. 2. World politics—1989- I. Weiss,
Thomas George. II. Series. III. Series: Emerging global issues.
JX1952.C576 1993
327.1'7—dc20   92-31965
                                                        CIP

British Cataloguing in Publication Data
A Cataloguing in Publication record for this book
is available from the British Library.

Printed and bound in the United States of America

The paper used in this publication meets the requirements
of the American National Standard for Permanence of
Paper for Printed Library Materials Z39.48-1984.

Contents

Part 1 The Case for Collective Security

Part 2 Collective Action to Deal with International Disputes

Part 3 Conclusions and Recommendations

Tables and Figures

Tables

Figures

Preface

RICHARD J. BLOOMFIELD & THOMAS G. WEISS

The World Peace Foundation and the Thomas J. Watson Jr. Institute for International Studies, Brown University, commissioned this study with the goal of assessing the effect of the dawning of the post–Cold War era on the prospects for improving collective action to maintain international peace and security.

This research effort is a continuation of an earlier collaboration between the two institutions that resulted in *Third World Security in the Post–Cold War Era,* edited by Thomas G. Weiss and Meryl A. Kessler (Boulder: Lynne Rienner, 1991). Shortly after that project was completed, the prospects for collective security appeared to improve for two reasons, both of which had been foreshadowed in the earlier research effort. First, it became clear that the end of the superpower confrontation of the past 45 years had, indeed, made possible a strengthened United Nations. This had been the fundamental question addressed in the earlier study, and the pursuit of the Gulf War through a combination of coalition forces and UN decisionmaking confirmed that our tentatively affirmative conclusions had been well founded.

Second, the actual implosion of the Soviet Union at the end of 1991 made perfectly obvious what had been becoming gradually more evident earlier, namely, that the United States was the only remaining "superpower," if that term still has any significance. As in 1918–1919 and 1945–1946, today's balance of power has been altered dramatically as a result of the end of a war, this time the Cold War. As in the previous periods, there is renewed hope for global collective security; unlike the previous periods, however, the present flux has not resulted from an armed conflagration among major powers. As a result, the global situation is more malleable than in the previous two postwar transitions. The term "collective security" has now come back into vogue in rhetorical terms, which distinguishes it from other outmoded labels that had until recently been part of the lexicon of international relations but that are no longer so: "North," "South," "East," "West," "superpower," and "Third World."

One of the main reasons that this research project was mounted was the conviction that the balance of power had been so transformed that the United States would be well advised to rethink totally the bases for its national security policies. More particularly, the goal of the study was to examine the range of responses by the United States to the opportunities to strengthen international collective security and, more especially, the feasibility of improving the UN's operational capabilities in this area. There is no reason to think that there will be any greater stability in the Middle East, Southern Asia, Africa, or the Americas than in the past. While US interests may not be as intensely engaged in as many regions as they appeared to be in the days of the Cold War, important and at times vital US interests are still at risk in a number of arenas. The specter of a disintegrating Yugoslavia has been a preoccupation in policy circles for several months and illustrates the logic behind and the timing of this study. Not only from a strategic point of view, such as to maintain stability in the Balkans and Europe, but also from a more traditional humanitarian vantage point, serious consideration of collective security options has become imperative for the United States and the international community. However, other than President Bush's periodic references to the prospect of a "new world order," there has been virtually no public discussion of the practical opportunities for and obstacles to collective security. This issue was, for example, totally absent from the primary and electoral campaigns of 1992.

Moreover, in the four and a half decades since the drafting of the UN Charter, the boundaries of state sovereignty have shrunk; any number of issues that formerly were considered purely domestic have become recognized as being the legitimate concern of other states and individuals. While a growing body of international conventions and norms to regulate the behavior of states has emerged, until recently the ability of the international community to respond when such norms are violated has been almost nonexistent.

While rethinking security is necessary, this project was not a Pollyannish inquiry into how the UN must be strengthened at all costs. As the following chapters will demonstrate, appropriate doses of cold water—both theoretical and operational—are necessary when approaching the subject of collective security. This was the case for the authors as well as a distinguished group of scholars and practitioners, who commented on drafts of the chapters during a conference at Brown University in May 1992.

The book is constructed in three parts. Part 1 considers "The Case for Collective Security." In the first chapter, Leon Gordenker and Tom Weiss provide a baseline for the rest of the book when we take a close look at "The Collective Security Idea and Changing World Politics." The examination of the development of this concept in the twentieth century precedes

Oscar Schachter's overview of international legal developments in "Sovereignty and Threats to Peace." A skeptical view of big power motivations and the feasibility of a new regime, from a distinctly Third World perspective, follows in Chapter 3, where Mohammed Ayoob argues "Squaring the Circle: Collective Security in a System of States." Part 1 closes with Ernst B. Haas's quantitative and prescriptive examination, "Collective Conflict Management: Evidence for a New World Order?"

This conceptual prelude sets the stage for some very concrete operational discussions in Part 2, "Collective Action to Deal with International Disputes." Chapters 5 and 6 respectively deal with the political and military shortcomings of the UN. James S. Sutterlin begins with "United Nations Decisionmaking: Future Initiatives for the Security Council and the Secretary-General." This analysis of a variety of political and management initiatives is followed by John Mackinlay's examination of the military lacunae of the UN, and of the international community more generally, in "The Requirement for a Multinational Enforcement Capability." Part 2 closes with Tom J. Farer's examination of "The Role of Regional Collective Security Arrangements."

Part 3 consists of "Conclusions and Recommendations." In Chapter 8, "Collective Security and US Interests," Lincoln P. Bloomfield examines prospective US approaches to collective security in the light of the present historical epoch. Chapter 9, entitled "Whither Collective Security: An Unsettled Idea in a Changing World," provides Gordenker and Weiss with the opportunity to review the most salient suggestions emanating from the preceding chapters as well as the discussion at the Brown conference.

The average shelf life of books in the field of international relations has been reduced drastically in the last half decade by the pace of world events. Nonetheless, this volume contains a host of valuable insights based on lengthy historical, legal, and political analyses; and they will be valid for quite some time. In fact, these chapters provide specific ideas and trenchant analyses to support many of the ideas in the report issued in mid-June 1992 by UN Secretary-General Boutros Boutros-Ghali. While this report falls short of calling for a collective security system, it nonetheless contains a series of related points, such as peace enforcement, preventive positioning of troops, and protection of humanitarian personnel in war zones. The book has been put together to reflect long-standing concerns with international peace and security within the context of contemporary developments. While events will continue to provide additional illustrations, the careful conceptual and practical arguments put forward and the conclusions drawn will remain pertinent.

R. J. B.
T. G. W.

Abbreviations

ASEAN	Association of Southeast Asian Nations
C^3I	Command, Control, Communications, and Intelligence
CBMs	Confidence-Building Measures
CIA	Central Intelligence Agency
CIS	Commonwealth of Independent States
CMEA	Council for Mutual Economic Assistance
CNN	Cable News Network
CSCE	Conference on Security and Cooperation in Europe
EC	European Community
ECOMOG	Economic Community of West African States Monitoring Group
ECOSOC	Economic and Social Council
ECOWAS	Economic Community of West African States
EFTA	European Free Trade Association
G7	Group of Seven
GATT	General Agreement on Tariffs and Trade
GCC	Gulf Cooperation Council
IAEA	International Atomic Energy Agency
IBRD	International Bank for Reconstruction and Development (The World Bank)
ICJ	International Court of Justice
ICRC	International Committee of the Red Cross
IGO	Intergovernmental Organization
ILO	International Labour Organisation
IMF	International Monetary Fund
MINURSO	United Nations Mission for the Referendum in the Western Sahara
MSC	Military Staff Committee
NAM	Non-Aligned Movement
NATO	North Atlantic Treaty Organization

NGO	Nongovernmental Organization
NIC	Newly Industrializing Countries
OAS	Organization of American States
OAU	Organization for African Unity
ONUC	United Nations Operation in the Congo
ONUCA	United Nations Observer Group in Central America
ONUSAL	United Nations Observer Mission El Salvador
ONUVEH	United Nations Observer Group Nicaragua
OONUVEN	United Nations Observer Group to Verify the Electoral Process in Nicaragua
ORCI	Office for Research and Collection of Information
PLO	Palestine Liberation Organization
SWAPO	South West Africa People's Organization
UNAVEM	United Nations Angola Verification Mission
UNDP	United Nations Development Programme
UNFICYP	United Nations Peacekeeping Force in Cypress
UNGOMAP	United Nations Good Offices Mission in Afghanistan and Pakistan
UNIFIL	United Nations Interim Force in Lebanon
UNIIMOG	United Nations Iran-Iraq Military Observer Group
UNIKOM	United Nations Iraq-Kuwait Observer Mission
UNITA	National Union for the Total Independence of Angola
UNPROFOR	United Nations Protection Force
UNTAC	United Nations Transitional Authority for Cambodia
UNTAG	United Nations Transition Assistance Group in Namibia
UNTSO	United Nations Truce Supervision Organization
WEU	Western European Union

■ Part 1 ■
The Case for
Collective Security

■ 1 ■

The Collective Security Idea and Changing World Politics

LEON GORDENKER & THOMAS G. WEISS

The extraordinary changes of the past several years in international politics suggest the possibility that the collective coercion to keep the peace foreseen in the United Nations Charter could at last become practical.[1] Yet, despite the magnitude of changes and rhetorical flourishes about a "new world order" following the Gulf War, little public or policy discussion of the practical opportunities for and obstacles to collective security has thus far evolved. The report issued by UN Secretary-General Boutros Boutros-Ghali in mid-June 1992 provides, as requested by the first-ever Security Council Summit, a number of suggestions pointing toward vastly strengthened UN machinery that merit careful scrutiny. [2]

The central concept of collective security itself emerged from international political systems so different from the present one that questions may be posed about the contemporary relevance of the idea and the tenability of its assumptions. This introduction, therefore, sets out the issues inherent in the concept of collective security and its application to contemporary world politics. Succeeding chapters of this book develop specific aspects of the inquiry. In this chapter, the concept itself is examined, as are its legal significance and institutional and operational issues; a final section frames questions about possible US responses to opportunities to strengthen collective security.

The Concept of Collective Security

While the roots of the concept of collective security reach back several centuries through a long series of proposals for maintaining international peace,[3] the central idea has remained the same: the governments of all states would join together to prevent any of their number from using coercion to gain advantage, especially conquering another. Thus, no government could with impunity undertake forceful policies that would fundamentally disturb peace and security. Any attempt to execute such policies

3

would, by definition, be treated by all governments as if it were an attack on each of them.

Perhaps because of the apparent simplicity of the central concept of collective security, the term has suffered a vast amount of misuse and imprecise reference. Somehow it summons up a beneficent and ethical set of supportive relationships among like-minded members of a community in a wicked world. Political debaters use the term to attribute both moral and material credence to alliances or to set out the reason for a plea to support a particular policy in a security crisis. It has been employed to characterize the UN peace-maintenance system as well as that of the League of Nations before it. At the same time, it was said to describe NATO and the Warsaw Pact, both alliances that defined an enemy. It seems obvious, therefore, that not every joint effort of governments to maintain peace, to avoid conflict, or to build an alliance against a presumptive enemy could be called collective security.

Inis Claude, for one, first warned nearly 30 years ago against the misappropriation of this term to describe almost any international arrangement whose aim is peace.[4] Only quite specific joint efforts by governments to maintain peace, prevent conflicts, and form alliances against an outlaw state should be described as collective security. It is a term of the art of international political analysis, not a catchall heading for various and sundry collective ventures of governments. Furthermore, the dearth of scholarly attention to the subject for the last three decades[5] requires serious effort to fill gaps in understanding.

The concept implicitly raises a series of important issues, including its actual definition. What is set out above as the nucleus of collective security hardly exhausts the potential for a sharper definition that specifies participants, boundaries, decisional and administrative procedures, and legal obligations. Nor does it plumb the possibilities of adaptation of the general concept for specific purposes or differing patterns of participation. Along with the effort to clarify the concept, renewed consideration of its historical development would enrich appreciation of its content and related expectations.

The unadorned concept of collective security, extracted from the ethical baggage that sometimes overwhelms it, involves certain assumptions that conceivably no longer can be squared with international politics. It assumes a world in which every government is prepared to use force to gain its will; in that world, restraint evolves from anticipation of the results of superior power. It is a world regulated not by a hegemonic power but rather by a collection of free actors that avoid domination from outside. It is a decentralized world in which central decisional organs have little or no place. If there are rules, therefore, they develop from explicit or implicit individual consent and usage, not from deliberate legislation. In fact, however, in today's world the rules of a collective security system most likely would be based on a treaty among the parties to it and would rely on the assumption that such consent would guide future behavior, although a collective security system does not aim at the general enforcement of law but rather at the maintenance of international peace.[6]

Such theoretical assumptions perhaps never modeled the actual world and, it is arguable, have scant relevance to the contemporary context. While military conflicts still abound, so does a much higher degree of centralized decisionmaking and international cooperation than ever before.[7] Statespersons everywhere acknowledge that the future of their realms depends not only on defense of territory but also on successful cooperation to protect the global environment and to cope with other general issues, such as economic development and the control of AIDS. The status quo can be defined only vaguely as new states blossom on the corpses of old empires. The development of nuclear weapons fundamentally changed expectations about the use of military force. If the fundamental theoretical bases of collective security have been undermined by actuality, then the concept either is merely a historical reminder or requires revised understanding as a guide to policy.

Beyond the primeval issue of theoretical bases and definition, the geographic extent of a collective security system also poses fundamental questions. If universality is intended, then every state, no matter what its policies and capacities, would be included. Would it then be necessary to pay strict attention to every existing state? or only those with considerable global significance (e.g., the Maldives as well as China)? Could a regional collective security system conform to the logic of the idea? If so, how is a region defined? Would the political character of the state (e.g., a repressive dictatorship or a military command system) fit into a collective security system?

Collective security assumes that aggression by any state will be met by "all against one," that is, by the combined power of the rest of the world to cut short a disturbance to the peace. If all governments are expected to react against a breach of international peace, they must be able to take note when a critical threshold has been surmounted. One possible benchmark is that of Article 2 of the UN Charter, which forbids the use of force in international relations. Along the lines of the League of Nations Covenant (Articles 12–13, 15–16), another might be the failure of a party to a dispute to conform to procedural rules of dealing with conflict. Yet another approach would call for centralization of perception of a reason to act, so that each government could be placed under a general obligation to oppose a disturbance; this is the approach of Chapter VII of the UN Charter. In addition, the threshold could consist of an act of self-defense by a government in the face of an actual or threatened military attack; this would be consistent with Article 51 of the UN Charter.

All but one of these tests for the invocation of a collective response to a breach of the peace involves two automatic phases of governmental decision. In order to act collectively, each government by itself would have to perceive the breakdown of peace as having an identical, or at least noncontradictory, form. Each individual government would also have to link its coercive efforts against the disturber with those of other governments. This, too, implies a necessity to act. A purpose of central decisionmaking would certainly include an attempt to mobilize the strength of component governments. The subsequent choices before governments would have to deal with how to react.

Collective security does not permit the advance designation of a putative enemy, as is the case with defensive alliances. In fact, collective security, directed against all aggressors, may better be contrasted with alliances, which have a particular foe.[8] The presumption in collective security is that any member of the system might at any time behave in such an aberrant manner that corrective measures would be necessary.

The assumption of preponderant force as the response to a violation has three important consequences. The first involves the premise that the collective security system really represents a deterrent to unacceptable coercive behavior. Collective security postulates that the use of violence or other threats to the peace would result in the mobilization of force so great that no reasonable policymaker would undertake such threats. Indeed the logic of collective security resembles that of nuclear deterrence, as the use of force in both situations should be prevented by fear of a forceful riposte.[9] Thus, a calculation with common assumptions on the part of all governments is implied, as is the expectation that a successful system would never actually need to resort to force.

The second consequence has to do with the strength of the participants. If the force available to a possible aggressor is to be overwhelmed by collective opposition, then no member could dominate the whole system or, perhaps, even exact very high costs for the repression of unacceptable actions. This raises the question as to whether a collective security system could exist in a world where governments had access to nuclear weapons and flexible delivery systems. A variation of this question arises in a world with one so-called superpower.[10]

The third consequence involves the geographic location of a dispute having no bearing on the collective response. Thus, any breach of the peace would impel a response throughout the world. While a response might be located primarily in a narrow geographic area, it need not be limited to that place and perhaps could not be.

A subsidiary conceptual issue relates to reducing the degree of automaticity in a collective security system by creating a process for centralized decisionmaking. Such a process clearly diminishes any presumed equality of the members and suggests the construction of a decisionmaking hierarchy, composed either of governments, transnational organizations, or individuals authorized to make decisions for states. A hierarchical arrangement of state relationships could conceivably be needed only when coercive measures are undertaken. The functions planned for the Council of the League of Nations have a close kinship to this latter approach.

The Margins of Collective Security

Like most explorations of collective security, this discussion so far has emphasized the use of armed force—the famed provision of "teeth" instead of mere persuasion. The emphasis may result partly from the apparent clarity of force and the appeal of its decisiveness when representing the pooled strength of all but the aggressor state. Yet other, milder forms of coercion could conceivably be more appropriate and less damaging to human life and the environment in the contemporary international political context. These coercive methods would include the familiar diplomatic, economic, financial, and communications sanctions mentioned in the League of Nations Covenant and in the UN Charter. They could precede the actual use of force or accompany it to make it more decisive and less destructive. Incentives to induce cessation of objectionable behavior also could be considered. At the same time, the concept of collective security could not be shorn of the possibility of military force without sapping its inner logic.

As it is usually treated, the concept of collective security rather blandly assumes that the goal of ending a threat to international peace is readily understood. That assumption brushes aside numerous difficulties. The first of these has to do with the policies of the aggressor government. If such policies strive to alter significantly the power rankings in international politics, they must be serious indeed. To change the policies the government involved must be either at least frightened by imminent defeat or actually damaged. Either probably would result in humiliation for the aggressor government and the reduction of domestic political support, both of which raise the possibility that the use of force in a collective security system would itself change the international strategic situation. It would reduce the political and military means that the offending government earlier possessed for redressing grievances or ameliorating what it thinks are intolerable relationships with the rest of the world. Indeed it would also usually sweep away that government as a reward for its failed policies.

As the rationale for drastic action under a collective security system is preservation of peace, presumably the causes of the disturbance would be subjected to an international political process aimed at adjusting difficulties. Such a process—for instance, negotiations or treatment by an international organization or court—would require cooperation by the aggressor government as well as by those just attacked. Whether a government can be deterred, threatened, or forced into good-faith negotiations remains a serious question. Whether its good faith would reliably be greeted with a similar attitude on the part of the injured also may give reason for skepticism, particularly given an emphasis on the perils of international politics.

If a collective security system engages in a considerable military action, heavy damages to the violator of the system as well as to those engaged in reversing aggression may result. A military response to aggression could in fact result in a war of long duration or of very damaging quality, although the hidden assumption of the system is that short work would be made of an aggressor. It could also be accompanied by large-scale violations of human rights, which constitutes another subject for international attention and, it may be hoped, correction. Furthermore, states located at a distance from combat may also be affected by the interruption of supplies of raw materials and familiar export dealing, not to speak of higher prices and other cascading economic costs.

To be entirely credible to its members, a collective security system would necessitate convincing provisions to deal with the ancillary effects of its ultimate utilization. The attempts to institutionalize the concept of collective security in the League of Nations and the United Nations include at least some effort to cope with these implications of the use of coercion. Article 16(3) of the Legal Covenant provides for mutual assistance in case of coercive measures. Article 50 of the UN Charter provides for consultation with the Security Council in case a member encounters special financial problems. Both documents, of course, include extensive provisions for pacific settlement of disputes that might lead to conflicts. Whether the results are satisfactory, either as a support for the system or in terms of outcome, remains open to question.

Legal Issues

In the four and a half decades since the ratification of the UN Charter, the boundaries of state sovereignty have become ever more porous, as repeated military, technical, economic, and environmental challenges demonstrate. Moreover, issues that yet recently were considered purely domestic, such as human and minority rights and even the character of a government, have been often included among the legitimate concerns of other governments.[11] This has led to a rapidly growing body of international conventions and associated practices aimed at regulating the behavior of governments in certain domestic matters,[12] a development that is not confined to the West.[13] The potential for an organized international response to violations of these norms and rules, however, remains undeveloped, and its use, fragmentary. Yet some of these issues may develop at the frontiers of collective security, either as the result of coercive action or as a cause for invoking corrective measures intended to maintain the peace. They therefore require further legal and political exploration.

In its more familiar form, the concept of collective security carries with it the necessity to create a set of legal provisions spelling out obligations for members and the limits on the system itself.[14] This follows from the assumption that states possess sovereign authority as well as from the likelihood that national bureaucracies would have to be deeply engaged in the execution of international policies to preserve peace. Without a legal structure, a collective security system would have to be based on the vague assumption that every government is committed to repressing disturbers. That would constitute hardly more than an idealized balance of power. A collective security system necessitates a high degree of specificity and certainty about the range of reactions to particular kinds of threats. As governments must be involved, this presumes the existence of a legal structure that they and their subjects will honor. It would therefore almost certainly have to include one or more elaborate conventions that set out the legal obligations and rights of its adherents.

The assumption that the existing international legal system is sturdy enough to bear the weight of a collective security system is, to say the least, problematic. Collective security involves radically reordering the traditional standard obligations of states. No longer would each government be authorized to make unlimited decisions about the use of force; rather, each would be obliged to limit the use of significant force only to the maintenance of international peace and security. The area of legal use of force would be reduced to those situations that would not threaten international peace generally—deciding what these might be would no doubt create much controversy.

In a collective security system without standing means for centralized decisionmaking, the legal obligation to perceive a breach of the peace would rest with each participating government. Consequently, legal tests for invoking the collective security system would be required. The League of Nations, which did have some centralized decisionmaking apparatus, nevertheless relied on what were largely obligations not to use force except in self-defense until a process of pacific settlement had been completed. That process was to begin with a complaint by a disputant or by another member of the League. In essence, members undertook a legal obligation to use the organization if its due process or they themselves could not settle a dispute. At least on paper, the League's Covenant embodied an institutional structure fitted to a working system of collective security.

The UN Charter imposes similar legal obligations with regard to pacific settlement of disputes. Moreover, it includes a legal obligation to avoid the use of force, except in self-defense, and to heed the decisions of the Security Council in case of a threat or breach of the peace. In addition, the Secretary-General has the right to call to the attention of the Security Council matters that either had led or could lead to a breach of the peace. Under this arrangement, the limiting and positive legal obligations reach much further than those of the League system and, in fact, further than those of any other international arrangement to maintain peace.

Aside from the tests for invocation of the collective security system, three other important legal issues arise. The first of these develops from the implicit premise that the inevitability of coercion, if a violation of the systemic norms occurs, will encourage pacific settlement of disputes between states. Such conciliatory proceedings would involve legal rights of the parties and perhaps would lead to judicial or arbitral settlement.

The second legal issue concerns the extent and depth of coercion to be applied. Presumably, if states are the basis of a collective security system, the inherent intention is to preserve the members. Under a collective security system, coercion would be used to persuade or force a breaker of the peace to change the policies that led or threatened violence. Would it be legally permissible then to destroy a government in order to preserve the international order? To what degree do members of a collective security system have the right to control the government of an aberrant member?

Finally, if permanent organizations were envisaged to manage a collective security system, they would need a constitutional basis. A host of legal issues arise here with regard to both the rights of members and the powers of the institution. The range of these issues is clearly suggested by the experience of the League of Nations and the UN.

Institutional and Operational Issues

Strictly speaking, the widespread acceptance of the idea of collective security would constitute an international institution. No permanent organization would be necessary if the requisite legal obligations were accepted by all members who acted accordingly on every occasion. Such a system presupposes that any joint efforts would occur spontaneously as a result of the coincidence of national policies.

As collective security was and remains an idea that has neither been completely tested nor entirely elaborated, contemporary governments would think a collective security system plausible only if it had an executive structure. How policies are to be formed, adapted to changing conditions, and executed, then, become central issues.

The experiences of the League of Nations and the UN in the use of coercion, as well as their constitutions, emphasize the central role of governments. They are expected to originate complaints concerning threats or breaches of the peace. Their representatives approve the common policies toward a state that interferes with peaceful relations or threatens to dominate the system. The secretariats of the two organizations have devoted their efforts mainly to the technical aspects of interstate meetings. In both organizations, the decisionmaking procedures either require or point toward consensus. The unanimity rule of the League and the veto power of the permanent members in the UN Security Council ensure not only that collective measures could hardly be conceived against a great power but also that such action would have the backing of the most powerful states.

Neither organization had, in fact, an executive capacity that would lend itself to carrying out decisions under a collective security arrangement. Were governments to agree that such a capacity, whether in being or in some form of reserve, should be constructed, the work of the executive head of the organization would be broadened beyond anything so far attempted. A military staff of considerable capacity would doubtless be needed to plan activities and to advise ongoing operations.

The UN secretariat has over the years accumulated considerable experience with protomilitary ventures, such as observation and peacekeeping.[15] However, in contrast to the "subcontracts" in the Korean War and the Gulf War, the actual role of the UN in what resembles enforcement actions has never surpassed the distant and rudimentary. No significant military advisory bureaucracy has emerged to assist the Secretary-General. Military advice has been obtained mostly in an ad hoc fashion by borrowing officers from national armies.

Two issues emerge from this experience. The first is whether it is indeed necessary and desirable to establish in the secretariat a permanent military advisory or operational capacity. A second issue has to do with how much independence from national governments such military capacities should have.

In order to overcome what was perceived as a central weakness in the League of Nations system, the UN Charter provided for a standing force to serve when the Security Council mandated military coercion to restore the peace. Antagonism between the United States and the Soviet Union prevented not only the constitution of such a force but also a precise definition of roles. Even if the Cold War had not blocked the creation of any standing UN force, it still is not clear what could have been approved by the Security Council.

The rhetoric of the unanimous declaration issued by the Security Council,[16] which met for the first time at the level of heads of state and government in January 1992, may augur well for change. Whatever the nature of the proposals made by Secretary-General Boutros-Ghali in June 1992, implementation is still problematic. Moreover, the UN's actual experience leaves unanswered questions as to whether the tools of an effective collective security system could be based on the provisions of the UN Charter and whether a modified system to meet the objective needs of the 1990s would, in fact, require the amendment or other adaptation of the provisions of the Charter.

The issues implied by an effort to create a coercive mechanism consistent with collective security are weighty enough to give pause to any observer. Every government contributing to international armed forces would have to hand over or throw open at least part of its existing command and control system for armed forces to a new central structure of some kind. The UN Charter provides for a Military Staff Committee (MSC) that would have the duty of consulting and negotiating about the creation of international armed forces. Decisions as to their composition were to remain in the hands of the Security Council, leaving open the questions of whether the Council might delegate a command function to the MSC and whether all armed forces would accept its orders in all circumstances.

A related issue involves financing. As long as collective security is conceived as pulling together the willing actions of national governments, financing would be the work of collaborating governments. Paying the assessment for past peacekeeping operations has always been a problem. With a more centralized organization, how to pay for forces and an increased demand for services could easily become an even more crucial organizational issue than the present crisis, with serious arrears coinciding with a quadrupling of the peacekeeping budget.

Institutional issues relate closely to operational contingencies. For example, establishing a permanent military advisory group of some kind in an international institution raises the question of the extent to which it might shape, or be turned to controlling, operations. Financing also would seriously affect operations unless a controlling international institution were sure of income, which has certainly not been the case in the past.

Other operational issues lie in the realm of command and control, intelligence, and provisioning. All three are necessarily intertwined in any successful military operation. The experience so far with international military operations devolves the major responsibility for these functions to the national commands that furnish the personnel. It is easy to imagine a collective security operation for which a great deal more centralization of these functions, as well as autonomy in taking decisions and action, would be thought desirable by the controlling international authority. In such circumstances, the operational issues would loom large indeed.

The UN experience with small military operations, such as peacekeeping, provide little comforting data. Not only have these been small-scale in comparison with almost all inter- or intranational conflicts, but also their aims and duration have varied greatly. Nor have they been numerous, compared with the historical incidents of military operations. UN undertakings have been mostly a series of ad hoc responses to occurrences in the field. Sometimes these led, as in the Congo, to fairly large military operations for which the command structure was hardly developed and the intelligence and supply functions improvised; operations under way in Yugoslavia and Cambodia continue this approach. Whether these experiences have become a useful part of institutional memory of the UN is at least doubtful, although a considerable number of military personnel from a large number of countries have participated.

Intelligence poses particularly difficult problems for operations within a collective security system. As the most comprehensive of the international organizations, the UN might be presumed by the innocent to have a useful strategic intelligence capacity. It does not, and efforts to create a more advanced capacity made slight progress during the last five or so years as the result of the establishment of a specialized bureau, recently abolished, within the office of the Secretary-General. Yet, strategic and operational intelligence form a seamless web during actual military operations. The lack of organization and experience with intelligence in existing international institutions (aside, perhaps, from NATO and the former Warsaw Pact) poses a broad set of challenges that so far has hardly even been formulated. These challenges include the contributions of national intelligence, the gathering of intelligence under international auspices, modes of analysis, determination of the ultimate user of processed intelligence, and possibly internationalization of advanced technological intelligence gathering.

Furthermore, the facilities of the UN and other international agencies for rapid communications have never even distantly approached the state of the art. Operations have been improvised, and at crucial moments communications could not be efficiently directed or secured. As a result, civilian control has remained rudimentary, raising the issue not only as to how messages concerning operations would flow but also as to whether they could be well considered.

In case civilian relief or temporary administrative control of territory and populations should be necessary in a collective security operation, parts of the UN system (e.g., the office of the UN High Commissioner for Refugees, the UN Children's Fund, and the World Food Programme) have substantial competence. Their work, however, has only rarely been geared to an active military action, suggesting that their adaptive capacities would become strained. In any case, as the UN system is characteristically highly decentralized, far more intense coordination would be necessary to bring even its fledgling potential to bear. It is possible that the recent creation of a high-level post in the UN secretariat for an emergency relief coordinator and the ongoing restructuring at the senior levels[17] could provide more coherence in the preparation and coordination for emergency relief when military and nonmilitary personnel are involved.

Any collective security system would face operational issues that are in fact basic in all military situations.[18] These are compounded by complications arising from the multinational character of such a coercive effort. Given the relatively slight institutional experience, a good deal of pioneering work remains to be done. Some of these issues, however, may yield to technical analysis by military personnel who have operational experience in conditions demanding improvisation, either in UN or national service.

US Foreign Policy and Collective Security

The end of the Cold War and the disintegration of the former Soviet Union obviously call for some fresh thinking about new security policies for the United States.[19] There is no reason to think that defeating Saddam Hussein's expansion into Kuwait presages a more peaceful Middle East or that any greater stability than that of the past will reign in Southern Asia or in other parts of the so-called Third World. The turbulence in Yugoslavia, Nagorno-Karabakh, and Albania also indicate that instability is no monopoly of lands in the South.

In fact, the international system at the dawn of the twenty-first century may well be characterized by levels of violence and unrest not even imagined when the UN Charter was drafted.[20] The search for order may be no less quixotic as the decolonization process continues in the former Soviet Union and as ethnic particularism elsewhere comes to dominate the global and local agenda.[21]

While the United States may not be as intensely engaged in as many places as it was during the Cold War, it will be challenged in many areas. Despite its success, albeit controversial,[22] Operation Desert Storm showed that the United States no longer can undertake such missions without the active collaboration of several other governments. This suggests that the United States has reason to seek reliable means of cooperating with other governments to cope with security threats whose scope and dimensions are difficult to forecast.

For strengthening collaborative arrangements and moving in the direction of collective security, the UN, which has been active in redrawing the line between sovereignty and domestic jurisdiction, has continuing attractiveness.[23] In fact, the outgoing Secretary-General, Javier Pérez de Cuéllar, went so far as to posit "an irresistible shift in public attitudes toward the belief that the defense of the oppressed in the name of morality should prevail over frontiers and legal documents."[24] Moreover, US attention to the UN, which has been gradually increasing in the last five years, is likely to continue as the end of the East-West conflict increases the capability of the United States to shape outcomes of decisions within the organization.[25]

While dramatic changes in governmental views that would transform the UN into a full-blown collective security system are unlikely in the near future, significant incremental decisions could move the UN closer to Chapter VII of its Charter. In addition to examining the decisionmaking potential of the Security Council and the leadership qualities of the Secretary-General, the papers in this research project distinguish among a variety of tasks within a putative collective security system. These tasks can be visualized as on a continuum: at the one extreme are the techniques of buffer-zone peacekeeping—really part of pacific settlement of disputes—and at the other, the exigencies of coercion—the heart of Chapter VII and enforcement.[26]

The relatively clear institutional and operational exigencies at either end of the continuum become very blurred for a host of security-related tasks that do not fit clearly into any conventional category and that are, in fact, traditional concerns for US foreign policy. In the middle are the protection of minorities and forced migrants threatened by communal violence or other fighting, the maintenance of peace in civil (not international) wars, the delivery of humanitarian relief, the safeguarding of law and order during elections, the monitoring of human rights violations, and the implementation of techniques to deny or guarantee rights of passage by land, sea, and air.

Past UN experience suggests important lessons and distinctions. While new activities may become possible as the international politics evolves and as a better-functioning peace system emerges, they are likely to constitute much more than basic peacekeeping. At the same time, the institutionalization and operationalization of these "Chapter VI 3/4" activities fall short of enforcement.

While the most active collaborative application of US foreign policy has focused largely on the UN, a larger security role for regional and subregional organizations should not be ignored. Perhaps the two might complement one another—regional diplomatic action, for example, at an initial phase and vigorous follow-up in the UN in the military sphere.

However the US response to collective security is formulated, the content of "security" must also come under review. Almost everywhere, national security is still conceived primarily in military terms, although a host of observers and distinguished international commissions have argued for a more comprehensive understanding.[27] In fact, what becomes clear in the chapters of this book is that there are at least two other Cs that characterize one debate about security in addition to collective security: common security, which proceeds from the need to reduce the insecurity of adversaries, and comprehensive security, which stresses nonmilitary dimensions of stability.

Finally, the research project addresses a range of doubts about the future of international collaboration in the security arena. Within the United States, arguments are heard that vital interests cannot be adequately protected with the limitations on freedom of action that genuine multilateralism entails. Another doubting attitude admits the need for some mechanism approaching collective security but emphasizes the many practical obstacles to its functioning in most instances of aggression. Particularly in the Third World, skepticism has been voiced about the durability of the US commitment to multilateralism in security affairs if it is not based on the hegemony of the United States.[28]

Notes

1. For a discussion of this overall landscape, see Thomas G. Weiss and Meryl A. Kessler, eds., *Third World Security in the Post–Cold War Era* (Boulder: Lynne Rienner, 1991); for more specific case studies, see Thomas G. Weiss and James G. Blight, eds., *The Suffering Grass: Superpowers and Regional Conflict in Southern Africa and the Caribbean Basin* (Boulder: Lynne Rienner, 1992); and for an emphasis on the emerging domestic situation of Third World countries, see Brian Job, ed., *The Insecurity Dilemma: National Security of Third World States* (Boulder: Lynne Rienner, 1992).

2. "Preventive Diplomacy, Peacemaking and Peace-keeping: Report of the Secretary-General Pursuant to the Statement Adopted by the Summit Meeting of the Security Council on 31 January 1992," UN document A/47/277, S/241111 (June 17, 1992).

3. For a discussion, see F. H. Hinsley, *Power and the Pursuit of Peace* (Cambridge: Cambridge University Press, 1963), 1–238; and S. J. Hembeben, *Plans for World Peace Through Six Centuries* (Chicago: University of Chicago Press, 1943).

4. Inis L. Claude, Jr., *Swords into Plowshares* (New York: Random House, 1971). His chapter 12 is the best short treatment of "collective security." See also Claude, *Power and International Relations* (New York: Random House, 1962); and Ernst B. Haas, "Types of Collective Security: An Examination of Operational Concepts," *American Political Science Review* 49, no. 1 (1955), 40–62.

5. Most of the scholarly literature was produced in the first two decades after the end of World War II and consists mainly of (1) historical analyses of the League of Nations and the United Nations (see, for example, Gilbert Murray, *From the League to the U.N.* [London: Oxford University Press, 1949]; and Roland Stromberg, *Collective Security and American Foreign Policy* [New York: Praeger, 1963]); (2) theoretical examinations of the difference between balance-of-power, alliance, and collective security systems (in addition to Inis Claude, see, for example, Hans Morgenthau, *Politics Among Nations* [New York: Knopf, 1960]; Arnold Wolfers, ed., *Discord and Collaboration* [Baltimore: Johns Hopkins, 1962]; and Quincy Wright, *The Study of International Relations* [New York: Appleton, 1955]); and (3) endeavors to evaluate the feasibility of collective security (see, for example, John Herz, *International Politics in the Atomic Age* [New York: Columbia University Press, 1959]).

6. See Morgenthau, *Politics Among Nations,* 5th ed., rev. (1978), 301–302, who mistakenly claims that "collective security envisages the enforcement of the rules of international law by all members of the community relations."

7. Harold K. Jacobson, *Networks of Interdependence,* 2d ed. (New York: Knopf, 1984), chap. 3; and Werner J. Feld and Robert S. Jordan, *International Organizations: A Comparative Approach* (New York: Praeger, 1988).

8. See Edward Gulick, *Europe's Classical Balance of Power* (Ithaca, N.Y.: Cornell University Press, 1955).

9. See Thomas C. Schelling, *The Strategy of Conflict* (London: Oxford University Press, 1960).

10. Charles Krauthammer, "The Unipolar Moment," *Foreign Affairs* 70, no. 1 (1990/91), 23-33; see also Robert W. Tucker and David C. Hendrickson, *The Imperial Temptation* (New York: Council on Foreign Relations, 1992).

11. See Cyril E. Black, "Challenges to an Evolving Legal Order," in Cyril E. Black and Richard A. Polk, *The Future of the International Legal Order* 1 (Princeton: Princeton University Press, 1969), 23-36; Richard A. Falk, "The Interplay of Westphalia and Charter Conceptions of International Legal Order," in

Black and Polk, *Future of International Legal Order, passim;* Richard A. Falk, *Legal Order in a Violent World* (Princeton: Princeton University Press, 1968); Wolfgang Friedmann, *The Changing Structure of International Law* (New York: Columbia University Macmillan, 1964); and Philip C. Jessup, *A Modern Law of Nations* (New York: Macmillan, 1951).

12. See Jack Donnelly, *Universal Human Rights in Theory and Practice* (Ithaca: Cornell University Press, 1989); and David P. Forsythe, *Internationalization of Human Rights* (Lexington, Mass.: Lexington Books, 1991).

13. UN Educational, Scientific and Cultural Organization, *International Dimensions of Humanitarian Law* (Dordrecht, The Netherlands: Nijhoff, 1988); and Marcel A. Boisard, *L'humanisme de l'Islam* (Paris: Albin Michel, 1979).

14. See Anthony A. D'Amato, *International Law: Process and Prospects* (Dobbs Ferry, N.Y.: Transnational Publishers, 1986), esp. chap. 2; Hedley Bull, *The Anarchical Society* (New York: Columbia University Press, 1977), esp. chaps. 2, 6, 10; I. L. Claude, Jr., *Power and International Relations* (New York: Random House, 1966), esp. chap. 4; Howard C. Johnson and Gerhardt Niemeyer, "Collective Security: the Validity of an Ideal," *International Organization* (February 1954), 19–35; Walter Schiffer, *The Legal Community of Mankind: A Critical Analysis of the Modern Concept of World Organization* (New York: Columbia University Press, 1954); and Quincy Wright, *A Study of War,* vol. 2 (Chicago: University of Chicago Press, 1942), esp. chaps. 23 and 25.

15. See UN Department of Public Information, *The Blue Helmets* (New York: United Nations, 1990); Alan James, *Peacekeeping in International Politics* (London: Macmillan, 1990); Augustus Richard Norton and Thomas G. Weiss, *UN Peacekeeping: Soldiers with a Difference* (New York: Foreign Policy Association, 1990); and a special issue of *Survival* 32, 3 (May/June 1990).

16. See the "Note by the President of the Security Council," UN document S/23500, January 31, 1992, which had the headline "New Risks for Stability and Security," *New York Times* (February 1, 1992), 4.

17. See UN documents ST/SGB/248 and 249.

18. For a comparison of UN and non-UN peacekeeping operations from the point of view of integrated military procedures, see John Mackinlay, *The Peacekeepers: An Assessment of Peacekeeping Operations at the Arab-Israeli Interface* (London: Unwin & Hyman, 1989).

19. For two sets of essays, see Charles W. Kegley, Jr., and Eugene R. Wittkopf, eds., *The Future of American Foreign Policy* (New York: St. Martin's Press, 1992), and *The Global Agenda* (New York: McGraw-Hill, 1992).

20. Brian Urquhart, "Learning from the Gulf War," *New York Review of Books* 38, 7 (March 1991), 34–37; James Rosenau, *Turbulence in World Politics: A Theory of Change and Continuity* (Princeton: Princeton University Press, 1990); and Augustus Richard Norton, "The Security Legacy of the 1980s in the Third World," in Weiss and Kessler, *Third World Security,* 19–34. See also the arguments made by a group of Third World intellectuals under the chairmanship of Julius Nyerere, *The Challenge to the South* (New York: Oxford University Press, 1990).

21. See Lawrence Freedman, "Order and Disorder in the New World," *Foreign Affairs* 71, no. 1 (1991/92), 20–37; James N. Rosenau, "Normative Challenges in a Turbulent World," and Charles W. Kegley, Jr., "The New Global Order: The Power Principle in a Pluralistic World," *Ethics and International Affairs,* vol. 6 (1992), 1–40.

22. See the reflections by Stephen Lewis, Clovis Maksoud, and Robert C. Johansen, "The United Nations After the Gulf War," *World Policy Journal* 8, no. 3 (Summer 1991), 537–574.

23. See Jarat Chopra and Thomas G. Weiss, "Sovereignty Is No Longer Sacrosanct: Codifying Humanitarian Intervention," *Ethics and International Affairs* 6 (1992), 95–117.

24. "Secretary-General's Address at the University of Bordeaux," UNDPI Press Release SG/SM/4560 (April 24, 1991).

25. See Leon Gordenker, "International Organization in the New World Order," *The Fletcher Forum of World Affairs* 15, 2 (Summer 1991), 71–86; and Bruce Russett and James S. Sutterlin, "The UN in a New World Order," *Foreign Affairs* 70, no. 2 (Spring 1991), 69–83.

26. This concept is spelled out by John Mackinlay and Jarat Chopra in "Second Generation Multinational Operations," *Washington Quarterly* 15, no. 3 (Summer 1992).

27. See, for example, Jessica Tuchman Mathews, "Redefining Security," *Foreign Affairs* 68, no. 2 (Spring 1989), 162–177. The reports of these commissions are, respectively; *North-South: A Programme for Survival* (London: Pan Books, 1980); *Common Security* (New York: Simon and Schuster, 1982); *Our Common Future* (London: Oxford University Press, 1987); and *Common Responsibility in the 1990's* (Stockholm: Prime Minister's Office, 1991).

28. See Edward C. Luck and Tobi Gati, "Whose Collective Security?" *Washington Quarterly* 15, no. 2 (Spring 1992), 43–56.

■ 2 ■

Sovereignty and Threats to Peace

OSCAR SCHACHTER

It is not surprising that there is a link between sovereignty and threats to peace. Contemporary events have made us acutely conscious of the limits of sovereignty as a principle of international order, which sometimes appears to be the major obstacle to collective security and to the rational management of world affairs. Moreover, as an ideal of self-rule and independence, this principle has fueled demands for new "sovereignties" and a proliferation of violence within and across established borders. There is a strong temptation to proclaim or predict the demise of sovereignty in the "new international order."

This chapter seeks to throw some light on this many-sided problem by examining sovereignty as it has developed and functioned in the relations of states, especially in regard to the maintenance of peace and order. Against this background, we shall also consider various contemporary threats to peace. Our discussion will not be value free, but we leave prescription to the other contributors to this volume.

Sovereignty, Nations, and Peoples

The idea of sovereignty is by no means as nebulous as sometimes suggested. As used in political and legal theory, it has had two distinct, if somewhat antithetical, meanings. With respect to the political structure within a state, it refers to the supreme political authority in that territorial community. It does not apply where there is no such ultimate authority. However, on the international level, with respect to the relations between states, sovereignty has the obverse meaning: it refers to the absence of an external superior authority. These two notions of sovereignty are not inconsistent. In fact, recognition of a supreme ultimate authority within a state tends to support the rejection of a superior external authority.

In the international context, sovereignty is generally accepted as the primary postulate of the modern state system. It has both a normative and a

19

descriptive application. In principle, each sovereign state has ultimate political and legal authority over persons, activities, and things within its territorial domain. Each is free to determine its form of government, and to pursue its own goals and interests, without dictation by any other state or superior political authority. The precepts of nonintervention and territorial integrity are the corollaries of sovereignty, expressed in the United Nations Charter and in general international law. Strictly construed, sovereignty implies that states are subject only to constraints necessary to ensure the reciprocal rights of other states and to such rules as they freely accept as obligatory. The vast body of international law and regimes are considered nationally to be manifestations of the sovereign wills of the individual states.

To be sure, these normative expressions of sovereignty are not wholly factual. Obviously, states are not free from external influences in their conduct of affairs. Large or small, they are constrained by the power of others and by their dependency on transnational factors. Economics and ecology do not respect territorial integrity. Communication and movement of people reduce the significance of territorial inviolability. Affinities grounded in ethnic, religious, and historical connections impinge on the state's autonomy. In law and in fact, a state's authority is subject to the numerous obligations of the international legal system, expressed through treaties, customary law, and juridical postulates accepted explicitly or implicitly by the community of states.

These limitations of sovereignty are well recognized. They have sometimes led political commentators to minimize state sovereignty as an operative principle. Indeed, some writers, with polemical fervor, have declared sovereignty to be fictional or outmoded. Many international lawyers have theorized for centuries that sovereignty is a conception or a "competence" determined by law and limited by it. Yet despite all of the qualifications of sovereignty as an operative concept, the reality of state power and authority cannot be ignored. The concept of world government is far from accepted; "great power" hegemony has neither been legitimized nor made effective. The world in its diversity remains incorrigibly pluralist. A system of self-governing states, mutually respectful of their independence, is widely considered by many the best foundation for stability and order. The dissatisfied are more inclined to seek their own sovereignties than to merge their identities in a global or regional authority. Many see national sovereignty as the effective way to achieve greater freedom and determine their own political destiny. Whether we like it or not, more people are ready to shed blood for their particular sovereignty than for the ideal of international community.

Sovereignty, though an abstract conception, is obviously part of political history, responsive to social forces and particular interests. In its European origins, it arose on the international level as a political response to the dissolution of ecclesiastical authority in the early fifteenth century. It was more than an abstract idea at that time. It expressed a specific jurisdictional development: territorial authorities replaced the church, assuming exclusive political and legal authority over defined areas and their inhabitants.[1] The critical international element was the reciprocal recognition of such exclusive jurisdiction. The citizens of one realm were not to be subject to the laws of another ruler. A legal maxim of Thomas Aquinas was cited in support: "Chacun est maitre chez soi; personne n'est maitre hors de chez soi."[2] (Each man is master in his own home; no man is master away from home.) In its origins and early development, sovereignty was not dependent on national identity or popular will. The question of legitimacy—that is, the international recognition of the rightful rulers and of succession of sovereigns—was judged by dynastic rules derived from feudal law. The monarch and the sovereign were the same. Not until the French Revolution was sovereignty attributed to the nation and linked to the will of the people.

Before considering how this profound transformation affected world order, it is worth noting that in the early period of state sovereignty—even before Westphalia—concern was expressed about the international anarchy of independent sovereigns and the need for collective security. In fact, the core concept of collective security that an attack on one is an attack on all can be found as early as 1454 in the pact for the Most Holy League of Venice and later in the 1518 Treaty of London and in the better-known Treaty of Munster of 1648 (part of the Peace of Westphalia).[3]

The joinder of the sovereign state and nationalism occurred dramatically in the French Revolution, a development profoundly subversive of the established order. It meant that the legal and historical state had to yield to the nation and, more subversively, the nation was identified with the people.[4] French revolutionary interventionism in other countries followed, but was soon transformed by Napoleon into imperialist domination, which in turn was overthrown by an alliance of powers that partly succeeded in curbing nationalist "excesses." But neither the Congress of Vienna nor the subsequent Concert of Europe (the "great powers") was able to prevent the linkage of national self-determination with state sovereignty. The ideology of national unity, expressed by Bismarck in Germany and eloquently by Mazzini in Italy, emphasized both the moral and the prudential value of the nation-state. It was morally right that every people should have its own state governing itself free of external authority. This would remove a principal cause of war and allow every nation to determine its own goals and develop in its own way. The principle of self-determination was thus tied to sovereignty. This was carried forward by Woodrow Wilson and more successfully by the anticolonialism that transformed the map of the world after 1945.

The logic of giving each people its own nation-state seemed compelling in the postwar period. Self-determination was declared a fundamental principle of international law in UN resolutions and lauded as a safeguard of the weak against the strong. Memories of imperialism and abusive intervention strengthened the emphasis on sovereignty. Democracy and nationalism were seen as mutually supporting.

It did not take long for this optimistic outlook to encounter the explosive force of nationalism, multiplied by emerging popular "wills." UN history is illustrative. The UN began with 51 member states. When its headquarters was planned in 1950, future growth was premised on a potential membership of 72, because that was the estimate of the number of nation-states given in international law treatises. Some four decades later, the UN members number 178, with more on the way. This population explosion of states was not foreseen by the proponents of national self-determination nor, for that matter, by academics.

On the whole, the state system has accommodated the UN's increased membership, though not without growing pains. However, the international community has not agreed on a governing principle to determine the "self" entitled to sovereignty. It has merely declared, solemnly and repeatedly in legal instruments, that every people is entitled to self-determination, without defining "people." At the same time, the UN and other international bodies have also affirmed the principles of territorial integrity and political unity of sovereign states.[5] These affirmations do not seem to have impeded the demand for new states and secession from existing states. The result has been a proliferation of internal conflicts and an unparalleled fragmentation of states that had long been perceived as stable entities. International order has been conspicuously shaken by these events. Not only have the internal wars fueled by secessionist demands spilled over into interstate conflict, but also the proliferation of new states has produced many disputes concerning territorial claims and minority rights. (I shall come back to this point in discussing threats to peace.)

Although the multiplication of new states and resurgent nationalism have thrown a bright light on the shortcomings of sovereignty, it is at least as important to recognize that nationalism has provided the strongest support of state sovereignty. Those inclined to dismiss sovereignty as outmoded tend to minimize the continuing strong hold of nationalist sentiment in sustaining the state system. Good reasons can be given as to why an emphasis on sovereign rights is dysfunctional in an interdependent world, but analysis and prescription are seriously deficient if they fail to recognize the power of political nationalism in sustaining state sovereignty. To deride this as a new "tribalism" has little effect.

The assertion that peoples have the right to self-determination is indicative of a general claim that sovereignty, as the term is now used, rests on the consent of the people. The idea of popular sovereignty is not new in regard to the internal government of a state.[6] The American and French revolutions most notably articulated the notion of the "sovereignty of the people"—it held sway in the rhetoric of both countries even though the majority of the people were actually excluded from the electoral process.

However, in international relations and law, consent of the people was never considered an essential element of sovereignty. It is only recently that the case is being made on the international level for conditioning sovereignty on the popular will. The principal legal argument for that position stems from the propositions of the Universal Declaration of Human Rights that "the will of the people shall be the basis of the authority of government" and that "this will shall be expressed in periodic and genuine elections."[7]

It is true that virtually all governments have professed approval of the Universal Declaration and many have adhered to binding treaties supportive of its democratic principles. This is certainly significant. Nevertheless, states with governments that clearly do not rest on the consent of the governed (as expressed through free elections) are treated as sovereign in their relations with other states. Dictatorial regimes do not forfeit state sovereignty. Even when a government is denied recognition on the grounds that it is a puppet of a foreign power, the state is not stripped of its sovereignty.[8] True, a nondemocratic regime may open itself to condemnation and even sanctions, but this is quite different from declaring that states with nondemocratic governments are no longer entitled to be treated as sovereign entities under international law.

I do not argue that popular sovereignty is entirely immaterial in international relations. Popular sovereignty has a sufficient degree of acceptance today to provide normative guidance in particular situations. For example, whether a state has consented to external intervention should be determined by reference to the people's will where that is ascertainable rather than by a nondemocratic government. (I will discuss this later in the section on civil wars.)

The Relativity of Sovereignty

The main problem posed by the principle of sovereignty (from the inception of the principle to the present time) has been to reconcile the independence of states with the practical requirements of coexistence and the generally accepted values of the international community. Some answers have been propounded in theoretical writing of a philosophical and juridical character as well as in governmental declarations. It is not appropriate for me to go into this complex body of ideas here; but it is pertinent to observe that the two main schools of juridical thought, while differing in important respects, have tended to agree that sovereignty in law, as in fact, cannot be absolute.

The older school, dating back to the sixteenth century (and including such eminences as Suárez and Grotius), took as its basis the "moral unity" of peoples and, more pragmatically, the necessities of a pluralist society.[9] The idea of a "society of states," which emerged most clearly in the eighteenth century, fortified the older conception of the primacy of "mankind" expressed through the law of nations.[10] Though this basic idea had many variations, its central core was—and still is—widely accepted by legal theorists and reflected in many international governmental declarations. Sovereignty, in this view, necessarily presupposes a body of rules and practice—that is, an international order—that defines its scope and limits. It cannot be left to the unlimited discretion of a state, as was asserted, for example, by the claim of *raison d'état*.[11]

The opposing school of thought denies that sovereignty is conceded to states by the international order or the law of nations.[12] Insofar as a legal order or international society exists, it is the creation of states and is dependent on its voluntary acceptance by them.[13] This doctrinal approach has had various expressions, but the common emphasis on the primacy of state sovereignty was broadly supported by jurists and political philosophers in Europe and the United States beginning in the eighteenth century. A historian of sovereignty has observed that by the nineteenth century sovereignty "became the central principle in the external policy and the international conduct of all the leading states of Europe."[14] It was taken for granted that with the exception of the high seas, every part of the world had to have a sovereign. The absence of a state (in the European conception) meant that territory was *terra nullius* open to acquisition by sovereign states. Indigenous political structures sometimes assumed statehood, but large areas were placed under the sovereignty of colonial powers. The idea of sovereignty, first supportive of imperial aims, was then turned against the European empires; it fueled demands for independence by subordinate peoples everywhere in the world.

The dominance of the principle of sovereignty in international relations did not mean the absence of legal restraints. On the contrary, the increase of sovereignties in the past 100 years has been paralleled by a great expansion of international law and institutions that imposed limits on state conduct. These limits were not generally viewed by statesmen or lawyers as inconsistent with sovereignty but rather as the collective expression of sovereign wills. In the prevalent positivist conception, states freely subjected themselves to obligations by treaty or custom. It was therefore unnecessary to denounce sovereignty in order to achieve greater limits on state autonomy; it was sufficient to recognize that the international community developed restraints through processes adopted by the member states.[15] The relativity of sovereignty was thus acknowledged in the practical working of the international system.

Renouncing the absolutist conception of sovereignty is helpful but not a complete solution. The basic problem still remains as to where the lines should be drawn and what process should be used for such line-drawing.

These issues arise sharply in respect to matters that are strongly believed to be elements of self-rule. Four such subjects are paramount. One is the relation between the state and the individual (i.e., human rights). A second, obviously, is the choice of rulers and governmental system. A third concerns the control and management of the natural resources within the country, and a fourth relates to the national security and defense.

These four subjects are surely central to the commonly held conception of independence and self-rule. It is also true that they may be of international concern and, under certain conditions, may affect peace and security. Put conceptually, the principle of sovereignty may compete with international obligation. We may hold that sovereignty is only relative, but that does not solve the particular problem of deciding how relative and where to draw the line. A quick survey of the four subjects mentioned is instructive.

I begin with the area of human rights that, most conspicuously, involves obligatory international norms regarding matters long regarded as within the exclusive competence of the state. Some international lawyers consider that the principle of sovereignty is no longer relevant in regard to the human rights that have been internationalized. But this broad conclusion involves some exaggeration. Recognizing obligatory human rights does not entirely eliminate respect for sovereignty. Two situations are cases in point. The first relates to the application of human rights in domestic law and practice. In many cases, the states concerned have maintained that local factors must be taken into account in applying rights and that each state should be entitled to a "margin of appreciation" in determining the implementation of the right. This principle has been recognized in the jurisprudence of the European Court of Human Rights and generally acknowledged as reasonable.[16] While some perceive this only as a sensible prudential rule, it is also an implied acknowledgment that the principle of self-rule should not be ignored in the application of international obligations.

A more controversial aspect of sovereignty and human rights concerns coercive action against a state that has seriously violated human rights. The argument has been made that in some cases sovereignty must yield to a right of "humanitarian intervention" by governments or international bodies that would allow the use of armed force.[17] On the whole, governments and legal authorities have not considered such intervention as a permissible exception to the prohibition of force in Article 2(4) of the Charter.[18] The memory of past abuses and the fear of intervention by powerful states remain strong deterrents to legitimizing armed intervention by governments in principle. This concern is less evident in respect to action by the UN or a regional organization, especially where a threat to international peace may be found.[19] Nonetheless, concern for sovereignty is still an important consideration for governments faced with demands to use armed force in another country without the consent or acquiescence of its government.

An even more obvious issue of sovereignty is raised by action to impose a regime or a constitutional arrangement on a state. This issue goes to the heart of political independence. It has come up in troubling ways whenever the UN has used armed force against a government, namely, in Korea and Iraq and in the internal conflict in the former Belgian Congo.[20] A basic question is whether the Security Council may determine the structure of government (e.g., unity or federalism) and even select the actual rulers (e.g., replace a ruler guilty of aggression) in order to secure international peace. While the Security Council is a political organ, it is bound by Article 24 to observe the principles of the Charter, even in regard to enforcement measures under Chapter VII. It may be plausibly argued that imposing a government would violate the basic Charter principle of "sovereign equality" found in Article 2(1).

But some would argue that the Council's responsibility to maintain international peace and security is a political matter left entirely to the discretion of the Council, particularly in regard to Chapter VII actions. Up to now, the Security Council has not expressly addressed this basic Charter issue. It has refrained from making a determination that a particular regime or individual must be ousted because of aggression or extreme human rights violations. It has gone only so far as to declare that a particular government or head of government is the legitimate authority for purposes of representation in the UN.[21]

A third sensitive area of sovereign rights relates to the use and exploitation of a country's resources. In this respect, "sovereignty over natural resources" is an acclaimed principle, affirmed by UN bodies and by most governments. While somewhat contentious in details, it is generally agreed that international law requires states to accord certain basic rights to foreign investors under customary law as well as applicable treaties.[22] Environmental concerns are also affecting absolutist ideas of sovereignty over resources. It is fairly clear by now that as a matter of broad principle, states should take into consideration the environmental harm to other states and to common areas caused by the exploitation of resources in their territory.[23] Claims of sovereignty are still important, especially in regard to development needs, but they are no longer regarded as ruling out constraints considered necessary to prevent or mitigate damage beyond the state's borders.

The fourth subject of self-rule concerns the highly sensitive areas of national security and arms. While states are subject to the Charter prohibitions on the use of force, they may resort to force in individual or collective self-defense. Their right to arms and related defense measures is regarded as an essential element of sovereignty. Nonetheless, legal restraints have been adopted in a number of international treaties, many multinational treaties, and some regional and bilateral treaties.[24] These have all been negotiated agreements, presumably freely accepted by the parties. Hence no derogation of sovereignty in a strict sense has been involved. However, constraints on sovereignty are implied by moves to limit armaments, particularly weapons of mass destruction (nuclear, chemical, and biological) without requiring specific treaty adherence or consent. A development of this character could be given effect by a concerted policy of denying materials for such arms to a noncomplying state and by other sanctions. This would, of course, effectively cut down on the sovereign right of a state to defense. Up to now, such action has been taken only in respect to Iraq under Chapter VII, and even there, with the coerced "agreement" of its government. A more general application has been discussed in official as well as unofficial circles. Objections will surely be raised on grounds of sovereignty, but these are not likely to be decisive if the restrictions are considered essential to international peace.

These comments on the relativity of sovereignty confirm that the Hobbesian and Hegelian notions of absolute sovereignty are remote from present conceptions and practice. But they do not show that sovereignty has lost its political and legal significance. Like other abstract concepts of law and politics, the law of sovereignty cannot be reasonably applied without regard to competing principles and the particular context of circumstances. Obviously, changing conditions and values affect its application, but it would be a mistake to conclude that they have removed its strong hold on the international system.

Divided and Joint Sovereignty

The general rule in international law is that the government of a state speaks for that state, whatever the national political structure provides. This is true of federal and confederal states that for internal reasons may have divided sovereignty. However, there are examples on the international level that depart from the general monolithic conception of sovereignty. Over time a variety of arrangements have been made by agreements of states, or unilaterally, under which sovereign authority of an area is divided or exercised jointly.[25] Such arrangements have usually been made to resolve disputes over territorial sovereignty, but in a number of cases they have been means to accommodate demands of powerful states or to limit sovereign claims in the general interest. An example common in the imperialist period of the nineteenth and earlier twentieth centuries is the dependent, "semi-sovereign" state—protectorates, states under suzerainty, neutral "buffer" zone areas. The Anglo-Egyptian condominium is another example. These examples of dominance of the more powerful states have largely vanished. All states are formally equal today.

Shared resources—such as rivers, lakes, maritime areas—while formally subject to sovereign rights, have often been dealt with by agreement as areas of joint administration involving mutual rights and responsibilities.[26] The Antarctic treaty regime is a more complex arrangement. It allows the various competing claims of sovereignty to be maintained in law, but it provides for uniform restraints on activities in the region (e.g., military activities or mineral exploitation) and for mutual inspection rights.[27] Sovereignty is, so to speak, put on ice.

Various forms of joint sovereignty have been proposed for disputed areas. A notable case for such proposals has been that of Jerusalem, but no proposal has been acceptable and the idea is strongly resisted by Israel. Dividing sovereign rights has also been suggested as a means of resolving the Falkland Islands territorial dispute, but it has not been adopted.[28]

The idea of separating some sovereign rights from others has been embodied in several important provisions of the Law of the Sea Convention. "Sovereign rights" for exploiting and managing the natural resources of the respective 200-mile exclusive economic zones are granted to coastal states, but this stops short of full sovereignty, thus denying the sovereign right to control navigation in that area.[29]

It has been suggested from time to time that claims for some degree of autonomy for national minorities within a state be granted by international agreements, in effect dividing sovereign rights over the area in question.[30] Reference is sometimes made to the agreement between Italy and Austria regarding Alto Adige (South Tirol), which gave a considerable degree of autonomy to the German-speaking minority.[31] The Camp David Treaty between Egypt and Israel promised autonomy for Palestinian Arabs on the West Bank; but, as of mid-1992, it has remained unfulfilled. The difficulty in this, as in other cases of minority rights, is not the monolithic nature of sovereignty but the difficulty of reconciling the incompatible demands of the parties.

Civil Wars as Threats to Peace

Civil wars have been far more numerous since 1945 than wars between states. They have raised issues of both sovereignty and collective security. The conflicts fall into two broad classes based on the ends sought. One category involves large-scale armed struggles for state power by opposing organized forces. The other includes the armed movements that seek secession or autonomy for a part of the state in question. In the first category the classic cases are the French Revolution of 1789 and the Spanish Civil War of the 1930s. In recent decades such internal armed conflicts have occurred in every part of the world except North America and Western Europe. Examples include the conflicts in Afghanistan, Angola, El Salvador, Lebanon, Mozambique, Nicaragua, Somalia, The Sudan, and Yemen. The second category, the wars of secession, include almost as many: in Bangladesh (East Pakistan), Biafra (Nigeria), Myanmar (formerly Burma), Ethiopia (Eritrea), East Timor, Sri Lanka (involving the Tamil), and

Yugoslavia, as well as Kurdish rebellions. The classic case in the past is, of course, the American Civil War.

The civil wars in both categories have been bound up with issues of sovereignty. International law generally concludes that internal conflicts are not limited by international law, although they are, of course, unlawful by national law. International law becomes relevant by prohibiting, in principle, intervention by a foreign power in an internal conflict. Thus, the armed intervention of German and Italian forces in support of the Franco rebellion in Spain was regarded as unlawful,[32] as was the comparatively minor assistance given by Britain to the Confederacy in the American Civil War (for which the British eventually were held legally liable for damages).[33] The legal bar on intervention in civil wars was reaffirmed by the International Court of Justice (ICJ) in the 1986 case of Nicaragua versus the United States.[34]

The idea of imposing a legal wall around internal conflicts—a kind of *cordon sanitaire*—has been difficult to maintain in many cases. An important reason is that the internal conflict tends to spill outside the territorial state when one or both of the warring sides has obtained external aid of a military or quasi-military character. When intervention has occurred on one side, a third state may counterintervene on the claim of collective self-defense to support the political independence of the state under prior external attack. Thus, in principle, counterintervention would support the sovereignty of the state in question.

Foreign military interventions in civil wars had been so common during the Cold War that the proclaimed rule of nonintervention seems to have been stood on its head. This is not new. Talleyrand quipped that "non-intervention is a word with the same meaning as intervention." Actually, no state would deny today that the people have the right to decide for themselves what kind of government they want and that a foreign state that supports one side with force in an internal conflict deprives the people in some degree of their right to decide on their government. It is therefore a use of force against their political independence in violation of Article 2(4) of the Charter.

The issue becomes murky where both sides have sought and received military support. There may be a presumption—and many so hold—that the recognized government has a right to receive foreign aid against an insurgency. On the other hand, the presumption that the government is entitled to foreign military aid may be questioned when that government faces a large-scale insurgency, with substantial support in the country. In those circumstances, outside support to the government would also violate the right of the people to decide by themselves. This conclusion would apply whether the insurgency were aimed at secession or at the overthrow of the government.

Of course, if one side gets substantial outside aid, the case can be made that aid to the other should be permitted to counteract foreign domination. This was essentially the argument of the United States in support of its military action on behalf of El Salvador against intervention by the Nicaraguan Sandinista regime.[35] It would, of course, be much better as a general rule to adhere to the nonintervention rule in any civil war. To achieve this, it would probably be necessary to have international mechanisms such as peacekeeping forces to monitor compliance and to bar the sending of arms, backed by sanctions against violators. Such UN measures are dealt with elsewhere in this book. Our specific point here is to emphasize that the principle of sovereignty supports a strong noninterventionist position in internal conflicts. Where intervention by a foreign state does occur, it opens the way to counterintervention and the consequential internationalizing of the civil war; this was borne out during the Cold War. It seems less likely today, but it cannot be excluded where ethnonationalism or economic interests impel a third state to take sides.

Even where the opposing forces do not invite or receive external support, a civil war may spill over into neighboring countries through the mass movements of displaced persons. This occurred in the course of the 1971 civil war in Pakistan, with Bengali (East Pakistani) war refugees entering India and giving India a reason to deploy its troops against Pakistan.[36] A more recent example can be found in April 1991 at the end of the war against Iraq when Kurdish inhabitants in Iraq were attacked by Iraqi troops. Many became refugees in the neighboring countries of Turkey and Iran. The UN Security Council declared that the repression against the Kurds constituted a threat to international peace and security and the Council demanded access for humanitarian aid.[37] The resolution was relied on by the United States, Britain, the Netherlands, and France as authorizing them to send troops to protect the Kurdish refugees.[38] The potential for armed conflict in a case of this kind is evident whether or not the UN has declared the situation to be a threat to peace. The exodus of refugees from the recent civil war in Liberia was also given as a reason for armed intervention by troops of the Economic Community of West African States.[39] The effect appears to have been a widening of the war.

A civil war of secession may be converted into an interstate war when the secessionist movement succeeds in obtaining significant recognition as a new state. Even before such recognition, the civil conflict may be generally viewed as international because of the national character of the opposing forces. This seems to have been the perception of the breakup of Yugoslavia.[40] Like treason, which if successful is no longer treason, a civil war is no longer "civil" when the seceding area receives formal recognition as a state. The more important point is that the breakup of a state through civil war may leave a legacy of antagonism and irredentism that endangers peace in the future. India-Pakistan is an example.

Finally I note that civil wars are often characterized by mass brutality and hardships of the civilian population. This engenders pressure for other states to intervene on humanitarian grounds, especially where they have ties of ethnicity, religion, or ideology. The antiapartheid conflict in South Africa, similar essentially to a civil war, was formally designated a threat to peace by the Security Council so as to enable the Council to take mandatory sanctions under Chapter VII.[41] This was justified on the grounds that the egregious racial regime of South Africa aroused such hostility among African states as to lead them to support armed action against South Africa.

Predictions about civil wars are as hazardous as they are about other wars. In 1988, *The Economist* wrote that wars of "national identity . . . are inevitably on the decrease, because most such breakaways have already taken place."[42] In fact, many more breakaways have occurred since 1988, and there is no good reason to believe that others (say, in Africa and Asia) are not on the way. The end of the Cold War has probably greatly reduced the probabilities of military intervention by major powers, but it may well make it more likely that new wars of secession will take place in countries, such as those in Africa, that have boundaries that were drawn by Europeans a century ago.[43] The reasonable way to avoid these breakups would be to improve the chances of peaceful settlement and genuine choices by the people concerned. This may be facilitated by modifying "monolithic" sovereignty and "unbundling" sovereign rights so as to make borders less important and movements of people and goods easier for all.[44]

Territorial and Resource Disputes as Threats to Peace

It is quite striking that nearly all wars between states in the recent decades have involved a territorial dispute. This does not mean that territorial disputes are themselves a significant threat to the peace. In fact, numerous conflicts of disputed sovereignty to territory (including boundary disputes) exist at the present time. Many are long-standing; many evoke strong nationalist sentiment and feelings of past injustice; some have important economic implications. Yet, most cannot be said to be threats to the peace.

With this important qualification, territorial conflicts must be included in the category of threats to the peace. I note two reasons. One is that territory may have significant value to a state, even if it is not the most important factor in its political or economic power. This is markedly evident where the territory has valuable resources, such as the oil deposits in the conflict between Iraq and Kuwait. It is also important in many parts of the world where water is scarce and sovereignty cuts across the sources of water.

The second reason we give as to why territorial conflicts are considered as threats to peace is that territory includes people, who may be more important than the land. The violent conflicts between Azerbaijan and Armenia and among Serbia, Croatia, and Bosnia over ethnic enclaves showed concern for the fate of the people more than for the land as such.

Other factors are also relevant to the outbreak of territorial disputes into violent conflict. In many cases, the popular emotions attached to territory play a critical role in domestic political affairs. Groups in power or seeking power find it very useful to take strong and uncompromising stands on territorial claims to win popular support. The Argentine use of force in the Falklands has been explained by the need of the military regime to strengthen its weakening internal rule.[45] And even on the other side, the resistance of the Thatcher government to proposals for peaceful settlement was attributed to its interest in winning the next election, and this was borne out by the popularity of the war despite its relatively large economic cost.[46] The emotional aspect of a territorial conflict appears repeatedly. Boundary disputes over maritime areas, such as those between Britain and Iceland and between France and Canada, have evoked local passions that made negotiated settlement difficult and even led to the use of naval force. That these states had long histories of friendly relations and cooperation was not enough to prevent popular anger over challenge to their sovereign rights.

It is also worth noting that armed conflict over territory has been functional in many cases—that is, it has resulted in fixing boundaries and settling old disputes in a definitive way. It is true that in some cases, irredentist claims remain alive. This seems to be the case for Pakistan vis-à-vis India and Argentina vis-à-vis the United Kingdom. It certainly applies to the territorial claims against Israel. But from the standpoint of the victorious governments, the armed conflict is not perceived as dysfunctional.

The use of international judicial and arbitral means to resolve territorial conflicts has perceptibly increased in recent years. The ICJ has become a principal arbiter of both maritime and land territorial disputes; in other cases ad hoc tribunals have been successfully utilized. This augurs well for the future. Nonetheless, it is likely that in areas of the globe where boundaries are perceived as the "artificial," arbitrary creations of foreigners, they will be disputed with a good chance that violence will erupt. This appears to be most probable in some areas of Africa. The effort of the Organization of African Unity to maintain the status quo for existing boundaries (fixed mainly by the European colonial powers) was successful for a couple of decades, but recent events indicate that it is unlikely to prevail and that violent means may be used in some cases to redraw the boundaries. That the Cold War has ended and both US and Russian involvement has greatly lessened is considered by some experts as likely to increase the use of force to redraw boundaries and create new sovereignties.[47]

Disputes over water resources, already mentioned, could merit a separate chapter. The underlying problem is that fresh water is increasingly a scarce resource and that many populations are in some jeopardy as a consequence of economic development and population growth. The Middle East and North Africa are areas where the problem has been most acute with strong political repercussions.[48] Egypt, with its extraordinary increases in population and economic growth, has little control over the Nile's upstream governments, which also face exploding needs for water. Not long ago an Egyptian minister declared, "The national security of Egypt is . . . a question of water."[49] Efforts to develop viable plans for sharing water have been made with regard to the Nile, the Euphrates, and the Jordan. However, the tensions in the region and the high stakes involved in water needs must qualify easy optimism that actual conflict will be avoided.

Armaments as Threats to Peace

Whether armaments are a cause of war has long been a subject of international debate. Nearly all states maintain armed forces for security against attack or intimidation. They have the sovereign right to do so without limit except as agreed by them or when the UN Security Council imposes mandatory limits. The actual use of arms against another state is prohibited by the UN Charter unless used for self-defense (individual or collective) under Article 51 or in accordance with a Security Council decision under Chapter VII. A significant number of multilateral and bilateral treaties have imposed limits on the size, number, and deployment of weapons and armed forces.[50] The Nonproliferation Treaty is the most notable example of arms limitation, but it has left nuclear weapons to the five nuclear powers; and it has not been ratified by several states with, or on their way to, nuclear weapons capability.

That states maintain armed forces against possible attack can be viewed quite rightly as supportive of international order. But there also is an element of irony in that a threat to peace arises only where there is likely resistance to threats of force. Clausewitz has a pertinent comment: "War takes place mainly for the defender; the conqueror would like to enter our country unopposed."[51] In other words, without defense, threats of force do not become threats to peace. Only a few pacifists and an exceptional government would follow this logic and eliminate national defense entirely. However, in a more limited way, and in a particular context, peace may be so compelling a value as to preclude armed resistance to threats of force, even though sovereign rights are lost.

Beyond these comments, I do not propose to discuss the somewhat theoretical question of whether armaments are per se a threat to peace. It is more realistic at the present time to consider the situations in which some regimes would have recourse to weapons of a particularly destructive character, especially on civilian populations. Biological, chemical, and nuclear arms fall into this category. Evidence of Iraq's activity in regard to these weapons and indications that Libya has similar ambitions have highlighted the issue of so-called poor men's weapons. It may be that these weapons will prove to be of little effect against organized military forces in developed countries, but they certainly could menace civilian populations and weak regimes. They are not only potential weapons of the poor but also weapons that can be used especially against the poor. In the hands of fanatical or unstable regimes, they would be weapons of terror. The UN Security Council took specific enforcement measures in Iraq in the aftermath of the Gulf War.[52] It is a safe guess that weapons of terror will make their appearance in various places. Threatened states are likely to take protective action. The menace to peace in that case may well be of large dimensions.

Treaties to outlaw such weapons have not been universally accepted, and there is continued fear of clandestine weapons whether or not covered by such treaties. Action may then be called for by the Security Council, employing its mandatory powers irrespective of consent, to outlaw such weapons and take enforcement measures. The Council took a step in this direction when it declared at the first-ever Summit in January 1992 that "the proliferation of all weapons of mass destruction constitutes a threat to international peace and security."[53] Presumably, claims of sovereignty and "sovereign equality" by the states in question would then have to give way to the Council's authority, provided, of course, that the requisite voting requirements of the Council have been met. In the absence of effective action by the Security Council, individual states may have recourse to measures, falling short of outright use of armed force, in order to compel a recalcitrant government to give up the proscribed weapons. At this point, we can do little more than speculate about the possible scenarios, though we can be quite sure that the problem of proliferation will have to be faced.

Illegal Activities that Endanger Peace:
Terrorism, Subversion, Genocide, Repression

A review of contemporary threats to peace would be incomplete without considering certain illegal activities that may provoke a government to react by using force outside its own borders. Terrorism, subversion, genocide, and flagrant repression are examples of such internationally illegal activities.

Terrorism is itself a form of warfare directed against a state. It involves the threat or use of violence to create extreme fear or anxiety in a targeted group or government so as to coerce it to meet political aims of the terrorists. Terrorist acts have an international character when carried out across national lines or directed against nationals or instrumentalities of a foreign state. Terrorism is defined by the act, whatever the motive and however idealistic in aim. Killing children, bombing airplanes, and abducting journalists are terrorist acts, even though those responsible see them as means to national liberation or some other ideal. Some terrorists act as agents of governments; many are not but receive support from governments in various forms, including territorial bases. A targeted or victim state may feel impelled to take retaliatory action by attacking the supporting state. Such retaliatory action has been rare up to now. The bombing of Tripoli by the United States in 1986 is one conspicuous example. The United States declared the bombing to be a "preemptive action," after an earlier terrorist attack on a Berlin nightclub patronized by US military personnel.[54]

It is open to conjecture whether state-supported terrorism will increase and whether the affected states will respond with force, as the United States did in Libya. The end of the Cold War may reduce support for international terrorism but will surely not bring an end to terrorist activity. The bombings by the Irish Republican Army in the heart of London in 1992 are indicative of the persistence of terrorist activity. The action of the Security Council against Libya this year suggests that collective measures may be used in lieu of individual retaliation.[55] A major concern is that new weapons—a suitcase nuclear bomb or biological toxin—will increase the power of terrorism and therefore precipitate warlike international retaliation.

Subversive activity against a regime by a hostile government has often been cited as a casus belli. Such activity has typically included provision of arms and logistic support to insurgents, often supported by propaganda attacks on the targeted government. Subversive activity has been motivated by support for oppressed minorities, by ideological opposition, and by historical hostility. It is illegal under international law.[56] The victim state may take countermeasures, but under the ruling of the ICJ in the Nicaraguan case, it may not have recourse to armed self-defense as long as the illegal acts do not amount to armed attack.[57] Whether this ruling will have an effect on the resort to force by the victim state is unclear. In any case, subversive activity is likely to continue in various parts of the world as an element of violent opposition to existing governments, whether caused by minority movements or struggles for power.

Genocide is sometimes referred to as a potential threat to the peace, recalling Nazi genocide as a factor in the causes of World War II. Since then, accusations of genocide have been made in respect to internal conflicts or repressive state action against minorities. Condemnation by organs of public opinion and on occasion by governments has not been effective in the most extreme cases. There have been calls for action by the UN—or, in lieu thereof, for unilateral intervention by concerned states—on humanitarian grounds. Some of the worst examples of mass killing (such as in Burundi, Cambodia, and Ethiopia) have not brought armed humanitarian intervention by international bodies or concerned states.[58] The French government's removal of Bokassa (the "Emperor" of the Central African Republic) is one of the rare clear cases of forcible military unilateral intervention on humanitarian grounds. The protection of the Kurdish refugees at the end of the war against Iraq pursuant to Security Council Resolution 688 is an example of collective action, as is the use of UN forces in Bosnia to safeguard relief supplies for a threatened people.[59]

No doubt genocide could be a threat to peace in that it might precipitate protective armed action by concerned states, resulting in war. That this has rarely occurred has sometimes been attributed to respect for the sovereignty of the culpable government, but the more realistic reason is that the material costs, especially in human lives, of an intervention are not perceived as justified by the national interests of other states. Concern that such humanitarian intervention would plunge the intervening state into a quagmire of internal conflict has usually been a deterring factor.

Like genocide, mass repression involving flagrant violations of human rights may bring international condemnation and calls for forcible intervention by concerned states and international bodies. Obviously, widespread human rights abuses can be important causes of internal conflict. Such conflicts may threaten peace on the international level when they result in interventionary action by a foreign state and counterintervention by another, as we noted earlier in our discussion of civil wars.

Are repressive governments likely to be more warlike than those that respect human rights? This has often been answered in the affirmative, generally on the grounds that a people enjoying freedom and democracy would not willingly choose war. Dictators, it is sometimes said, tend to choose or risk war to win popular support or to divert attention from their repressive acts. In Marxist ideology, the ruling classes sought war for markets and other economic gains, whereas the people, the proletariat, were presumed inherently peaceful. Kant more persuasively argued that self-governing peoples acting reasonably would avoid wars that impose hardships on them and that freedom of speech and the institutional limits on power are effective restraints on waging war, contrary to popular will.[60] Empirical studies pursuing Kantian views indicate that liberal democracies rarely engage in wars with one another but that they have behaved aggressively toward nonliberal regimes.[61] Kant, by the way, did not favor armed action by "republics" against despotic regimes.

I may surely conclude that despotic regimes and egregious violations of human rights give rise to international tensions and that, in some circumstances, they gravely threaten peace. Such threats to peace arise not simply because human rights are violated but because the violations are perceived to harm specific interests of other states, as, for example, injuries to their nationals, to common ethnic and religious groups, or, in extreme cases, to security and vital economic interests. Even if democratic states do not generally threaten peace at least among themselves, both past and recent experience show that popular passions have resulted in mass violence across, as well as within, borders. In contrast to Kant, Thucydides observed on the basis of Athenian experience that popular rule engendered expansionist moves in order to expand commerce, maintain employment, and enhance glory—and that this leads to war.[62] History is not without examples of popular wars. Still, skepticism that people are always peace-loving should not lead to ignoring the historical evidence that despotic regimes have a greater tendency to instigate or invite international violence. There is good reason to conclude that, as UN Secretary-General Boutros Boutros-Ghali recently stated, "there is an obvious connection between democratic practices—such as the rule of law and transparency in decision-making—and the achievement of the peace and security."[63]

Micronationalism and Splintered States

Earlier in this chapter, I noted the emergence of the revolutionary idea that every people is entitled to its own nation-state, thus joining sovereignty and nationalism under the concept of self-determination. To its supporters, the principle was both morally just and politically wise. It upheld the ideal of equality of peoples; it met the claims of self-conscious territorial communities to control their own destinies. Moreover, granting self-determination to all would remove a major cause of international conflict. So argued Mazzini, Woodrow Wilson, and the leaders of independence movements after World War II. The largely peaceful dissolution of the colonial empires fitted into this conception of orderly self-determination, as did, at least initially, the breakup of the Soviet Union.

However, the optimistic projection of self-determination as a force for peace has obviously been called into question by the frequent clashes between rival ethnic communities as well as by the use of armed force against liberation movements. This is not new. Military historian Michael Howard recently wrote: "National self-consciousness far more than any aspirations towards social justice or economic equality has fueled international conflict in the nineteenth and twentieth centuries."[64]

Now, toward the end of the twentieth century and after the Cold War, "national self-consciousness" has exploded into a virtual epidemic of demands for self-rule by territorial communities based on ethnic, religious, and historical identities. Many, perhaps most, of the demands have come from peoples not hitherto perceived as "nations." They have included small indigenous folk communities, obscure pockets of transplanted peoples, large populations sharing a religion or language distinct from the state in which they found themselves, and many other varieties. It is no exaggeration to say that nearly every nation-state in the world includes some groups claiming the status of a separate "nation" or self-governing people.

There is irony in that this contemporary outburst of nationalism, or, more aptly, "micronationalism," has occurred in the same period as state boundaries have diminished in significance for the lives of most people. Economics, ecology, communications, technology, and education have created a more interdependent and integrated world. The contradictory tendencies of micronationalism and integration are striking and appear paradoxical. However, they may well be causally related. When the national state appears to be diminished by globalization and new structures of authority, it can appear to its citizens as a loss of their control. We see this even in Western Europe, where integration has gone furthest. It is not surprising that people everywhere are made uneasy by a perception of remote anonymous authority controlling their lives, whether through supranational organizations, multinational corporations, or the influx of foreigners. One attempt to allay such anxiety would involve an assertion for demands for more autonomy of respective states or subnational groups. Micronationalism then flourishes, sustained often by legacies of historical injustices and violence.

In some cases, it has been possible to resolve the group conflicts within existing states or across state lines by negotiation or political processes. However, in a substantial number of cases, violence erupted especially when secession or far-reaching autonomy was demanded. Armed conflicts also arise between the communities within a state, competing for power or benefits. The UN Secretary-General summed up this situation in June 1992:

> National boundaries are blurred by advanced communications and global commerce, and by the decisions of States to yield some sovereign prerogatives to larger, common political associations. At the same time, however, fierce new assertions of nationalism and sovereignty spring up, and the cohesion of States is threatened by brutal ethnic, religious, social, cultural or linguistic strife. Social peace is challenged on the one hand by new assertions of discrimination and exclusion and, on the other, by acts of terrorism seeking to undermine evolution and change through democratic means.[65]

The same report noted that the UN had not closed its doors to new states, but it added: "Yet if every ethnic, religious or linguistic group claimed statehood, there would be no limit to fragmentation, and peace, security and economic well-being for all would become more difficult to achieve."[66] The conclusion often drawn is that the answer to such fragmentation and its attendant violence lies in the observance of human rights and in effective protection for minorities, preferably enforced by international mechanisms. This would meet the legitimate demands of minorities and, it is hoped, enhance the stability of existing states. It may be too optimistic, however, to conclude that a regime of minority rights would provide a solution in all cases. Autonomy for some, or special privileges, may not be acceptable to the majority or be consistent with democratic principles. Deeply rooted mistrust and animosities may not yield to genuinely negotiated solutions. The result would be continued internal tensions, with an added international dimension that would spread conflict beyond the state's borders. In such cases, the prudential solution would be separation, with protection for remaining minorities in each state. These considerations suggest the futility of seeking a single formula for all situations. Economic conditions, cultural factors, and security concerns vary from case to case. They need to be taken into account in seeking viable solutions.

This practical political approach seems to bypass the normative and legal effect of the right to self-determination. But ignoring that right may not be quite practical or wise in view of its recognition in law and its powerful appeal in actuality. Moreover, a regulative principle is important if the international community is to avoid the extreme fragmentation threatened by the potential demands of numerous ethnic, religious, and linguistic communities for international status.

At present, the international law of self-determination contains two major principles. One recognizes the human right of each people to self-determination—that is, to choose independence or autonomy.[67] It is similar to other human rights: an entitlement imposed on the territorial state. The second principle, asserted with equal force in UN declarations, affirms the territorial integrity of national states.[68] This principle may appear incompatible with the first, but they can be reconciled by considering the second as an affirmation of the basic prohibition against intervention and particularly against coercive intervention in support of separatist movements in other states. On this interpretation, the right of a people to self-determination is a human right, but foreign states may not forcibly intervene to support secession against the territorial sovereign.

However, these principles of self-determination do not provide a regulative norm to determine which peoples are entitled to self-determination. The extraordinary influx of new member states in the UN indicates that no general normative criterion has been applied and that the actual test is simply the new regime's effective control over territory. This offers little normative guidance and leaves the UN door open for any self-defined "nation" to claim sovereign rights based on the universal right of self-determination. At the same time, the spread of micronationalism has highlighted the danger of sovereignty "on demand." Very few states have ethnic homogeneity, and it has been estimated that at least 2,000 self-conscious ethnic communities exist. To recognize a right of secession by all such communities would be totally disruptive of peace and security.

The question then remains whether states can develop a consensus on standards for determining which people or communities are entitled to independence, allowing secession for peoples demanding such status. The following criteria find support in UN declarations and practice and in the views of scholars:[69]

1. The claimant community should have an identity distinct from the rest of the country and inhabit a region that largely supports separation.

2. The community has been subjected to a pattern of systematic political or economic discrimination.
3. The central regime has rejected reasonable proposals for autonomy and minority rights of the claimant community.

Other criteria have been proposed that are more controversial. One is that the secession would not be likely to result in armed conflict between the old and new states or generally threaten international peace more. The implications of a rule of this kind may be far-reaching. A second criterion that may find support is that the seceding areas should not have a disproportionate share of the country's wealth; but this, too, will be contentious.

The solution to the phenomenon we have called micronationalism is not likely to come quickly or to be neatly packaged as new law. It is, however, a problem that affects a great number of countries and it has a salient impact on the maintenance of peace and security. In one way or another, it will be high on the international agenda.

The Deeper Roots of Conflict

A discussion of threats to peace would not be complete without some reference to the underlying causes of violence and insecurity. This is a vast subject, extensively treated in scholarly literature. Official declarations and rhetoric in international bodies have abundantly declaimed that peace and security cannot be ensured in the absence of the following conditions: economic and social progress, observance of basic human rights, respect for international law, and, broadly, the attainment of the major purposes enshrined in the UN Charter. These generalities have been commonplace for some decades, but there is reason to believe that they have acquired a fresh urgency at present.

The marked increase in violence within national units and across borders is a key factor in the current concern with the sources of unrest. In many countries, there is a sense of crisis in governance and social cohesion. The gap between generations appears greater than ever, unsettling expectations of progress. These sociopsychological factors are seen by many as linked to economic distress and "the growing disparity of rich and poor."[70] The unchecked population growth in many countries, the spread of drugs, and the perception (and reality) of ecological damage are relatively recent phenomena that exacerbate social tension. Migration, whether by displaced persons, victims of persecution, or so-called economic refugees, appears to evoke increased hostility and often outright violence.

It is fair to say that these phenomena are indications of deeply rooted instabilities likely to produce conflict and disorder. Advances in technology may help in some respects (e.g., increasing material goods and human skills), but they also may have a destabilizing effect (e.g., increasing dangerous weaponry and the opportunity for terrorism and other lawless activity).

The range and enormity of these underlying causes of insecurity indicate how difficult it will be for the main structures of authority—states, substate groups, and international institutions—to provide adequate stability. The end of the Cold War has reduced some dangers, but subsequent events have highlighted new tensions and menaces to peace. We cannot expect that these problems will be solved by merely recognizing them and preaching cooperation. But it is at least a large step forward to see the necessity of international action and a greater collective responsibility. The sphere of state sovereignty might then be diminished, but we can expect that a more secure world will strengthen the social cohesion of communities and add the freedom of individuals.

Notes

1. See M. Wight, *Systems of States* (London: Leicester University Press, 1977), 132–136.

2. *Ibid.*, 135; quotation of Aquinas is from *Summa Theologia.*

3. G. Mattingly, *Renaissance Diplomacy* (Baltimore: Penguin Books, 1955), 75–76, 144–145.

4. C. De Visscher, *Theory and Reality in Public International Law,* 2d ed., Corbett translation (Princeton: Princeton University Press, 1968), 31–32.

5. UN General Assembly Resolution 46/182 (1991).

6. See F. H. Hinsley, *Sovereignty,* 2d ed. (Cambridge, Mass.: Cambridge University Press, 1986), 153–155.

7. Article 21(3) of the Universal Declaration of Human Rights, UN General Assembly Resolution 217 (III 1948).

8. For example, countries occupied or annexed in World War II were not extinguished as states though they were governed by the conquering power. See J. Crawford, "Criteria for Statehood in International Law," *British Yearbook of International Law* 48 (1976–1977), 173–176.

9. See A. Nussbaum, *A Concise History of the Law of Nations* (New York: Macmillan, 1947), 66–68, 104–105.

10. See T. Nardin, *Law, Morality and the Relations of States* (Princeton: Princeton University Press, 1983), 45–46, 60–61.

11. See H. Lauterpacht, *The Function of Law in the International Community* (Oxford: Oxford University Press, 1933), 422–423; and M. Virally, *Panorama du droit international contemporain recueil des cours* (Hague Academy of International Law), Tome 183 (Dordrecht, The Netherlands: Nijhoff, 1983), 77–79.

12. See De Visscher, *Theory and Reality in Law,* 104–105, quoting Judge Anzillotti, "To States, nothing is more repugnant than the idea of exercising a power conceded to them by the international order."

13. International judicial tribunals have tended to treat sovereignty as the basic regulative principle, holding that states are free to take any action not prohibited by positive international law. This is often referred to as the "Lotus Case principle" based on a judgment of the Permanent Court of International Justice in 1927 (PCIJ Ser. A. No. 10). The present International Court of Justice has also tended to the same doctrinal principle in several decisions. See, for example, "North Sea

Continental Shelf Cases," *ICJ Reports* (1969), 23. For criticism of this view, see Lauterpacht, *Function of Law*, 94–96.

14. Hinsley, *Sovereignty*, 204.

15. See O. Schachter, *International Law in Theory and Practice* (Boston: Martinus Nijhoff, 1991), 35–38, on the "inductive science of law."

16. R. Higgins, "Derogations Under Human Rights Treaties," *British Yearbook of International Law* 48 (1976–1977), 281, 296–297.

17. F. Teson, *Humanitarian Intervention* (Dobbs Ferry, N.Y.: Transnational Publishers, 1987), 130–137.

18. Schachter, *International Law*, 124–126; L. Henkin, "The Use of Force: Law and US Policy," in *Right v. Might*, 2d ed. (New York: Council on Foreign Relations, 1991), 37–42.

19. T. Farer, "An Inquiry into the Legitimacy of Humanitarian Intervention," in L. Damrosch and D. Scheffer, eds., *Law and Force in the New International Order* (Boulder: Westview Press, 1991); and D. Scheffer, "Towards a Modern Doctrine of Humanitarian Intervention," *University of Toledo Law Review* 12 (1992), 253–293.

20. Schachter, *International Law*, 397–400, 407–408.

21. Such decisions have been required when rival claimants to governmental authority present themselves as entitled to represent a member state. The General Assembly has generally acted in such cases through its credentials procedure. It also adopted a general resolution stating that such cases "should be considered in the light of the Purposes and Principles of the Charter and the circumstances of each case," UN General Assembly Resolution 396 (V), 1950.

22. Schachter, *International Law*, 300–325.

23. *Ibid.*, 362–388. See also O. Schachter, "The Emergence of International Environmental Law," *Journal of International Affairs* 44(a) (1991), 457–493.

24. See UN publication *The United Nations and Disarmament, 1945–1985.*

25. See F. Kratochwil, P. Rohrlich, and H. Mahajan, *Peace and Disputed Sovereignty* (Lanham: University Press of America, 1985), 3–23; and R. Lapidoth, "Sovereignty in Transition," *Journal of International Affairs* 45(2) (1992), 325–345.

26. See O. Schachter, *Sharing the World's Resources* (New York: Columbia University Press, 1977), 64–83.

27. G. Triggs, ed., *The Antarctic Treaty Regime* (Cambridge, Mass.: Cambridge University Press, 1987)

28. See Kratochwil et al., *Peace and Disputed Sovereignty*, 51–58.

29. Article 56 of the UN Convention on the Law of the Sea, 1982. See W. Riphagen, "Some Reflections on Functional Sovereignty," *Netherlands Yearbook of International Law* 6 (1975), 121–165. Although the Convention of 1982 is not yet in force, its provisions on the exclusive economic zones and on navigation are accepted as customary law binding on all states.

30. See H. Hannum, *Autonomy, Sovereignty and Self-Determination* (Philadelphia: University of Pennsylvania Press, 1990).

31. See Kratochwil et al., *Peace and Disputed Sovereignty*, 130–131.

32. See N. Padelford, *International Law and Diplomacy in the Spanish Civil Strife* (Princeton: Princeton University Press, 1939).

33. Alabama Claims Arbitration 1892. See J. G. Wetter, *The International Arbitral Process* 1 (Dobbs Ferry, N.Y.: Oceana Publishers, 1979), 27–57.

34. Case Concerning Military and Paramilitary Activities in and Against Nicaragua, Merits, *ICJ Reports* (1986), 14.

35. *Ibid.*

36. See T. Franck and N. Rodley, "After Bangladesh," *American Journal of International Law* 67 (1973), 275.

37. UN Security Council Resolution 688 (April 5, 1991). The resolution "insists" that Iraq allow immediate access by all humanitarian organizations to all those in need of assistance in all parts of Iraq.

38. See O. Schachter, "United Nations Law in the Gulf Conflict," *American Journal of International Law* 85 (1991), 452, 468–469.

39. See D. Scheffer, "Towards a Modern Doctrine," 274, n. 80.

40. See Weller, "The International Response to the Dissolution of Yugoslavia," *American Journal of International Law* 86 (1992), 569.

41. UN Security Council Resolution 282 (1970).

42. *The Economist* (March 12, 1988), 13.

43. C. G. Widstrand, ed., *African Boundary Problems* (Uppsala, Sweden: Institute of African Studies, 1969).

44. See Kratochwil et al., *Peace and Disputed Sovereignty,* 130.

45. F. Teson, book review, *American Journal of International Law* 81 (1987), 558–559. See also D. Kinney, *National Interest, National Honor: The Diplomacy of the Falklands Crisis* (New York: Praeger, 1989), 61–71.

46. See H. Young, *The Iron Lady: Margaret Thatcher* (New York: Noonday Press, 1989), 279–288, and M. Charlton, *The Little Platoon: Diplomacy and the Falkland Dispute* (New York, Oxford: B. Blackwell, 1989), 76–98.

47. See B. Davidson, *The Black Man's Burden: Africa and the Curse of the Nation State* (New York: Times Books, 1992).

48. See J. Starr, "Water Wars," *Foreign Policy* 82 (1991), 17–36.

49. *Ibid.,* 21. The Egyptian minister quoted is Boutros Boutros-Ghali, then Minister of State.

50. See n. 24.

51. Quoted in M. Howard, *The Lessons of History* (New Haven: Yale University Press, 1991), 166.

52. UN Security Council Resolution 687 (1991). The safeguards system of the International Atomic Energy Agency and the Nuclear Nonproliferation Treaty are the major international instruments for limiting the spread of nuclear weapons. An optimistic recent study is D. Fischer, *Stopping the Spread of Nuclear Weapons* (New York: Routledge Publishers, 1992).

53. Note by the President of the Security Council, UN document S/23500 (January 31, 1992).

54. See C. Greenwood, "International Law and the United States Air Operation Against Libya," *West Virginia Law Review* 89 (1986–1987), 911 et seq.; and A. Sofaer, "Terrorism and the Law," *Foreign Affairs* 69 (1986), 921.

55. UN Security Council Resolution 748 (1992) imposed mandatory trade and communication sanctions against Libya until Libya surrendered named individuals accused of bombing a civilian aircraft to concerned governments for prosecution and also committed itself to cease all forms of assistance to terrorist groups.

56. The UN General Assembly Declaration on Principles of International Law adopted unanimously in 1970 condemns intervention as illegal and, specifically, refers to subversive activities in that connection. General Assembly Resolution 2625 (XXV) (1970). See also n. 34, 107–108, 123–125.

57. *Ibid.,* 126–127.

58. See M. Bazyler, "Reexamining the Doctrine of Humanitarian Intervention," *Stanford Law Journal* 23 (Stanford: Stanford University Press, 1987).

59. Security Council Resolution 752 (1992).

60. See F. R. Teson, "The Kantian Theory of International Law," *Columbia Law Review* 92, no. 1 (1992), 74–81.

61. M. W. Doyle, "Liberalism and World Politics," *American Political Science Review* 80 (1986), 1151.

62. *Thucydides, Book VI* (The War in Sicily), par. 24 in M. I. Finley, *Greek Historians* (New York: Viking Portable, 1960), 311–312.

63. UN Secretary-General report, "An Agenda for Peace," UN document A/47/277, S/24111, par. 59 (June 17, 1992).

64. Howard, *Lessons of History,* 170.

65. "An Agenda for Peace," par. 11.

66. *Ibid.,* par. 17.

67. The UN Declaration on Principles of International Law General Assembly Resolution 2625 (XXV) (1970) expressly declares, "The establishment of a sovereign and independent State, the free association or integration with an independent State or the emergence into any other political status freely determined by a people constitute modes of implementing the right of self-determination by that people."

68. The UN Declaration (see n. 67) also includes the following paragraph, "Nothing in the foregoing paragraphs shall be construed as authorizing or encouraging any action which would dismember or impair, totally or in part, the territorial integrity or political unity of sovereign and independent States conducting themselves in compliance with the principle of equal rights and self-determination of peoples as described above and thus possessed of a government representing the whole people belonging to the territory without distinction as to race, creed or colour. Every State shall refrain from any action aimed at the partial or total disruption of the national unity and territorial integrity of any other State or country."

69. For a helpful discussion of normative criteria for entitlement to secession, see A. Heraclides, "Secession, Self-Determination and Nonintervention," *Journal of International Affairs* 45, no. 2 (Winter 1992), 399–420. For more extensive analysis, see A. Buchanan, *Secession* (Boulder: Westview Press, 1991); and L. Buchheit, *Secession: The Legitimacy of Self-Determination* (New Haven: Yale University Press, 1978).

70. See "An Agenda for Peace," par. 13.

■ 3 ■

Squaring the Circle: Collective Security in a System of States

MOHAMMED AYOOB

The most appropriate way to address the issue of the relevance of the concept and ideal of collective security to the contemporary international system is to pose and attempt to answer two important definitional questions:

1. What do we understand by the concept of the international system as it is currently organized?
2. What do we mean by collective security?

Then, two other questions extremely relevant to the ongoing discussion about collective security need to be posed and answered:

3. Why has the idea of collective security once again come to preoccupy the minds and absorb so much of the energies of both international statespersons and political analysts?
4. Given the inequality in the distribution of power within the international system, can and should the idea of collective security be made operational?

This chapter will attempt to answer these four questions.

The International System

When analyzing the contemporary international system, it is clear that this system is composed primarily of political communities called states, which are juridically sovereign and legally equal. Although the terms *sovereignty* and *equality* need to be qualified—the first because of the economic and technological permeability of the state and the second because of the existence of a hierarchy of powers—there is enough residual strength left in the concept of the sovereign state for one to argue successfully that the state continues to be the major organizing principle of international political life.

Even a writer as skeptical of the continuing efficacy of the sovereign state as Joseph Camilleri has been forced to admit that in the contemporary world there is, "on the one hand, a growing web of international interdependencies and, on the other, increased centralization of national institutions and decision-making processes. . . . The centralization of state power goes hand in hand with the internationalization of economic activity."[1] Robert Gilpin has countered the argument that economic interdependence and the proliferation of transnational corporations have reduced the importance of politics and of the primary political institution, the state, by pointing out that

> politics determines the framework of economic activity and channels it in directions which tend to serve the political objectives of dominant political groups and organizations. Throughout history each successive hegemonic power has organized economic space in terms of its own interests and purposes. . . . [T]ransnational economic processes are not unique to our own age and . . . the pattern of international economic activity reflects the global balance of economic and military power.[2]

A strong argument can, in fact, be made that statehood is a more popular commodity today than ever before. Compared with the 25 or so full members of the (European) international system in 1900 and the 50 or so at the end of World War II, there are approximately 175 members of the international system today, with a few more waiting in the wings either to successfully demonstrate their political independence or to gain the international recognition that they already consider their due. The large majority of the new members of the international system belongs to the Third World, and these members value their autonomy of action (however circumscribed in practice) far too much to relinquish their newly acquired statehood.[3] The most recent entrants into the system are beneficiaries of the breakup of the Soviet empire and are, therefore, also expected to guard their newly acquired sovereignty jealously.

Additionally, technological advances and the increasing complexity of economic interactions have augmented the role of the state in the economic sphere. This is particularly true of the Third World, where the state is often both the major engine of economic growth and the major dispenser of acutely scarce resources. Nowhere has this proved more true than in the case of the East Asian NICs, especially Taiwan and South Korea, where the state by a judicious mixture of encouragement, cajoling, and systematic pressure has propelled the economies of these countries in directions mapped out by state elites.[4]

The frequent meetings of the political leaders of the major industrialized countries, in the form of the G7, to discuss salient problems of the international economy and evolve strategies to address and manage these problems in light of their individual and collective interests, are clear indications of the actual and potential interventionist capabilities of the industrialized states in the international economic sphere. Furthermore, the current economic debate among the major industrial powers demonstrates mercantilist attitudes more overtly than had been the case in the recent past when the existence of a universally recognized and benign hegemonic economic power and prospects of uninterrupted and unilinear economic growth had allowed mercantilist tendencies to be shrouded in the rhetoric of the free liberal market.[5]

The decline of US economic hegemony and the prevailing uncertainties in the industrialized world regarding uninterrupted economic growth can be expected to increase rather than reduce state interventionist policies in the economic sphere within the industrialized world. Stephen Krasner captures the complexity of the international economic system and the role of the state (especially of the major economic powers) within it in an extraordinarily insightful manner in concluding that

> the structure of international trade changes in fits and starts; it does not flow smoothly with the redistribution of potential state power. Nevertheless, it is the power and policies of states that create order where there would otherwise be chaos or at best a Lockian state of nature. The existence of various transnational, multinational, transgovernmental, and other nonstate actors that have riveted scholarly attention in recent years can only be understood within the context of a broader structure that ultimately rests upon the power and interests of states, shackled though they may be by the societal consequences of their own past decisions.[6]

Despite the proliferation, therefore, of transnational and nonstate actors during the last several decades, one would still be correct in arguing that the international system as a whole and the international political system in particular are still essentially centered around states that continue to be the primary actors within that system. Arguments for impending systemic change often underestimate much of this evidence in favor of overdrawn scenarios of turbulence and discontinuity and thereby end up drawing premature or distorted conclusions regarding the speed, if not the direction, of change in the contemporary international system.[7]

Collective Security Defined

Having established that the international system is still principally state-centric in character (and nowhere more so than in the sphere of political and military security, which forms the central concern of this chapter), I am now in a position to define collective security and distinguish it analytically from related but discrete concepts. The failure to make such distinctions has often led to a great deal of confusion in discussions about collective security, especially about the applicability of the concept and the appropriateness of the ideal to a system principally composed of juridically sovereign and legally equal entities called states.

"The principle of collective security," according to the definition of the term provided by Hedley Bull, "implies that international order should rest not on a balance of power, but on a preponderance of power wielded by a combination of states acting as the agents of international society as a whole that will deter challenges to the system or deal with them if they occur."[8] Similarly, Stanley Hoffmann, in a somewhat more pointed definition of the term, has argued that the notion of collective security is one "in which all or most states will come to the rescue of a state that is the victim of aggression and punish the wrongdoers through sanctions or even force."[9] The working definition of collective security provided by Leon Gordenker and Thomas G. Weiss echoes the definition provided by Hoffmann, in that the concept of collective security revolves around the central idea that "governments of all states would join together to prevent any of their number from using coercion to gain advantage over the rest."

These definitions taken together make several things very explicit. Above all, they make clear what is not covered by the idea of collective security. First, collective security does not mean peacekeeping. Peacekeeping operations are undertaken only when parties to a conflict agree that UN (or other multinational) observers or peacekeeping forces should be deployed to separate warring states or factions or generally to keep the peace in potentially conflict-prone areas. Often such agreement requires the use of persuasion, sometimes arm-twisting, either by UN representatives or by interested great powers. Nonetheless, peacekeeping activities cannot be initiated unless parties to conflicts explicitly agree to the introduction of UN (or multinational) observers or other forces. This assertion is borne out by case studies of peacekeeping operations in as diverse contexts as Kashmir, the Middle East, Cyprus, Indochina, and Yugoslavia.

An enterprise related to peacekeeping that has become quite fashionable in the last three or four years is the use of the UN Secretary-General's office for the provision of mediation or good offices, or "peacemaking," in the settlement of regional disputes. Despite the recent spate of qualified successes that such efforts have achieved with the winding down of the Cold War, these efforts cannot be classified as falling within the ambit of collective security. Like peacekeeping operations, these efforts, in the final analysis, are dependent for their success, or even their initiation, on the voluntary acceptance of such good offices by the parties engaged in conflicts. They do not have the coercive sanction of the international community behind them.

Second, collective security does not mean alliance-building, which is, rather, despite the rhetoric of interested parties desirous of selling alliance systems in the garb of collective security, *selective* security. At best, alliances provide security to member states from threats emanating from sources outside particular alliance systems. At worst, they contribute to political and military polarization and thereby heighten the sense of insecurity either regionally or globally or both. In other words, alliances are blocs usually established to confront other blocs politically and militarily.

Third, collective security has no demonstrated positive correlation with interdependence. In fact, interdependence does not necessarily contribute to collective or any other form of security. Interdependence, especially if it is asymmetrical in character (as is most interdependence), is as often the cause of conflict between states and groups of states as it is a contributor to cooperative interstate relationships. Asymmetrical interdependence is a potential contributor to conflict because asymmetries "are most likely to provide sources of influence for actors in their dealings with one another. Less dependent actors can often use the interdependent relationship as a source of power in bargaining over an issue and perhaps to affect other issues."[10] Such asymmetries can, therefore, be the cause for conflict especially if the weaker party feels that it has been pushed too far and its vital interests face the threat of significant erosion, if not outright extinction.

Recent concerns with problems of global management, above all of ecological matters, have been touted by members of the international system as major reasons for collective action. Even where imperative, such action should not be equated with collective security. International cooperation for the management of nonsecurity problems or issues is not new. International regimes to manage the flow of international communication and travel (e.g., through the Universal Postal Union and the International Civil Aviation Organization) have long been in place. Similarly, the international regime for the exploration of Antarctica without despoliation has been evolving. An international regime to manage issues relating to the global commons, while temporarily stalled as a result of US unwillingness to accept the international consensus on this issue, is all but in place through the medium of the Law of the Sea Convention.

There is no reason why ecological problems, like those of ozone depletion, cannot be similarly managed through the construction of international regimes along with the natural proclivity of states (especially of the great powers) to compete with each other in the political-military and economic spheres. Such international regimes may help to mellow strategic and economic competition but cannot aspire to replace the latter.

Daniel Deudney, a sympathetic advocate of global ecological management, has explicitly warned against confusing the ecological and security realms and has concluded that, while

the degradation of the natural environment upon which human well-being depends is a challenge of far-reaching significance for human societies every-

> where . . . this challenge has little to do with the national-security-from-vio-
> lence problem that continues to plague human political life. . . . The pervasive
> recourse to national security paradigms to conceptualize the environmental
> problem represents a profound and disturbing failure of imagination and politi-
> cal awareness.[11]

Global environmentalism is an arena of action distinct from the sphere of
collective (or any other form of) security that is intimately linked with the
political and military balance of power.

Collective security implies several notions that are very different from
the concepts and issues discussed above. In particular, if one goes by Bull's
definition, collective security must consist of four essential elements: (1)
the exercise of "preponderance of power" (2) by a "combination of states"
(3) acting as "agents of international society" (4) in order to maintain
"international order." In essence, it suggests the idea of the legitimate
enforcement of the will of the international community by coercion where
necessary against recalcitrant states. One hopes that this careful scrutiny of
the definition of collective security will help to clarify much of the confusion that has come to surround the concept and also to set the stage for a
systematic analysis of its relevance to the evolving international situation.
But before we begin such an analysis, we need to look at the reasons why
the idea of collective security has come to enjoy such a remarkable revival
in the last few years.

Revival of the Collective Security Idea

International relations during the twentieth century have reflected the international community's preoccupation with the notion that collective security
increases dramatically when the global balance of power is in radical transformation, when the contours of a new balance are blurred, and, therefore,
when the level of uncertainty regarding the nature of the future balance as
well as its stability is high. In this fluid context, collective security appears
to statespersons and analysts alike as the panacea for the multiple insecuri-
ties afflicting the international system.

This assertion is borne out by studies of the periods immediately following the end of each of the world wars. The immediate postwar years led
not only to the flowering of collective security discourse but also to the
founding of the League of Nations and the UN. These two experiments in
international organization were explicitly based on the notion of collective
security especially against the aggressors (or, to be more exact, the vanquished) of the last major conflict. In both cases the collective security
mechanisms of the Covenant and of the Charter could not become operational, except very partially and in isolated cases. New balances of power
came to dominate the international political landscape and soon rendered

them marginal, if not totally irrelevant, to the then-prevailing political and military status quos.

As in 1918–1919 and 1945–1946 as a result of the end of the world wars, today the old balance of power and, therefore, the political and military certainties that accompanied it have been transformed dramatically because of the termination of the Cold War. The collapse of Moscow's sphere of influence in Eastern Europe and the unraveling of the Soviet Union itself have removed the second pole of power in what had been commonly assumed to be a bipolar global balance and has given rise to what Charles Krauthammer has termed America's "unipolar moment."[12] It is no wonder, therefore, that in this situation there should once again be a fixation with the notion of collective security among both the practitioners and analysts of world politics.

However, the current situation is unique in that the international balance of power has not been changed as a result of a major war among the world's great powers or even as a result of the threat of great-power conflict. In fact, the nuclear revolution in weaponry has effectively ruled out war between the superpowers (as distinct from wars by proxy in the Third World) as an instrument of state policy for the last four decades. The current fluid situation is the result of the unilateral collapse (or, more appropriately, contraction) of one of the superpowers under the weight of its own economic and political problems that resulted in a system overload of gigantic proportions.

This does not mean that the Russian Republic (the successor to the Soviet Union) has been rendered totally marginal in strategic terms, as the vanquished powers were at least for a while after the two world wars. It is still in control of much of the Soviet territory and resources as well as almost all of the Soviet nuclear arsenal. Furthermore, despite recent arms reduction agreements, the Russian Republic has the continuing capacity to inflict unacceptable damage on the United States in case of a war between the two countries. In a narrow sense, therefore, strategic bipolarity is still a fact of international life, and this is demonstrated by the continuing concern in Washington and Moscow with nuclear arms control.

What has changed is the explicitly political dimension of the balance of power, namely the capability and, even more, the will to project power globally in order to protect and enhance worldwide interests. It is in this dimension of power that first the Soviet Union under Gorbachev and then the Russian Republic have retrenched dramatically. This political, as opposed to the narrowly defined strategic, retrenchment has provided the opportunity for the United States to project its image as the only superpower in the international system—an image considerably augmented by the recent Gulf War and the continuing crusade against Iraq.

An analysis of the US-led war against Iraq is, consequently, necessary to provide the answer to the question: What is the connection between the unipolar moment and the current preoccupation of statespersons and analysts with collective security? The Gulf War demonstrated the efficacy, however temporary, of the rhetoric of collective security, especially as embodied in President Bush's "new world order" pronouncements, as an instrument through which the political unipolarity enjoyed by the United States in the context of the Soviet Union's imminent demise could be legitimized. In fact, one could argue that the significance of this rhetoric went beyond US objectives in the Gulf War and that it was deliberately employed to extend the duration of the unipolar moment by persuading the international community to underwrite a world order largely manufactured in Washington principally to serve US interests. In other words, it could be seen as an exercise in promoting US hegemony under UN auspices.

The way in which the UN was cajoled into endorsing objectives and strategies before, during, and after the war with Iraq provided adequate proof that Washington was using the UN to achieve its own objectives in the Gulf under the pretext of building a new world order. The most important of these objectives was to prevent a single major Arab state (especially one, like Iraq, that could become a pole of attraction for radical Arab nationalists around the region) from controlling, directly or indirectly, the vast exportable oil resources of the Arab world of the Gulf and thereby dominating the process that determined oil prices, production levels, and the direction of oil exports. From Washington's point of view, this would have been a worst-case scenario, especially because future rounds of conflict between Israel (the major recipient of military aid and Washington's leading Middle Eastern ally) and one or more Arab parties could not be ruled out in the absence of a resolution of the Palestinian problem. The possibility of such a scenario, with Iraq dominating the oil resources of the Gulf at a time of Arab-Israeli war, was enough to make the Arab oil embargo of 1973 pale by comparison.

This reading of US objectives has been corroborated by Washington's insistence after the war that Iraq's war-making capabilities be decimated so totally that Baghdad is prevented from attempting to dominate the Arab littoral of the oil-rich Gulf for the next half century. This objective is now being achieved in the guise of implementing UN resolutions demanding the destruction of all facilities remotely connected with Iraq's future capability to launch a major war. These resolutions have resulted in the violation of state sovereignty, in this case that of Iraq, to an extent unprecedented since the occupation of Germany and Japan at the end of World War II.

The Iraqi violation of Kuwait's sovereignty provided a considerable degree of legitimacy for US actions, especially since it reminded most Third World states of their own multiple vulnerabilities in the face of internal and external challenges to their juridical sovereignty. Even more important, however, was the universal perception that, after the contraction of Soviet commitments and in the context of the Soviet Union's impending demise, the United States was the only superpower left in the international system. It was further perceived that it would be unwise to defy Washington on a matter that the latter considered to be of vital concern to itself at a time when it was at the zenith of its power after having finally "won" the Cold War. This perception was shared in equal measure by members of the Western alliance (some of whom had reservations about the Gulf venture), by the traditionally nonaligned states of the Third World, and even by China, which wanted to rebuild its bridges with the United States that had been damaged as a result of the Tiananmen Square massacre. It was the fortuitous convergence of these perceptions both within and outside the UN that allowed the US-led war against Iraq to be portrayed as a success of a revitalized UN that was once again in a position to fulfill its original collective security mission.

However, discerning observers quickly realized that the war against Iraq was conducted in the name of the UN but not by the UN. Command and control of operations rested securely in the hands of the United States and, to a much lesser extent, its allies that also continued to set the military and political objectives of the war. The UN was reduced to the role of an endorsement agency that merely legitimized the military venture against Iraq without allowing the international community any major input into the direction of the war, which was extolled as an example of collective security at work.

This realization led two scholars to characterize the conduct of the war against Iraq as "a procedure in which action is taken on behalf of the [Security] council but without any council control over the nature, timing or extent of the action." The same scholars asserted further that "none of the 12 Security Council resolutions called for eliminating Iraq's war-making capability or deposing Saddam Hussein. But the former clearly became a goal of some coalition members, and the latter was widely suspected." They further raised the pertinent question: "In any operation, if the Security Council has asserted no control over the military action authorized, will it be possible for it to assert control over the terms of peace?"[13] If the Gulf War is the prime example of collective security and is the trendsetter in international enforcement action for the post–Cold War era, a legitimate question arises as to whether the notion of collective security has not been stretched to such lengths as to render it meaningless.

The Future of Collective Security

What then does the Gulf War convey about the future of collective security as a mechanism for the maintenance of international order? If it means, to quote Theodore Draper, that "the UN was used both to get into the war and to get out of it,"[14] but without the world body and the international community exercising control on the enterprise, then to term it an example of collective security and to deduce that collective security's time has come demonstrates less than complete comprehension both of the basic character of that war and of the essential nature of collective security.

Furthermore, if a major power was able to appropriate the authority to define the content of collective security on behalf of the international community and to implement its military strategy without any supervision (let alone control) on the part of the UN, then the question arises whether it is possible to make the idea of collective security successfully operational in an international context marked by both tremendous inequalities in the distribution of power and the total concentration of military and political decisionmaking at the national level. The answer has to be negative at the level of analysis immediately relevant to the post–Gulf War context as well as at the deeper level related to long-term structural factors. The United States will not be easily able to repeat its Gulf success elsewhere because the unique combination of two crucial elements in the run-up to the Gulf War cannot be replicated unless the same exceptional circumstances come to prevail once again in a future crisis.

The first element was the clear perception in Washington that vital interests were at stake, which made military action imperative to reverse Iraq's annexation of Kuwait. Despite the United States's current lone superpower status, the financial and domestic political constraints on resources and responsibilities would seem to rule out an open-ended commitment to the indiscriminate deployment of US forces around the world to reverse aggression by a powerful regional state against a weaker neighbor. Even in 1990 the US response to the Indian annexation of Bhutan or an Indonesian attack on Papua New Guinea would have been markedly different from its response to Iraq's move into Kuwait.

Moreover, even if there is the perception in Washington that major strategic and economic interests are involved in a future hypothetical instance comparable to the Iraqi invasion of Kuwait, it is unlikely that the president will receive as free a hand, as he did in 1990, to deploy massive US troops to a Third World region, not excluding the Gulf and the Middle East. Financial costs, which were inadequately comprehended at the beginning of the Kuwait crisis and were compensated by generous payments from Japan and Germany, are expected to play a strong part in any future decision. More rigorous cost-benefit analyses will be made with the clear understanding that Germany and Japan may be either unwilling or unable, or both, to foot such bills for future US-led ventures.[15]

The second element in the run-up to the Gulf War was the coincidence of the crisis with the United States's ascension to unipolar status. The suddenness of the Soviet collapse (first of will and then of structure) had left the international community too astounded, and too impressed by what was perceived as the US victory in the Cold War, for important countries to fashion their responses to the Gulf crisis independently of this dramatic transformation of the global balance of power. Many were numbed into inaction, and several others decided that there was no alternative but to comply with US wishes on the Iraq-Kuwait episode. Several votes in the UN Security Council during the Gulf crisis, especially those cast by Third World members, can be explained in light of this factor. Now that the world has had time to adjust to the changed balance of power and has taken stock of US strengths and weaknesses (especially that the United States would have been very hard put to undertake such a colossal military mission without Japanese and German, as well as Saudi and Kuwaiti, financial subsidies), it would be extremely difficult for the United States to construct the sort of international consensus that existed during the Gulf crisis, which helped give international legitimacy to US objectives and strategies vis-à-vis Iraq.

The problems of replicating international enforcement action necessary for the success of a collective security strategy à la the Gulf War are likely to be even more difficult if we analyze them at the level of structural forces that underpin the contemporary international system. These structural imperatives can be best analyzed in the context of three likely scenarios based on the end of the Cold War (and the subsequent bipolar balance of power), which would be relevant to projected attempts at collective security.

The first scenario would be the reemergence of a multipolar world with three or four major centers of power. These centers would be in possession of nuclear weapons either overtly or in terms of their generally acknowledged technological capacity to do so, and they would compete for power and influence in the international system. Such a multipolar world has been clearly in existence for the last two decades in the economic sphere. What is novel is that it seems to be in the process of materializing in the political arena as well. The flexing of the German political muscle in relation to Eastern European issues, particularly those related to the breakup of Yugoslavia and the disintegration of the Soviet Union, is but an early indication of the reassertion of German primacy in central and eastern, if not western, Europe. It is no coincidence that major Western European powers and the United States and Russia have evinced great interest in the retention of NATO, this time as an instrument to control growing German power and influence in Europe and abroad.[16]

At the other end of the globe, the increasingly acrimonious trade dispute between the United States and Japan can be expected to have significant fallout on the explicitly political and military dimensions of Japanese foreign policy. Normalization of Russian-Japanese relations and a settlement of the northern islands issue will further free Tokyo from its security dependence on the United States and can be expected to augment Japanese inclinations toward strategic and political autonomy.[17] Such a projected fracturing of the international power establishment can be expected to provide Russia, already in control of the overwhelming proportion of Soviet nuclear and missile capabilities, with greater room for political and economic maneuver and help in Moscow's reemergence as a major international player in its own right.

A multipolar world comprising three or four major political-military centers of power, more or less corresponding to the major economic centers of power and keeping in check the hegemonic tendencies of each of them, cannot be ruled out in the next century. One can argue, therefore, that despite the best efforts of the Pentagon,[18] the international system is headed toward another era of multipolarity and that the bipolarity of the post–World War II epoch was merely an aberration in the midst of a continuing saga of multipolar balances. A major problem hindering the operation of a collective security system in such a multipolar world would be the question of defining aggression and identifying the aggressor in every interstate war. As is well known, it is very difficult in most cases to define aggression because of the complexity of the conflict-initiation process and differing perceptions of who was responsible for starting a particular war. A genuinely multipolar world would make the determination of aggression and of the aggressor even more difficult as the divergent interests of major powers would dictate different interpretations of the same events. In such a multipolar world, therefore, collective security is unlikely to remain at the top of any major power's international agenda.

The second likely post–Cold War scenario may turn out to be somewhat more favorable to one version of collective security. This scenario has been described best by Barry Buzan as unipolarized multipolarity, "multipolar in the sense that several independent great powers are in play, but unipolarized in the sense that there is a single dominant coalition governing international relations."[19] Such a multipolar but unipolarized system, dominated collectively by the great military-industrial powers and led by the United States,[20] may find itself in a position occasionally to use the collective security mechanism provided in the UN Charter. These would be suitably adapted to the interests and circumstances of the dominant coalition against recalcitrant Third World states that may appear to be threatening the strategic and vital economic interests of the industrialized world.

Much would depend, however, on the future composition of the Security Council (including the induction of new permanent members) and on the attitudes adopted by Russia and China toward such ventures. Third World reactions are bound to be extremely critical, if not fundamentally hostile, compared with their largely pliant behavior during the war against Iraq. This would be particularly so because of the overtly discriminatory nature of international enforcement action, which would have to exempt the major veto-wielding powers and their allies from international chastisement. In short, it will be viewed as a new form of collective imperialism.

Recourse to humanitarian justifications for international intervention, as in the case of the Kurds in Iraq following the Gulf War, would be greatly resented by Third World states, above all because the logic of humanitarian intervention runs directly counter to the imperatives of state-making, defined as "primitive central state power accumulation,"[21] the primary political enterprise in which Third World countries are currently engaged.[22] The dominant powers could persist in collective enforcement and international intervention selectively, despite the opposition of the majority of Third World states (a majority of the membership of the international system). However, such actions, even if ostensibly termed "collective security," would lose much of their legitimacy and could, in fact, seriously erode the idea of international society itself.

In the context of the current contrived enthusiasm about collective security, one needs to emphasize the danger that attempts to enforce selectively the idea of collective security (often in murky and contested situations in the Third World and possibly in Eastern Europe and certain regions of the former USSR) may pose to the notion of international society. Such a society undergirds the routinely pacific interactions, symbolized above all by economic and political exchanges in the form of trade and diplomacy, among states. These routine interactions form the overwhelming proportion of all interactions within the international system and are the fundamental hallmarks of the existence of international order.

The concept of international society is integral to any framework devised for the maintenance of international order and incorporates the notion of common interests and common values among members of the international system. These shared values and interests among states are, in turn, essential prerequisites for them to "form a society in the sense that they conceive themselves to be bound by a common set of rules in their relations with one another, and share in the working of common institutions. . . . An international society . . . presupposes an international system, but an international system may exist that is not an international society."[23] An international system that is not a society, or is so in very diluted form, will obviously suffer from greater disorder and lack of legitimacy than one that approximates the idea of international society more closely. Playing out the second scenario described above would be likely to decrease drastically the societal component of the international system and, therefore, contribute to greater anarchy in interstate relations.

Neither of the above scenarios rules out the operation of international organizations as institutions of international society in matters relating to international peace and security. However, the first scenario more than the second assumes that international organizations, especially the UN Security Council, will be subject to the logic of state sovereignty and will, therefore, concentrate on the functions prescribed for it in Chapter VI rather than Chapter VII of the UN Charter. The second scenario, because of its relative ambivalence regarding the use of collective security instruments provided under Chapter VII, is much more contingent than the first for its success upon the coordination of policies and interests among the major, and especially veto-wielding, powers. Such coordination would, in fact, be essential for the creation of an international security directorate as envisaged by this scenario. It is the difficulty, if not the impossibility, of continuing security coordination among the major powers over the long haul that is likely to form the Achilles' heel of unipolarized multipolarity.[24]

A third scenario would be based on radically strengthening the UN system, especially as it pertains to collective security. For such a scenario to become operational, two major forms of sacrifice on the part of member states, especially on the part of the major powers, would be essential: (1) the surrender to a UN decisionmaking body, subject to some modified version of majority control, of important aspects of national decisionmaking in the sphere of security and the use of force and (2) the voluntary or enforced abdication on the part of the permanent members of the right to veto enforcement action against themselves.

It is extremely doubtful if this version of collective security will be acceptable to the major powers in the international system, even if most of the weaker states agree to sacrifice a large proportion of their sovereignty to achieve a greater degree of security that a strengthened UN system may be able to provide. For great powers to sacrifice their autonomy of decisionmaking in the security sphere and hand over segments of their command, control, communications, and intelligence (C^3I) functions to an international body responsive to majority opinion in the international system would be tantamount to committing political and military suicide.

However, in the extremely unlikely event that great powers genuinely agree to transfer important portions of their C^3I functions to an international security agency and a collective mechanism is put in place to punish aggressor states in the context of interstate conflicts, it will still leave the majority of conflicts around the world outside the purview of this collective security system. If the post–World War II experience is any guide, most conflicts will continue to take place in the Third World. Most of these conflicts have not been, and are not expected to be, clear-cut interstate wars that provide the basis for much of the theoretical literature on war in the international system and, therefore, determine the nature and definition of the collective security enterprise.

The overwhelming number of conflicts in the international system since 1945 have occurred in the Third World and have been, to quote K. J. Holsti, "a ubiquitous corollary of the birth, formation, and fracturing of Third World states."[25] A majority of these conflicts has been intrastate, although several have also acquired an interstate dimension and become internationalized civil wars. If the civil war in Yugoslavia is any indication of things to come, the incidence of such conflicts is likely to increase following the unraveling of the Soviet Union and the drastic change in the status quo in Eastern Europe. Collective security, as envisaged by the UN Charter and by the proponents of a strengthened collective security system, does not have, and will not have, much relevance to these categories of wars that will provide the bulk of armed conflicts well into the next century.

Furthermore, if, as envisaged in the third scenario, the great powers agree to surrender sovereign control over decisions of war and peace to an international body over which they would have at best imperfect control and at worst limited influence, they would be signing the death warrant of the system of states as presently constituted. Such a surrender of authority would signal a fundamental transformation of the international system, which major powers, and indeed other states, would be loathe to contemplate short of a cataclysm threatening human survival. If the system of states was able to survive the nuclear and thermonuclear revolutions, as well as the proliferation of intercontinental ballistic missiles and spy satellites, without undergoing a major transmutation, there is no reason to believe that its members (especially its more powerful members) would be willing to sacrifice the essence of political and military sovereignty at the relatively abstract and untried altar of collective security.

We are, therefore, left with the first two scenarios of a future world order. The first, which envisages competing great powers, will be able to restore a substantial degree of equilibrium to the international system while still providing weaker states with a considerable degree of political and military autonomy in the context of continuing but managed great-power rivalry. It may be more difficult to sustain global equilibrium under the second scenario of unipolarized multipolarity because of the contradiction built into the scenario and, indeed, into the concept itself. However, if such an order does prove sustainable over the long run, it is bound seriously to circumscribe the political, military, and economic autonomy of the weaker members of the system—this may prove to be its greatest drawback. According to a Swahili aphorism, although the grass suffers when elephants fight, it suffers immeasurably more, in fact to the point of obliteration, when they make love.[26] As stated earlier, the naked political (in addition to the already prevailing economic) domination of the international system by a concert of major industrial-military powers for any length of time would be likely to detract from the legitimacy of the existing international order and, therefore, from the international consensus underpinning the notion of international society.

Both the likely scenarios presented here do not leave much room for the inclusion of collective security—defined as the use of legitimate preponderant power on behalf of the international community against recalcitrant states—as a principal component of a future world order. While in the first scenario it would be next to impossible to achieve the goal of preponderant power, in the second it would be almost as improbable to achieve the equally important objective of legitimate power necessary for the enforcement of the will of the international community.

This does not mean that leaders of major powers (and of some not-so-major powers) will not continue to pay verbal homage to the idea, and the ideal, of collective security. However, such verbal obeisance must not be equated with any tangible commitment to the translation of that ideal into reality. Collective security will continue to be a chimera as long as the essential features of the international system do not undergo fundamental metamorphosis. There is no reason to believe that the system is as yet ready for, or is in urgent need of, such a basic transformation.

Notes

1. Joseph A. Camilleri, "Rethinking Sovereignty in a Shrinking, Fragmented World," in R. B. J. Walker and Saul H. Mendlovitz, *Contending Sovereignties: Redefining Political Community* (Boulder: Lynne Rienner, 1990), 33, 38.

2. Robert Gilpin, "The Politics of Transnational Economic Relations," in Robert O. Keohane and Joseph S. Nye, Jr., *Transnational Relations and World Politics* (Cambridge, Mass.: Harvard University Press, 1971), 53, 55.

3. For a discussion of the Third World's place and role in the international system, see Mohammed Ayoob, "The Third World in the System of States: Acute Schizophrenia or Growing Pains?" *International Studies Quarterly* 33, no. 1 (March 1989), 67–79.

4. For details of this argument, see Robert Wade, *Governing the Market: Economic Theory and the Role of Government in East Asian Industrialization* (Princeton: Princeton University Press, 1990).

5. According to a recent UNDP estimate, 20 out of the leading 24 industrial countries are "now more protectionist than they were a decade ago." For details, see "Why the Poor Don't Catch Up," *The Economist* (April 25, 1992), 48.

6. Stephen D. Krasner, "State Power and the Structure of International Trade," *World Politics* 28, no. 3 (April 1976), 343.

7. For one example of this genre of writing, see James N. Rosenau, *Turbulence in World Politics: A Theory of Change and Continuity* (Princeton: Princeton University Press, 1990).

8. Hedley Bull, *The Anarchical Society: A Study of Order in World Politics* (New York: Columbia University Press, 1977), 239.

9. Stanley Hoffmann, "Delusions of World Order," *New York Review* 39, no. 7 (April 9, 1992), 38.

10. Robert O. Keohane and Joseph S. Nye, *Power and Interdependence: World Politics in Transition* (Boston: Little, Brown and Co., 1977), 11. For an interesting study of asymmetrical interdependence promoting conflicts of interests and policies, see Stephen D. Krasner, *Structural Conflict: The Third World Against Global Liberalism* (Berkeley: University of California Press, 1985).

11. Daniel Deudney, "The Case Against Linking Environmental Degradation and National Security," *Millennium: Journal of International Studies* 19, no. 3 (Winter 1990), 474.

12. Charles Krauthammer, "The Unipolar Moment," *Foreign Affairs* 70, no. 1, (1991), 23–33. To be fair to Krauthammer, I note here that he gives collective security short shrift by stating explicitly that "our best hope for safety in such times, as in difficult times past, is in American strength and will—the strength and will to

lead a unipolar world, *unashamedly laying down the rules of world order and being prepared to enforce them.*" (emphasis added), 33.

13. Bruce Russett and James S. Sutterlin, "The UN in a New World Order," *Foreign Affairs* 70, no. 2 (Spring 1991), 76–77.

14. Theodore Draper, "The True History of the Gulf War," *New York Review* 39, no. 3 (January 30, 1992), 45. Also, see Theodore Draper, "The Gulf War Reconsidered," *New York Review* 39, no. 1–2 (January 16, 1992), 46–53.

15. For a scathing attack on the United States' new "imperial" role in the guise of collective security, see Robert W. Tucker and David C. Hendrickson, *The Imperial Temptation: The New World Order and America's Purpose* (New York: Council on Foreign Relations Press, 1992).

16. For a perceptive prediction of the multipolar nature of the future balance of power, especially in Europe, see John J. Mearsheimer, "Back to the Future: Instability in Europe After the Cold War," in Sean M. Lynn-Jones, ed., *The Cold War and After: Prospects for Peace* (Cambridge, Mass.: MIT Press), 141–192.

17. For a major example of the increasing assertion of Japanese autonomy from the United States, see Shintaro Ishihara, *The Japan That Can Say No: Why Japan Will Be First Among Equals* (New York: Simon and Schuster, 1991). Karel von Wolferen, after a careful analysis of the Japanese power structure and its impact on Japanese policy toward the West in general, and the United States in particular, has come to the conclusion that "the [Japanese] phoenix appears stuck on a collision course," in Karel von Wolferen, *The Enigma of Japanese Power* (New York: Vintage Books, 1990), 407.

18. For the Pentagon's valiant effort to ensure the indefinite extension of the US unipolar moment, see details of the "Defense Planning Guidance for the Fiscal Years 1994–1999" as published in *New York Times* (March 8, 1992), 1, 4, under the heading "US Strategy Plan Calls for Insuring No Rivals Develop: A One Superpower World."

19. Barry Buzan, "New Patterns of Global Security in the Twenty-first Century," *International Affairs* 67, no. 3 (July 1991), 437.

20. Such a course of action has, in fact, been identified by Secretary of State James Baker as the United States's best possible approach to foreign policy in pursuit of a new world order: "a straightforward policy of American leadership called 'collective engagement'" for the building of a "democratic peace" around the globe. Thomas L. Friedman, "Baker Spells Out US Foreign Policy Stance," *New York Times* (April 22, 1992), A6.

21. Youssef Cohen, Brian R. Brown, and A. F. K. Organski, "The Paradoxical Nature of State Making: The Violent Creation of Order," *American Political Science Review* 75, no. 4 (December 1981), 902.

22. This contradiction between humanitarian impulses and the requirements of state-making is adequately borne out by the history of state-making in Europe going back to at least the sixteenth century. For a comparative analysis of state-making in Europe and the Third World, see Mohammed Ayoob, "The Security Predicament of the Third World State: Reflections on State-Making in a Comparative Perspective," in Brian Job, ed., *The Insecurity Dilemma: National Security of Third World States* (Boulder: Lynne Rienner, 1992), 63–80.

23. Bull, *The Anarchical Society*, 13–14.

24. For a contrary view advocating the merits of a new concert of great powers, see Richard Rosecrance, "A New Concert of Powers," *Foreign Affairs* 71, no. 2 (Spring 1992), 64–82. The main problem with the Rosecrance thesis is aptly summed up in his own conclusion, which seems to be based, ultimately, on wishful

thinking: "Despite historic precedents, this time the central coalition does not have to collapse." May one ask, why?

25. K. J. Holsti, "International Theory and War in the Third World," in Job, *The Insecurity Dilemma,* 38.

26. See Thomas G. Weiss and James G. Blight, eds., *The Suffering Grass: Superpowers and Regional Conflict in Southern Africa and the Caribbean Basin* (Boulder: Lynne Rienner, 1992).

∎ 4 ∎

Collective Conflict Management: Evidence for a New World Order?

ERNST B. HAAS

Toward a New World Order?

There is more than the rhetoric of the US government to suggest that we may be living in a brand new era as far as the collective and multilateral management of international conflict is concerned. The waning of the Cold War seems to have brought with it a rebirth of the collective security practices advocated and designed in 1945 by the victors in World War II. The fortunes of intergovernmental collective security organizations (IGOs) were at an abysmal low in 1985: referrals of new disputes were at their lowest point since 1945, as was the effectiveness at managing disputes on the agendas of IGOs. The number of unimplemented decisions was at an all-time high: on a scale of 1 to 100 (where 100 = perfect performance of all management tasks for all disputes on the agenda), the UN stood at 10 and the major regional IGOs at 15.[1]

This chapter combines theory-based analysis with advocacy, a genre of argumentation we call "policy science." I base my analysis of the state of multilateral conflict management on a particular theory of international politics, a theory that seeks to derive change in behavior from changes in actors' collective calculations and from their collective learning. The theory eschews notions of system and structure, of balancing and bandwagoning; it avoids value judgments about desirable outcomes and morally preferable orders. The second part of the chapter, however, offers moral judgments that are in no way derived from the analysis—they represent the kind of world order I personally prefer. These judgments determine some normatively based suggestions for changes in US policy. What is the link between the personal preferences and the value-neutral theory? I try my best not to advance suggestions that I know to be incompatible with my analysis, that might therefore be of interest to people who do not share entirely my ideological persuasion. It remains, of course, that the theoretical and normative portions of the enterprise remain subject to the strictures of the social construction of reality.[2]

Increased IGO Authority and Relevance

All IGOs, except for the OAU, increased their effectiveness in the last five years as compared with the prior cumulative record (see Table 4.1), though the sharp increases on the part of the OAS and the Arab League must be discounted because so many of their cases appeared simultaneously on the UN's agenda. It was in the UN that most of the action took place.

However, UN performance during the most recent period reverses a downward slide that had gone on steadily since 1960. Ten new peacekeeping and truce observation missions, many with legally unprecedented mandates, were launched between January 1, 1986, and December 31, 1990, whereas only 13 such initiatives were mounted in the previous 43 years. Two election-monitoring operations were also launched. As Secretary-General Javier Pérez de Cuéllar proudly announced in 1991, "Today the Organization is conducting some missions that were unthinkable in the previous era."[3] But in the case of the regionals, performance actually represents a decline over the previous and over several other quinquennia in the histories of these organizations.

Since 1985 the number of disputes that have involved fighting and have been referred to IGOs has increased sharply and the number of such

Table 4.1 Success in Conflict Management: 1945–1985 vs. 1986–1990

	1945–1985			1986–1990		
IGO	Total Disputes	Disputes at Once on UN and Regional Agenda	% Success	Total Disputes	Disputes at Once on UN and Regional Agenda	% Success
United Nations	159	—	23	32	—	32[a]
Organization of American States	34	7	31	5	4	33[b]
Arab League	27	6	20	4	2	25
Organization of African Unity	28	7	22	2	1	56[c]

Notes:
a. Includes 7 disputes referred earlier but settled during this period.
b. Scored before the deterioration of solutions in Haiti and Nicaragua.
c. Success misleading because the breakthrough in one case was scored by the ICJ.

disputes not so referred has gone down proportionately, suggesting that the legitimacy of IGOs as conflict managers is improving (Figure 4.1). For the first time in the history of the UN, the rate of success and the rate of referral have gone up together (Figure 4.2), an achievement not duplicated by the regional organizations whose aggregate effectiveness during the last five years has declined, in line with an overall erratic performance (Figure 4.3). The practice of unilateral intervention in civil wars on the part of the most powerful industrial states has declined markedly, as illustrated by events in Nicaragua, Angola, Ethiopia, The Sudan, Cambodia, Afghanistan, and Chad. The legitimacy and authority of the UN appeared to increase spectacularly as the organization took on the mandate to monitor elections as an essential component in multilateral mediation of civil wars and in transitions to democracy, to give relief to refugees and victims of civil strife, and to take more aggressive steps than in the past with respect to the protection of human rights.[4]

Finally, there were no complaints against the Soviet Union, Britain, and France, and only one against China, in marked contrast to earlier periods in the history of the UN. Unimplemented decisions in the UN went down to 45 percent of all decisions from 54 percent for the previous 40 years.

Figure 4.1 Disputes Involving Armed Conflict Referred and Not Referred to Five Intergovernmental Organizations

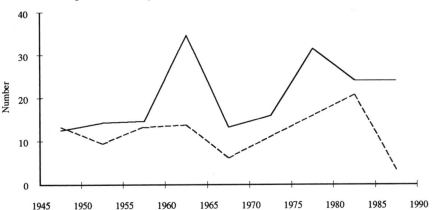

Referred to UN, OAS, AL, OAU, and Council of Europe
Not Referred

Figure 4.2 United Nations: Referrals and Success Rate

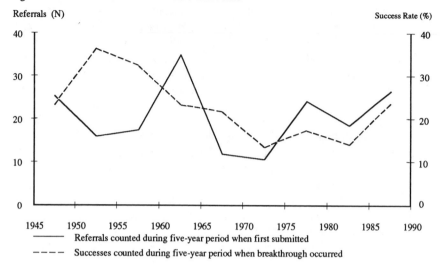

Referrals (N)   Success Rate (%)

——— Referrals counted during five-year period when first submitted
– – – – Successes counted during five-year period when breakthrough occurred

Figure 4.3 Four Major Regional Organizations: Referrals and Success Rate

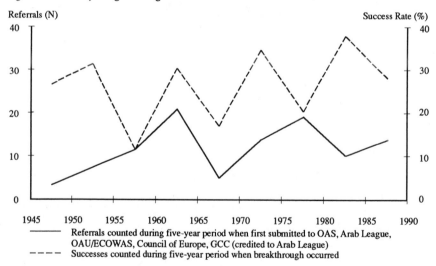

Referrals (N)   Success Rate (%)

——— Referrals counted during five-year period when first submitted to OAS, Arab League,
OAU/ECOWAS, Council of Europe, GCC (credited to Arab League)
– – – – Successes counted during five-year period when breakthrough occurred

Lost IGO Authority and Relevance

The trends in increased authority and relevance of IGOs were not the only trends of interest, however. Disputes on IGO agendas were markedly less intense and dangerous than was true in previous periods (see Table 4.2). This slight decline in relevance is also evident in the number of civil wars that were not referred to multilateral agreement since 1985 (see Table 4.3). In addition to the unilateral interventions noted in Table 4.3, I call attention to the incursions and support given by Libya, Syria, Israel, North Korea, and Morocco, activity mostly reflected in disputes that were referred to IGOs. I have already noted that the overall role of regional organizations declined during the last five years because the regionals were overshadowed by UN activities in situations when both types of organizations were called upon to manage conflict jointly. During the last five years, the United States, the leader of the coalition against Iraq and the champion of a new world order, was the target of complaints no less than nine times, followed by Israel (five times) and South Africa (four times). The United States also used the veto more frequently than any other Permanent Member of the Security Council to ward off complaints against itself and to protect Israel.

Table 4.2 Intensity of Old and New Disputes (%)

Intensity of Disputes	United Nations	Five Regionals
1945–1985	(N=137)	(N=92)
Insignificant	36	59
Low, moderate	31	25
High, very high	33	16
1986–1990	(N=32)	(N=11)
Insignificant	65	62
Low, moderate	18	23
High, very high	18	15

Why Improvement in Performance? Correlates of Success

My scheme to explain the improvement in IGO performance is based on a simple model. The dependent variable—success in managing conflict—is thought to be immediately explained by four "management variables":

Table 4.3 Civil Wars Not Referred to Multilateral Organizations: 1985–1990

Civil War	Outside Intervention by:
Afghanistan	Pakistan/US/Saudi Arabia to insurgents; USSR to government
Burma	
Colombia	US to government
Ethiopia	USSR to governments; Arab countries to Eritrean insurgents
Fiji	
Guatemala	
India (three separate ones)	Pakistan to Kashmiri insurgents
Kurdistan/Iraq	Western coalition to insurgents
Kurdistan/Turkey	
Maldives	India to government; Sri Lanka to insurgents
Mexico	
Mozambique	Republic of South Africa to insurgents; also Malawi
Papua-New Guinea	
Peru	US to government
Philippines	US to government
Romania	
Rwanda	
Somalia	
South Africa	
Sri Lanka	India to government; Tamil Nadu to insurgents
Sudan	Ethiopia, Kenya to insurgents; Arab states to government
Tibet	
USSR (four separate ones)	

organizational decision, field operations, leadership, and consensus.[5] These variables, however, are associated with, and embedded in, six "contextual variables": the degree of intensity of the dispute, the seriousness of the hostilities (from simple riots to efforts to eliminate the antagonist), the extent of the geographic spread (from bilateral confrontation to global involvement), the relationship of the conflict to such global issues as the Cold War and the decolonization movement, the power dyad of the disputants (from conflict among superpowers to confrontations among the smallest states), and the alignment with power blocs of the antagonists. Figure 4.4 illustrates the model.

Some contextual variables were chosen because of a core hypothesis embedded in the research design taken from the cognitive international relations theory informing most of this study: states are able to change their policies as a result of realizing that earlier policies failed. The extent of geographic spread provides a way of observing whether states take disputes likely to escalate more seriously than those confined to bilateral border squabbles. Global issues are relevant because they afford a chance for determining whether Cold War and colonial disputes are perceived differently by states as requiring multilateral management. The power dyad and the Cold War alignment of the parties tells us something about who is

Figure 4.4 Causal Model of Conflict Management

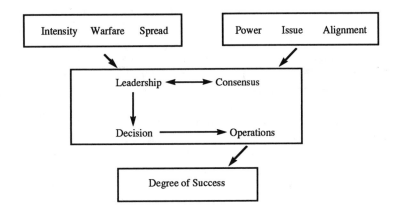

learning to build a coalition against a strong state, or who learns to mediate a conflict that involves a superpower. Other contextual variables—disputes, intensity, and seriousness of hostilities—reflect the influence of structural theories of international politics, allowing us to code the importance of a dispute in terms of presumed salience to the potential dispute managers.

Contextual Variables as Correlates of Success
One plausible explanation for the rise in organizational success is the possibility that there was some systematic difference between the character of the most recent disputes that found their way to IGOs and the character of the disputes before 1986.[6] The UN improved its ability to manage the more threatening disputes; success was achieved more frequently, as compared with the first 40 years, when disputes were intense and featured heavy fighting. As to power dyads, the most recent era differs from earlier ones in that the United States is more frequently cited as a threat to the peace, whereas the Soviet Union is targeted less often than before. In the regional IGOs, the same trends show up with respect to intensity and type of warfare, but in addition the geographic spread is widening. Members of opposing alliances and alignments challenged each other more often in recent years in regional fora. Disputes pitting a superpower (the United States) and such middle powers as Iran, Iraq, or Egypt against small states have

risen sharply in number. In short, the salience of disputes to world and regional peace has gone up.

As salience to world peace rises, so does the success of the UN in managing disputes.[7] Since 1986, success in management of the UN is disproportionately associated with high intensity, violent warfare, and geographic spread to the neighbors of the antagonists; with Cold War issues as well as issues unrelated to any global meta-issue; with parties in opposing blocs as well as among allies (whereas bloc opponents earlier usually did not resolve their disputes, despite efforts at IGO management); and with dyads of small-power antagonists (as opposed to larger degrees of success associated with large and middle powers earlier).

The contextual explanation that jumps to mind is that the Cold War's ebbing made it permissible for countries that had been allies but that also entertained grievances against each other to take these to an international forum. Similarly, the ebbing facilitated conflict management among members of formerly opposing blocs. As the Soviet–US confrontation receded, disputes that had originally arisen, or been globalized, because of that confrontation lost their salience and thus allowed for collective management. The positive association of high-intensity/violent warfare disputes with management success resulted partly because situations previously tainted by the Cold War now permitted collective solutions that had not been conceivable before, as we shall see when management variables are examined. Small-power dyads became more prominent than dyads including large and middle powers because of the shrinking of the decolonization issue.

The picture is quite different when we turn to regional organizations, whose overall effectiveness declined markedly during the most recent period. No significant changes in the association of the contextual variables with management success are in evidence, except when we turn to bloc alignment.[8] Such successes as were scored were very disproportionately associated with disputes in which the antagonists were not aligned at all, whereas performance in dyads among allied disputants declined markedly. These trends are due to the numerous sharp confrontations in the OAS between the United States on the one hand and Nicaragua and Panama on the other. More basically, we suspect, the decline in organizational effectiveness is associated with a weakening of consensus in all regions, which in turn is associated with changes in bloc alignments that also reflect the waning of the Cold War.

Management Variables as Correlates of Success
Improved performance by the UN was closely associated with the end of the Cold War as a meta-issue and with the growing irrelevance of the alignments associated with that conflict, with higher average intensity and wider spread of the disputes on the organization's agenda.[9] These changes are in line with striking changes in behavior of the member states inside the UN.

The very profiles of the disputes were different. In the most recent era the organization was much more likely to launch large field operations than in the earlier periods, to make decisions that were approved by smaller majorities, and to rely much more on the leadership of the Secretary-General in shaping decisions and managing operations. Decisions to launch operations that were ultimately to prove successful, especially large operations, were far more common in recent years; no single form of leadership proved especially successful before 1986, whereas the leadership of the Secretary-General, often exercised jointly with a coalition of states including one or both superpowers, was the most prominent form of leadership associated with successful operations thereafter. In earlier eras, success demanded very wide consensus among the member states, but in the most recent period weaker forms of consensus often sufficed.

Disputes submitted to regional organizations showed exactly the same differences in profile in the most recent era as compared with earlier cases. However, unlike the situation with the UN, the change in profile is associated with an overall decline in effectiveness. As the context in which disputes occur, despite the decline of the Cold War and its alignments, moves toward more violence and a wider geographic scope, the ability to make unambiguous decisions declined too. While success today is more prominent in situations in which regional organizations managed to mount large operations, their earlier good record in mounting small successful operations fell off sharply. However, here too, success is clearly associated with leadership by executive heads, which was emphatically not the case in earlier periods and with smaller majorities. These differences are graphed in Figures 4.5 and 4.6.

Improvement Analyzed in Terms of Task and Mission

Conciliation without large operations. The UN's achievements in peacekeeping were not matched in efforts at mediation and conciliation that did not involve any field operations of major scope. The 22 cases of that type were distributed as shown in Table 4.4. Six successes in a field of 22 cases is not a very impressive rate, though much of the failure is attributable to the United States being the victim of the complaints, in order to side with Israel. The actual percentage of success (16 percent) is substantially less than the average during the pre-1986 history of UN small operations, while the record for attempted conciliation without any operations is as bad now as it was earlier. The adage that without substantial effort no impact is scored holds now as it did before, as does the finding that the membership makes little effort to mediate or conciliate in low-intensity local disputes. Conciliation efforts by the OAU to settle the Aouzou Strip and Agacher disputes came to nothing, as bilateral mediation helped ease one and an appeal to the ICJ the other. The OAS was unable to mediate or conciliate

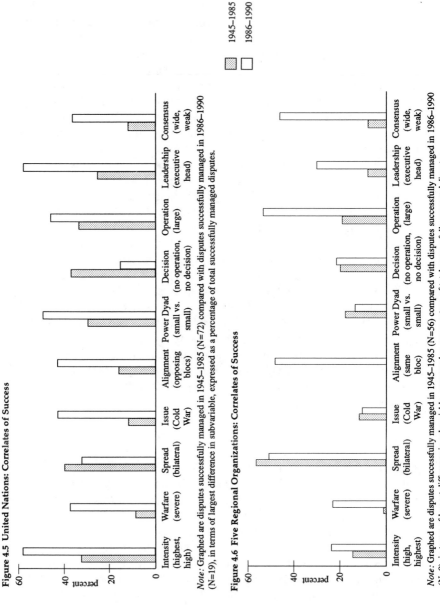

Figure 4.5 United Nations: Correlates of Success

Note: Graphed are disputes successfully managed in 1945–1985 (N=72) compared with disputes successfully managed in 1986–1990 (N=19), in terms of largest difference in subvariable, expressed as a percentage of total successfully managed disputes.

Figure 4.6 Five Regional Organizations: Correlates of Success

Note: Graphed are disputes successfully managed in 1945–1985 (N=56) compared with disputes successfully managed in 1986–1990 (N=9), in terms of largest difference in subvariable, expressed as a percentage of total successfully managed disputes.

1945–1985

1986–1990

with the help of small secretariat missions, as it had done very often in past years, except in one trivial case. The Arab League scored only one such success since 1985, in its role in the Lebanese peace process.

Table 4.4 Characteristics of Disputes Conciliated Without Large Field Operations: 1986–1990

Type of Resolution/Operations	No Success	Success
No resolution, no operations	11 disputes (US, Israel, RSA sole defendants)	None
Weak resolution, no operations	Chinese human rights; Al Wazir assassination; Panama elections	Lebanese peace process; RSA death penalty
Strong resolution, small operations	Intifada; Temple Mount	Iranian airliner downing; Guatemalan peace process; Albanian human rights; ending Pacific trust

Judicial settlement and the ICJ. Like the Security Council, the ICJ came into its own after 1985 in terms of number of submissions. Before that date, the Court had heard 23 cases that involved political, territorial, military, or resource issues featuring states rather than private parties; since 1985, eight new cases were referred to it. (See Appendix 4.2, Table G.) Seven of the original cases were not settled for procedural reasons; in eight others one of the parties either failed to participate or declined to implement an adverse award. As if this record were not bad enough, nine advisory opinions were in effect decisions adverse to specific governments; none of the "defendents" paid any attention to the rulings. It is hardly surprising that judicial settlement of major international disputes by the world's most prominent court had a bad reputation. A number of politically very sensitive cases are now before it, the kinds of cases that, prior to the Nicaraguan complaint against the United States for supporting the contras, the Court had rarely been called upon to hear. Mali implemented an adverse decision; Libya and Malta settled their maritime boundary dispute bilaterally, with the Court's help. One careful student of the Court's impact on the peaceful settlement of international disputes writes that "the record of international adjudication suggests that there has been a recent and significant decline in the respect nations accord the Court. This decline is found in states' resistance to submit important matters to the Court, their refusal to appear or participate in cases brought to the Court, and their refusal to abide by the determinations of the Court. Furthermore, the number of states bound by the Optional Clause under Article 36(2) of the Statute has declined."[10] It is too soon to tell whether this judgment will stand.

From peacekeeping to peacemaking? Pre-1986 truce observation and peacekeeping efforts resembled one another in that the mandates given by the Security Council or the General Assembly did not go beyond ending hostilities and monitoring the resulting truce, although UNIFIL when prevented from carrying out its mandate, also assumed some humanitarian duties. Typically, the mandates called for separating the belligerent forces, creating buffer zones, patrolling truce lines, reporting violations, and mediating local disagreements among the parties.

Things are different now.[11] Large military and civilian forces are also given the task of disarming guerrilla groups and stopping the arms traffic (UNGOMAP, UNTAG, ONUCA, UNAVEM 2, UNIKOM, MINURSO); monitoring elections and the observance of human rights (UNGOMAP, UNTAG, OONUVEN, ONUVEH, ONUSAL, MINURSO); administering relief operations for civilians (ONUVEH, MINURSO); as well as mounting a full-scale administration of the area (UNTAG). Similar extended duties are planned for Cambodia (UNTAC) and Croatia (UNPROFOR). Situations work out better, on the whole, if there is full agreement among all parties and organs of the UN about mandate and duration before the operations begin. There is a growing consensus that the Secretary-General alone has the power to determine the composition of the forces. While approximately 70 member states furnished personnel for these operations, a few countries stood out as consistent, continuous, and experienced participants. Many were the same as before 1986: Norway, Sweden, Denmark, Austria, Finland, Ireland, and Canada; these were joined after 1986 by Spain, Argentina, Yugoslavia, and India as core participants.

The growing autonomy of the UN Secretary-General is striking. Javier Pérez de Cuéllar, though lacking Dag Hammarskjöld's charismatic qualities, will be recognized as the most innovative executive head of the UN as far as conflict management is concerned. His active intervention has much to do with the increasing scope and versatility of UN peacekeeping, whether through personal intervention or by the regular use of his personal representatives. He reports that in January 1987 he came to an agreement on "a remarkable coordination between the work of the Security Council and the Secretary-General."[12] The most innovative of these "coordinating" measures is his active role in negotiating a generally accepted constitutional order for countries racked by civil war; such was his role in contributing to constitutional settlements in Namibia, El Salvador, Afghanistan, and Western Sahara, and it may become a role in Guatemala, Cambodia, and Croatia.

The Secretary-General, along with others, has eloquently and repeatedly called for "peacemaking" in addition to peacekeeping. The most recent operations aim at much more than separating the warring parties—the mandates included humanitarian tasks as well as measures to aid in the introduction of democratic governance. In many cases the mandate called for intervention in civil wars and the introduction of democratically elected national governments to succeed the parties in conflict, a task by no means foreseen by the drafters of the UN Charter who insisted on excluding matters "essentially within the domestic jurisdiction" of member states from the rules governing collective security and the peaceful settlement of disputes. Peacemaking came to mean, in the 1980s, that the UN has some role in mediating an end to civil strife, monitoring elections, protecting human rights in order to make free elections possible, disarming and resettling guerrillas and their families, and making sure that democratic constitutions be written and implemented.[13] Whether the organization also has a responsibility for intervening if and when violations of such constitutions occur is still being debated. The OAS, which claims such a right, has had indifferent success in making democracy prevail.

In any event, peacemaking by UN-run democratization remains controversial. Alvaro de Soto, the UN's "man in Central America," insists that the Nicaraguan and Haitian events were not a precedent, that the UN has no regular mandate to monitor elections or assure democratization. There is a loophole, though: intervention in favor of democracy may be permissible when explicitly requested by the parties, thus waiving Article 2(7) of the Charter, when it is part of a larger peacekeeping mission and when it is approved by the Security Council or the General Assembly. In other words, only when civil wars appear to shade into interstate conflict (as in Central America) can the mandate be expanded to include measures to implant democracy.[14]

Enforcement measures and the liberation of Kuwait. The UN's victorious war against Iraq and the subsequent effort to make President Saddam Hussein's government carry out the terms of Security Council Resolution 687 represent the first full-scale enforcement measures since the Korean War, and the first ever to conform to the Charter's definition of collective security. What concerns me for present purposes is not the now-familiar sequence of events and decisions that led to the current situation. Rather, I want to address these issues: What was truly innovative about the liberation of Kuwait, and how likely is it that the innovations will be institutionalized?

Enforcement did not occur until gradual collective measures of warning, separate negotiations by the Soviet Union and by the Arab League, and an economic blockade (eventually enforced with naval forces) had proved unfruitful to bring about an Iraqi withdrawal from Kuwait. The authorization to use force was given six weeks before Operation Desert Storm began, thus allowing more time for peaceful measures to resolve the crisis; but after the deadline—January 15, 1991—had passed without any move by Iraq to honor UN demands, the operation was executed exactly as threatened. Article 51 was never invoked; decisions were made unanimously by the permanent members; no UN military command was created, because the Security Council in effect delegated Operation Desert Storm to a coalition of states willing to do the fighting. The procedure, in short, followed the rules intended by the drafters of the Charter *and* used innovations added later under Cold War conditions but allowed under Articles 48 and 106.[15] The most striking innovation, however, was Resolution 687, which orders stringent arms control and disarmament for Iraq, imposes the duty to pay reparations, and continues the trade embargo in order to compel Iraqi compliance. In addition, it creates a Special Commission to supervise the disarmament of Iraq in cooperation with IAEA and WHO and gives the Secretary-General new authority to demarcate and demilitarize the Iraq-Kuwait border (the operation that became UNIKOM), repatriate refugees, and provide monitoring mechanisms for the Special Commission. Nothing like this had ever been approved by the Security Council, and not everyone was happy about it.

The oddities of decisionmaking that authorized these innovations ought to be considered before we can conclude that these measures define collective security and enforcement for the foreseeable future. The United States took the leadership role from the beginning and retained it. There is some evidence that Washington planned the complete military defeat of Iraq, not just the liberation of Kuwait, as early as September 1990. Moreover, the United States never had any intention to follow the preference of those, especially the Soviets, who wanted to have a UN enforcement machinery utilizing the revived Military Staff Committee. Typically, the United States elbowed such suggestions aside. Nor did the Secretary-General take a leading role in the Iraq-Kuwait episode; in fact, his staff advised him to distance himself from the directorate of the Permanent Five, who ran the show, in order to show his agreement with the Third World states that objected to this collective hegemony. Pérez de Cuéllar went out of his way to negotiate a compromise with Saddam Hussein. He insisted that the enforcement was not intended to compel "surrender but the righting of the wrong that has been committed."[16] He did nothing to stimulate the institutionalization of the enforcement procedures. Typically, the United States would seek first the support of the Soviet Union, France, and Britain before offering a resolution. Afterward and with their help, Washington lined up a sufficient number of supporters from the nonpermanent members of the Security Council (offering side payments if necessary), and only then approached the most reluctant supporter of sanctions, China, whose support for the crucial Resolution 687 also required a side payment.

The continuing difficulty experienced by the UN in getting Iraq's cooperation in implementing Resolution 687 is ample testimony to the gaps in the collective security system and the reluctance of many UN members to undertake further enforcement to compel compliance. In fact, the consensus among the governments that authorized or participated in Operation Desert Storm grew weaker as the rout of the Iraqi forces became evident. There was no consensus on matters beyond the liberation of Kuwait. Even the official finding that aggression had been committed and had to be repelled failed to convince many people in the Third World who believe that this was just another imperialistic war by the West, a position also taken by a segment of the political left in the West. The lesson is inescapable: A war, even if relabeled as collective enforcement to repel aggression, is still seen as an illegitimate use of force when employed by a strong Western country against a weaker, non-Western foe. In February 1991 Libya wrote to the Security Council that Iraq was "being subjected to a deliberate process of humiliation . . . an operation designed to debase the Arab community, through Iraq, in the eyes of the world."[17]

The spotty fortunes of peacekeeping by regional organizations. The OAU was upstaged by ECOWAS in a large operation seeking to end the Liberian civil war. ECOWAS lurched from conciliation to peacekeeping to enforcement against one of the warring groups, and back to peacekeeping between the two surviving factions, in its long effort to end the turmoil. Most observers agree that ECOWAS's first foray into collective conflict management was a great improvement over the OAU's failures in these endeavors. OAU, however, was accepted by the UN as a junior partner in monitoring the upcoming referendum in Western Sahara. The Arab League was unable to influence the course of events in the Gulf, because of the deep split in its membership over whom to support. The crucial resolution condemning Iraq and demanding the liberation of Kuwait was adopted by the 12 members who attended the meeting of August 10, 1990, while 9 other members failed to attend. The GCC, on the other hand, lined up solidly with the UN without undertaking a collective intervention of its own.

The OAS, however, enjoyed a modest revival of its waning fortunes because of its new role as election monitor. The organization was requested by some governments to monitor elections designed to choose successors for regimes of disputed legitimacy in the Dominican Republic, Guatemala, Panama, El Salvador, Paraguay, and Suriname. In addition, it joined the UN in observing and certifying the election of President Jean-Bertrand Aristide in Haiti, as well as the Haitian legislature. More important, the member states, under the prodding of Venezuela's President Carlos Andres Perez, expressed a commitment to intervene collectively on behalf of democracy when Aristide was overthrown by the army, first by offering conciliation and then by mounting an embargo on all commercial transactions; as of mid-1992, neither intervention has been effective. The OAS was asked to help in the implementation of the Esquipulas agreements by demobilizing and resettling contras operating in Nicaragua (the bulk of the contras in Honduras were disarmed by ONUCA), but the operation was not wholly successful. OAS observers joined UN observers in OONUVEN, though coordination between the two teams was poor. On the whole, one gets the impression that OAS election monitoring has been less than energetic unless augmented by observers from other organizations.[18]

Even though sporadic efforts were made in 1987 and 1988 by members of the Rio Group of Latin American states to reform OAS collective security procedures to allow the organization a role in the Esquipulas process, nothing happened until the UN entered the area. The Central Americans had sought the support of both organizations as early as 1986 in their regional efforts at peacemaking. Mexican opposition to an OAS role foiled the intervention in Manuel Noriega's Panama urged by the United States. When the unilateral US invasion came in December 1989, the OAS condemned it ineffectively by a vote of 21 to 1 with 9 abstentions.

Lasting Improvements?

Improvements in collective conflict management were by no means uniform in the last five years. In summary of the findings just reported, regional efforts at the peaceful settlement of disputes did not improve; those of the UN probably deteriorated unless they were backed up by field operations eventually. The end of the Cold War and the disintegration of voting blocs associated with it combined with the leadership of the secretariat to bring about very impressive improvements in peacekeeping and peacemaking under UN, but not regional, auspices. Judicial settlement remained as marginal to conflict management as it had always been. Collective security by means of enforcement measures has been added to the international arsenal as a new and potentially powerful technique. I now ask: Are the improvements in UN peacekeeping, peacemaking, and enforcement likely to remain with us as institutionalized practices?

Integrating Aspects of Conflict Management: Three Modes of Organizational Change

Feeding and caring for refugees threatened with genocide, separating warring armies, disarming guerrillas, ending a civil war, monitoring respect for human rights and certifying elections as honest, writing democratic constitutions, intervening to protect fledgling democracies, and fighting a war to end aggression—all are aspects of multilateral conflict management. They need not be integrated into a single organizational task labeled "peacemaking"; nor need they be tied to one another by a single causal theory about war and peace. No government, until now, ever thought of so linking these activities to each other. My concern with the institutionalization of steps toward fully integrated peacemaking is an outgrowth of my cognitive approach to international politics. I theorize that states can change multilateral organizations of which they are members, and in changing them also change their perceptions and practices to become even more multilaterally committed. I hold that collective learning is possible in international life, that the recent progress of peacemaking may become an instance of collective learning to manage interdependence.[19]

A UN that "manages interdependence" in peacemaking bases action on an agreed notion of cause and effect about war and peace, on a consensual knowledge base. The membership understands that political goals are interacting and interdependent, not separate and achievable in isolation. Decisions are made on the basis of analytic techniques, not merely by counting votes or by consensus. Issues are linked to one another by taking inherent interconnections into account, not merely by means of logrolling or by exchanging substantively unrelated concessions, such as the side payments in the Kuwait war. Analytically justified solutions must be supported with appropriate means. Thus, ever more ambitious peacemaking by the UN must be accompanied by adequate and assured financial and personnel resources to constitute credibly learned management of interdependence. States especially willing and skilled at peacemaking are given special representation, as are NGOs friendly toward the organization's goals. The secretariat is independent and not polluted by unprofessional personnel quotas. Financial commitments are met by capital subscriptions proportional to GNP, and they are honored. International administrators are permitted full access and authority on the soil of member states; international monitoring of national obligations is smooth and continuous. The executive head is recognized as the supreme crisis manager; she or he plays that role to the hilt.

Clearly, only a few of these conditions have actually been met since 1986. Financially, the UN limps along from crisis to crisis. Administratively, no standing machinery has been developed for recruiting personnel needed for peacemaking, for training them, and for making sure that only the most qualified are selected. Personnel and voting practices continue to be less than optimal because the UN has not yet managed to digest all of its variegated members. Member states insist on equality of representation. The secretariat is penetrated by member-state appointees of dubious merit. Some outside experts are independent; others merely front for governments. On the whole, UN administrators do not enjoy untrammeled access on the soil of member states, and monitoring of international obligations is rudimentary—and widely resented. Voting tends to be by simple majority (except in the Security Council). Budgeting still retains some logrolling and disjointed incrementalism. The executive head is sometimes reactive and self-effacing, unwilling consistently to oppose the coalition of states that actually dominates decisionmaking.

The UN has survived for 45 years even though its mandate, membership, leadership, and decisionmaking styles have changed dramatically during this time. It has survived by following two modes of change we call "incremental growth" (operative mostly before 1965) and "turbulent nongrowth" (operative between 1970 and 1985). Neither involves much learning; both are reactive to outside stimuli. They differ from managing interdependence by failing to integrate newly accruing tasks into coherently linked metatasks, thereby disappointing the expectations of many member states. Improvements in performance since 1986 remain episodic, incremental, unintegrated, and not based on agreed knowledge or on consensual goals. Following is an illustration of this state of affairs, via an examination of the extent to which the components of peacemaking are in fact treated as portions of a metatask.

Peacemaking and Humanitarian Intervention
One consequence of the defeat of Iraq was the outbreak of a revolt in Kurdistan. The Iraqi army had no difficulty in defeating the Kurdish guerrillas, whereupon up to 2,000,000 Kurds fled into the mountains where the borders of Turkey, Iran, and Iraq meet. Allied troops then occupied northern Iraq to provide food, shelter, and medical aid for the refugees and to keep the Iraqi military from advancing, all the while calling for UN humanitarian intervention to relieve the allies from acting unilaterally.

The Secretary-General was most reluctant to accept the challenge, even though some members of his staff urged him to do so in order to be able to invoke humanitarian intervention as a justification for disregarding the Charter's strictures against intervening in the domestic affairs of member states. Pérez de Cuéllar pointed to the absence of authorization by any major UN organ, denial of access by Iraq, lack of clarity about what the mandate of a UN force ought to be, the reluctance of China and the Soviet Union (neither wanted to create a precedent for such an excuse), and the active opposition of many Third World countries.

Yet some Western European countries supported the allied initiative. They went some way toward endorsing the most radical argument for disregarding national sovereignty and vesting the right of intervention in a collective effort imposed on the local government. That argument holds that there is a right to interfere. It "means that a request from those who are suffering is sufficient to justify crossing a boundary without authorization from a nation's leaders; the humanitarian imperative takes precedence over non-interference and sovereignty."[20]

The UN General Assembly, always given to hyperbole, responded by announcing the creation of a "new international humanitarian order." Yet the content of that "order" remains elusive. On the one hand, the Assembly held that in the event of emergencies, "the principles of humanity, neutrality and impartiality must be given utmost consideration by all those involved in providing humanitarian assistance;" but on the other hand, it emphasized "the sovereignty of affected States and their primary role in the initiation, organization, coordination and implementation of humanitarian assistance within their respective territories."[21] We are a long way from a consensus on the primacy of a right to intervene on behalf of refugees, starving people, or democracy.

In mid-1992 a new type of multilateral humanitarian aid operation appeared: "armed humanitarian intervention." Peacekeeping forces were redeployed by the Security Council to reopen the Sarajevo airport to bring relief supplies to Bosnia; others were being discussed for Somalia to keep such supplies from being seized by bandits and guerrillas.

How Solid the UN Consensus on Peacemaking and Peacekeeping?
There has been some opposition from nonpermanent members of the Security Council on most of the successful peacekeeping and peacemaking operations of the last five years. In each case, however, the unanimous agreement of the permanent members, linked to considerable autonomy for the Secretary-General's mediatory activities, prevailed quite easily. In the Kuwait case, however, the dominance of resounding majorities in the Security Council (not counting the frequent opposition by Cuba and Yemen) is very deceptive. It took a long time to assemble the majority for Resolution 678 that authorized the attack, and even then China abstained. In November 1990, Cuba, Yemen, Colombia, and Malaysia wanted to deploy UNTSO in the West Bank to protect Palestinians against the Israeli army and settlers. In December, a few days after Resolution 678 had been adopted, the same countries wanted to outflank it by deploying a peacekeeping force between Iraq and Kuwait, lift the sanctions, and withdraw all foreign forces from Saudi Arabia if only Iraq would first withdraw from Kuwait and agree to conciliation by the Secretary-General.[22] China, India, and Yemen abstained from voting on Resolution 686, which outlined the 12 principles Iraq had to accept before military operations would cease, presumably because the terms were considered too harsh and too intrusive. Ecuador and Yemen abstained from voting on Resolution 687, apparently for similar reasons. Before we can assume the permanence of a new commitment to collective security, it is wise to analyze the character of the consensus on which such a commitment would have to be based.

I use the unprecedented UN administrative role in Cambodia (UNTAC) as my opening example. It is an operation in which the risk of failure is high even if we presuppose the continuity of the consensus among Indonesia, Vietnam, France, China, Russia, the United States, and Britain that has made possible the agreement in place now. UNTAC's job, in cooperation with almost all other agencies in the UN family, is to organize and conduct the election that will determine the composition of the government of a post–civil war Cambodia. The UN is also to reintroduce a normal life for Cambodians. Because of the centrality of the election as a way of permanently reconciling the four contending factions, the UN has the power to second-guess all government agencies involved, supervising the police, the courts, and the ministry of the interior. Human rights monitors will play ombudsperson roles. Other units will repatriate and resettle up to 400,000 civilian refugees. Military units will monitor the cease-fire; disarm, regroup, and house the guerrillas; and prevent the reintroduction of imported arms.[23]

Success depends crucially on the willingness of Vietnam and the Khmer Rouge to accept defeat. But suppose such an act of submission is resisted by either or both? Their continued cooperation depends—as before—on the positions taken by China, Russia, and the United States. Will the perceptions of interest of these governments continue to converge? True, Russia is not in a position to influence events in Southeast Asia any longer; therefore, Vietnam lacks the power to act decisively. But no such constraints apply to the United States and China. Each might find reason to reactivate and rearm its local allies.

Other events also ought to be recalled to put the post-Kuwait euphoria into perspective. It required more than a shaky consensus among the Permanent Five to translate Resolution 598 on the Iraq-Iran war into UNIMOG; the military defeat of Iran almost two years after the adoption of the resolution had to occur first. UNGOMAP ceased operations in part because of lack of agreement on how to force an end to the Afghan civil war, until Pakistan decided to quit aiding the guerrillas. Consensus in the Security Council cannot be translated into an agreement between the parties in Cyprus as long as the Permanent Five are unwilling to intervene strongly. The same can be said of the Arab-Israeli conflict about which the big powers are not in complete agreement.[24]

Nonetheless, in the crunch Britain and France always supported the United States in recent UN conflict management efforts. In a European Community in which Germany will increasingly outweigh them in making common foreign and defense policies, this state of affairs cannot be taken for granted. Our sole test of this suspicion is the Yugoslav operation. Germany insisted that the EC countries recognize the independence of Croatia and Slovenia even though UN circles and the United States preferred a more neutral approach and thought that UN intercession depended on evenhandedness. Initial British and French agreement with the United States did not prevent Germany from having its way. In general, we may expect a reduction of British and French interest in Third World disputes in which no immediate economic interests are at stake, and hence a growing indifference to UN interventions, which may translate into withholding material support.

China is an even more serious source of discord. Chinese arms sales violating UN policy have been routine. So have challenges to the nuclear nonproliferation regime. The Chinese have given evidence of opposing any policy or principle that might at some time be turned against them, and they have been zealous in shoring up the principle of nonintervention. It is very doubtful that Washington can buy Chinese support for conflict management operations in the future in situations Beijing sees differently. In fact, given the irritant of differences over democracy and human rights, opposing interpretations of any salient set of events is the more likely development.

Before the Soviet Union reemerged as Russia, Moscow had inundated the UN with suggestions for improving and institutionalizing peacekeeping and peacemaking. The architects of the "new thinking" in international affairs seemed to love the UN, offering a standing force of Soviet military personnel for observation, peacekeeping, and border patrol duties in trouble spots. A UN naval force was proposed as well.[25] None of this proved acceptable to Washington. The extent to which Boris Yeltsin continues to endorse these Gorbachevian initiatives is unclear. We cannot take for granted that the new Russia will embrace everything multilateral on principle. Instability in the Middle East may assume a new salience when ethnic and religious conflicts within and among the newly independent republics endanger the lives of Russians or the security of Russia. The former USSR may soon be a source of problems for the UN, not a repository of new solutions.

Nor is unflinching commitment to the multilateralism of collective security to be taken for granted in Washington. Gone is the old internationalism that identified US global interests with support for international organizations and with fighting the Cold War. With the waning of the Cold War and internationalist consensus has gone an agreed national interest undergirding foreign policy.[26] The Reagan administration was ideologically opposed to multilateralism and downgraded US support for the UN with a vicious vigor. The United States threatened to use unilateral means on several occasions when the Security Council was slow to go along with the lack of institutional control over Operation Desert Storm that Washington demanded. The unclear and hesitating language found in all Security Council resolutions authorizing sanctions was the result: Washington wanted carte blanche, while Russia and China were, for different reasons, reluctant to authorize the use of any UN force.

The UN: Not an Independent Actor Yet
Could the UN practice "coercive diplomacy, achieve objectives in a crisis without bloodshed, avoiding the costs of war"?[27] To do so would require the carefully calculated mixture of threat and promise, as well as incrementally augmented deadly force, the very ladder of escalation not consistently

climbed against Iraq. In terms of a political consensus it would require either a stable coalition of supporting states or an autonomous, strong, and respected secretariat headed by a charismatic and brilliant executive head. I have tried to show why, despite appearances, we do not now have a predictably stable coalition of core states on which institutionalized conflict management can rely. Nor is there evidence of a global public opinion that will hail UN conflict management as authoritative and legitimate irrespective of who the parties may be, no matter what the cause in question is perceived to represent.

Still, many innovations in conflict management were the result of adaptations triggered by the Cold War, by the absence of a permanent consensus among the Permanent Five. The UN never functioned according to the Dumbarton Oaks blueprint and never will; the present renaissance of conflict management by no means implies the apotheosis of the founders. Past successes were achieved as a result of ad hoc and shifting coalitions producing temporary majorities. Entrepreneurial states, most often the United States, had to build these coalitions, just as the United States built the coalition that opposed Iraq. Dag Hammarskjöld worked in close cooperation with the hegemon; no executive head ever operated successfully in opposition to that power. That situation has not changed. A heavier agenda, the demand for new tasks and mandates, and the hope for multilateral solutions do not add up to that new order everyone talks about and nobody defines.

Institutionalization of the Management of Interdependence: A Possibility?

The remarkable record of the UN since 1985 is a case of adapting to new challenges and opportunities without rethinking the basic rules of international life or considering the very foundations of international order. To adapt is to make do, to improvise, to benefit in the short run from not repeating a recently recognized error. International conflict managers have been practicing adaptation since the adoption of the "Uniting for Peace" resolution in 1950. But in order to conclude that conflict management has evolved to something more coherent than mere adaptation, we would have to find that actors agree to reject an earlier causal scheme about war and peace as inadequate and adopt a new comprehensive way of thinking about cause-effect and ends-means relationships. To learn means that such a cognitive breakthrough has taken place. Few governments think as yet in terms of a truly "new" international order.

In the remaining sections of this chapter, I shall probe the kinds of values, and the means necessary for their attainment, that might be said to constitute a new international order. I shall be inquiring into the kinds of issues

I want governments to learn about collective conflict management. The new order I shall now describe is the one I prefer to the established one. I advocate the change in institutions that I consider necessary for the effective management of interdependence, having first demonstrated by using value-neutral analytical means, that past practices of bringing about organizational change have not rested on a strong base of consensual knowledge. I admit the reality and utility of incremental growth and of turbulent nongrowth. I prefer managed interdependence. After reviewing the record of the major activities of international organizations, I make suggestions on how to bring this about.

Lessons of Peaceful Settlement Reviewed
Pérez de Cuéllar put the issue of the UN's role in this way:

> Over long years, there has grown a view of the United Nations itself. . . as a place of litigation that is likely to result in a negative verdict for one or the other party. I believe that we need now actively to foster the perception that, except in . . . matters dealt with in Chapter VII, the United Nations is more an instrument of mediation that can help reconcile legitimate claims and interests.[28]

Peacemaking has been added to peacekeeping as a multilateral response. Yet this augmentation of multilateralism is built largely on sand. We know that it is made possible by the revolution in the former Soviet Union and by the consequent realignment of global political forces and priorities, by the disappearance of the Cold War as the meta-issue. More concretely, the augmentation in multilateral authority is associated with a new consensus, with new coalitions of states backing specific operations and giving the executive head ample new space for independent initiatives in facilitating peaceful change. So far, however, the only fixed coalitional support for the mandates has been the agreement of the Permanent Five. Because this agreement cannot be considered as lasting and because Big Five hegemony is not acceptable to many other members, we conclude that institutionalized support for the larger mandate is lacking.

Institutionalization is weak not just because of the perennial financial crisis, the weakness of the secretariat engendered by its recruitment practices, and the absence of a standing military machinery on which new operations can be based. At one time the General Assembly indulged its penchant for hyperbole in announcing ambitious new norms of conduct for its members, only to see them disregarded at practically the same moment. Nor is the somewhat clouded legal basis for "intervention" a major reason for the weakness of institutionalization.[29] These complaints are no longer wholly apposite, because of major improvements in UN decisionmaking practices instituted in the 1980s. In fact, as experienced an international

civil servant as Sir Brian Urquhart is confident that these additional innovations are now feasible: creating an early-warning capability to alert the
world to upcoming troubles, linked to a Security Council ability to intervene preemptively upon receiving such warnings; creating standby military
forces (a standing reserve) with a regularized budget for its immediate
deployment; reviving the Military Staff Committee and its enlargement by
adding other major militarily powerful states; and upgrading UN abilities to
deal with terrorism by giving the Secretary-General a Delta-type force and
a panel of experts.[30] All of this would contribute to institutionalization.
None of it can be discussed without first understanding the relevant past
experience of the UN in three related fields: decolonization; arms control
and disarmament; and human rights, humanitarian intervention, and
democratization.

Decolonization. Some of the most striking UN successes in the field of
peaceful change and pacific settlement have occurred in the context of
decolonization. This meta-issue is now history. The patterns of consensus,
bloc alignment, and leadership that once prevailed are no longer relevant
today. The case of Namibia is thoroughly atypical because the international
position of South Africa is unique normatively and in terms of its political
dynamics, external as well as internal. The remaining territories subject to
Article 73 of the Charter are anomalies, not instances of peaceful change
that can teach us something about institutionalization of procedures and
norms. These territories do not raise the issue of national self-determination
because their populations wish to retain their "colonial" status; to consider
them useful precedents is to confuse colonial subjection with the quite different issue of multiethnic states and the special rights, if any, of ethnic
minorities in them. The formal declaration by the General Assembly that
the 1990s are the "International Decade for the Eradication of Colonialism"
can be excused only by considering it quixotic.

Arms control and disarmament. The disarmament field is not going to
teach us much more than that of decolonization. Multilateral organizations
devoted to peaceful settlement and collective security have always been
marginal with respect to such negotiations. Bilateral dealing between
Washington and Moscow resulted in the most important agreements;
regional organizations were significantly involved in Europe only. The one
striking success of the UN system is the Nuclear Nonproliferation Treaty.
The UN's Conference on Disarmament represents little more than the effort
of Third World and so-called nonaligned states to influence, without success, the direct talks among the former Cold War blocs about such global
conventions as those demilitarizing outer space and banning nonnuclear
weapons of mass destruction. While the General Assembly's ceremonial
announcement of the "Third Disarmament Decade" is rhetorical posturing,
we should note that the concern is less with weapons reduction and more

with the redirection of resources to peaceful uses, and that a consensus procedure is now employed for making decisions. Such innovations as new Missile Technology Control Regime owe no more to UN action than does the London Nuclear Suppliers' Conference agreement.[31]

Human rights, humanitarian intervention, and democratization. The basket of issues represented by these labels is the new growth area in multilaterally aided peaceful change. Hitherto these have been considered separate and separable—institutionally, legally, and financially. Before we look at them as a single issue, some points about the UN's role in the human rights field have to be made.

The General Assembly continues to write global conventions, as it has since the inception of the UN. The most recent include texts defining the rights of migrant workers, of children, and of ethnic minorities, as well as outlawing the use of torture. Such conventions, with one major exception, lack any UN monitoring role or complaint procedure. They are not self-enforcing and therefore create no new rights in fact unless ratification is followed by the adoption of appropriate national legislation. It is doubtful that they contribute to the institutionalization of norms. Much the same is true of the two covenants on human rights even though there is available a complaint-and-reporting procedure. However, the UN Commission on Human Rights is increasingly active in investigating complaints it receives from individuals and NGOs. It may be a participant in a norm-creation process that will legitimate multilateral intervention to protect human rights. Several Latin American countries actively espouse such a role for the UN as well as for the OAS, which they see as giving multilateral protection to newly established and insecure democratic governments. In fact, several see the future role of the OAS as a protector of weak democracies by way of monitoring the civil and political rights of citizens, though Mexico strongly opposes this policy.[32] The Geneva-based UN Center for Human Rights, the secretariat of the UN Commission, is possibly becoming the monitoring arm of the Commission in the investigations of complaints.

The indifferent success of free-standing human rights regimes has given rise to the hope that a melding of three activities—monitoring of human rights and elections, refugee relief, and peacekeeping—in ending civil wars can upgrade the impact of these intrusions into national sovereignty. The impressive mixture of these objectives and activities is illustrated by the UNTAG and ONUSAL experiences, to be reenacted, if all goes well, by MINURSO and UNTAC. ONUSAL, even before the cease-fire went fully into effect, acted as an ombudsman in human rights complaints on the part of ordinary citizens with respect to allegations of torture, illegal imprisonment, and assault. Such measures were considered necessary as confidence-building steps to make possible the eventual cease-fire and the disarming of guerrillas and their reintegration into normal political activity, including elections. The work of the UN High Commissioner for Refugees is intended, in some places, to empower refugees, once they are resettled, to take part in the political life of their countries as citizens rather than remain inert and exploited subjects.[33]

I doubt that the amalgamation of these formerly separate activities constitutes a genuine case of learning to manage interdependence. These experiences rest on consensual quicksand.[34] There is no agreement among states that suggests the acceptance of a new view of causation and more complex vision of instruments appropriate for effective multilateral action. Regional institutions that enjoy legitimacy and authority exist under the auspices of the Council of Europe and the OAS, while the OAU machinery has not yet displayed much life. These institutions should go their separate ways. It seems unlikely, given the lack of general consensus, that the UN's various commissions and committees will soon reach that level of attainment. In the meantime, however, harm can be done if they continue their activities under an aura of high promise and ever-loftier declarations not backed by a solid consensus among the members. Neither the invention of new basic rights nor the launching of numerous new investigations is likely to be helpful unless member-state performance is more responsive to these impulses. To argue that every shortcoming of the state and every threat to human freedom must become subject to UN intercession is to condemn the UN to failure, not usher in a community based on recognized interdependence. Interdependence must be experienced, not asserted as a matter of faith. For most people, the denial of human rights to someone thousands of miles away is a direct experience only if it appears in all its gory detail on the evening news.

Task Aggregation to Be Avoided
Do not create a metaregime for peacekeeping and peacemaking. Peacekeeping in the restricted sense of separating parties to an international war is a familiar and generally successful UN activity, one that regional organizations do not do well. Until the most recent period, such peacekeeping had nothing to do with introducing and protecting democracy and human rights, although refugee relief occasionally figured in such operations. At the same time, merging electoral supervision (in the context of multilaterally ending civil wars) with protecting civil and political rights most germane to the integrity of the electoral process makes a great deal of sense. This is a "natural" substantive combination of objectives and activities in which the protection of key civil rights is one means for the attainment of the key aim, stopping war. Institutionalization of the Salvadoran experience, therefore, is a reasonable objective for those of us who want to perfect the multilateral management of interdependence.

Peacekeeping, an activity so well understood, is so important in augmenting the management of disputes that have escalated to violence that it ought not be complicated with new assignment. Marrack Goulding wants to restrict peacekeeping to "UN field operations in which international personnel, civilian and/or military, are employed with the consent of the parties and under UN command to help control and resolve actual or potential international conflicts or internal conflicts which have a clear international dimension."[35] Nothing is said about democratization; civil wars are eligible for peacekeeping only if they are part of an international conflict as well. Obviously the special mediatory role of single powerful states is compatible with this conception, such as the US role in settlements in Cyprus, Angola, Namibia, and Rhodesia. Peacekeeping in this traditional and restricted sense does not require a firm "concordat" of the Permanent Five if one or more are willing to abstain from voting on measures they do not like instead of voting negatively. However, such an agreement would certainly help to institutionalize the practice further. Nor would peacekeeping be impaired if suggestions for monitoring borders or troop deployment were authorized prior to the outbreak of hostilities. An early-warning system is also consistent with the further institutionalization of old-fashioned peacekeeping.[36]

Democratization should not be attempted by any international organization unless all relevant parties show commitment to freedom and pluralism. The annual Freedom House surveys of the global diffusion of democracy disclose that between 1981 and 1990 the percentage of the world's population living under the institutions of freedom has increased from 36 to 39 percent; the number of "free" countries, from 51 to 61. The remainder are classified as either "partly free" or "not free." Since 1990 many more African countries have held free elections and have abolished single-party rule.[37] Nonetheless, democracy remains the form of government of a minority of countries. Whether its introduction in Africa and Latin America in the last few years betokens a permanent change remains debatable. Clearly, the passing of single-party rule and the holding of free elections once or twice does not a democracy make.

All parties must request the monitoring of elections and of human rights, humanitarian intervention, refugee relief, and aid to police and the courts in order for such operations to be authorized. Hence the activities of ONUSAL and UNTAG are models of what ought to be done. MINURSO and the Cambodian relief operation are much more ambiguous; if they turn out to be offering democracy in an inhospitable setting, then both freedom and the UN become the victims of disillusionment. To encourage a permanent OAS role in intervening on behalf of democracy even though a coup against an elected government has massive support is to force democracy down the throats of unwilling consumers.[38]

Aid to national self-determination by means of peacemaking ought not to be attempted unless a failure to act would result in genocide, as in the Kurdish case. If there is a danger of genocide or mass famine, then intervention is justifiable and international organizations ought to be prepared for mounting it. Peacemaking in Yugoslavia may still turn out to have been a mistake, because to determine who or what areas belong to which "nation" is often impossible. Are Croats or Serbs the more authentic nation to whom the Krajina ought to belong? How can any outsider determine this? Intervention makes sense only if the contending nations have agreed to abide by the results of a plebiscite conducted by the organization.

No intervention in any civil war ought to be attempted unless requested by all parties and/or unless genocide and famine are threatened in the absence of organizational intercession. It is not clear that this condition was fulfilled in the Yugoslav case. It certainly was not met in the case of the ECOWAS intervention in Liberia. This means that the organization is not clearly contributing to the establishment of a consensus-based government even though it may manage to separate and disarm the contending factions. The war is likely to resume as soon as the peacekeepers withdraw. Organizational intervention in civil wars makes sense only if the war is stalemated and the parties have given up hope of victory over one another.[39] In the absence of this condition, an enhanced democratization-peace-making-humanitarian intervention task is to be fostered only in situations threatened by genocide or famine, and then irrespective of consent.

New Task Aggregations to Be Encouraged

Heading off resource wars. We hear more and more about the likelihood of resource wars, especially among Third World countries.[40] Three Gulf conflicts, all involving Iraq as the core belligerent, illustrate the phenomenon. The prolonged Libyan conflict with Chad over the Aouzou Strip demonstrates how an interstate resource issue can become inseparable from domestic civil war and interethnic strife. Peaceful change and the peaceful settlement of disputes—international and domestic—must, in the future, take into account that the source of the grievance may involve a natural resource that might become a divisible "private" good or an international public good. The welfare aspects of the good, if they are part of the grievance, must also be considered in devising a multilateral solution.

The failure to reconcile such claims by dividing the resource might then be followed by the payment of "compensation" to the aggrieved party. This payment may take the form of loans from the World Bank, increased assistance from UNDP, or new services from specialized agencies. I suggest that true learning occurs when the parties and the organization can so reconceptualize their quarrel as to nest territorial and legal solutions in an economic one, to amalgamate territorial and economic problems into a single causal schema to resolve the quarrel peacefully.

An arms sales regime. Lasting democratization is heavily dependent on lasting demilitarization. Without access to modern arms, most Third World countries would be unable to fight wars, civil and international. Massive arms control negotiated by NATO and former Warsaw Pact states makes possible a rethinking of the arms trade in general. However, it also necessitates thinking about how one may compensate Third World exporters of arms for giving up on the deadly trade. Brazil, India, Argentina, Israel, Iran, and North Korea are unlikely to sacrifice their foreign exchange earnings for the love of peace, especially when arms sales provide a kind of substitute mission to military establishments running out of wars to fight. No regime would be acceptable unless the major merchants of death—the United States, the successor states to the USSR, France, and Britain—take the initiative in getting out of the arms trade. This requires the refusal on the part of these exporting states to extend credit for arms sales. But more important, such a regime must be tied to the economic-development ambitions and demands of Third World countries. It must offer compensation, in the form of some other economic benefits, for sales foregone. Learning must take the form of linking arms sales control to economic development much as we are already doing in the environmental policy field.

Unless the peacemaking and enforcement measures of the Charter become fully legitimate and routinized, it is not realistic to expect such countries as those of the Middle East to accept restraints on arms purchases. Simple coordination of arms export policies by means of information exchanges, a step the Permanent Five are now taking, is at best a first step, which must culminate in a more comprehensive prohibition on sales.

Why Enforcement Should Remain a Separate Task

The reversal of the UN's fortunes has encouraged many of us to heave a sigh of relief because the realist doomsayers of a Hobbesian world seem finally to have been confounded. Contemporary idealists tend to feel that because Hobbes has finally been vanquished we should now redefine collective security as something more comprehensive and melioristic than the definition enshrined in Chapter VII of the UN Charter. Instead of merely deterring and, if necessary, reversing acts of aggression, the practice of collective security ought to be expanded to bring about peaceful change before aggression becomes a temptation for the dissatisfied.

This sense of relief should be resisted. We need not juxtapose the Hobbesian view to recent history because its basis in theory and fact has always been weak. Interdependence, and the consequent recognition that unilateral state action is not likely to be effective, is undoubtedly much more strongly experienced now than in the past; but the picture that Hobbes drew and that the modern realists perpetuated was always a grotesque exaggeration. States did not always posture toward one another as if they were gladiators in the arena; nor did they calculate every ounce of power in terms of relative advantage over potential antagonists. The extreme condition in international politics was mistaken for the normal one.

There surely is now more opportunity for expanding actions to bring about peaceful change. But these opportunities ought not lead us to expect the end of aggression. Even if the UN becomes a more successful agent of peaceful change, with a mandate for intervention broader than a strict interpretation of Charter Article 2(7) allows, then we would be very foolish to expect the end of all temptation to belligerence. Therefore, the procedures for mounting sanctions and enforcement must be not only retained as now defined but also strengthened.

It is better not to redesign institutions on the assumption that everything interacts with everything else, that all processes are linked by complex feedback loops, even if this is in fact true. To postulate the nondecomposability of the global system is to be tempted to do nothing. Institutional effectiveness demands some decomposability of issues and policies because of our inability to comprehend and run human systems of unprecedented complexity.[41]

I discuss possible improvements of Chapter VII by focusing on reviving regionalism, reforming the Security Council, augmenting the leadership potential of the Secretary-General, and committing the United States to a consistent multilateralist emphasis.

Regional Organizations Revived?

Speaking generally, regional organizations are unable to do tasks better than the reborn UN; in most cases they cannot do them as well as the new UN. While some improvements are conceivable, the main justification for seeking better regional conflict management—escape from global meta-issues and big power hegemony—are no longer valid. Hence I do not share the hopes of some commentators that a revival of regionalism is possible and desirable.

The Organization of American States. In the past, and before the OAS was discredited in the eyes of many Latin Americans as essentially a front for Washington, the organization excelled at stopping externally supported civil wars.[42] Success is explained by US hegemony and the acquiescence, on the part of most Latin American governments, in the inter-American system's role as part of a Cold War alliance. Since the late 1960s there has been no such consensus; therefore, the United States has been unable to use the OAS in the same way. Hemispheric collective security since 1986 became more and more intertwined with the protection of human rights and the transition to democratic regimes, as in Central America, Chile, Suriname, and Haiti. If the OAS today has a comparative advantage in conflict management, it is in the new complex area of ending civil wars, protecting human rights, easing the introduction of democracy, and giving humanitarian aid. Some commentators note the OAS command over flexible procedures, its ability to appeal to the parties' declared commitment to OAS principles, the absence of the veto, and an informal negotiating environment. With the exception of the veto, the UN matches these characteristics. Their availability has done little for the OAS in the 1980s. More and more resource-related disputes arise among the members, but very few are referred to the organization for settlement. However, the impact (possibly unintended by the member states) of the Inter-American Commission on Human Rights has been growing consistently, and its services have become an important constituent in transitions to democracy. If the OAS is to be given a new lease on life at all it must be as the core agent in processes such as Esquipulas and Contadora. Hence it is striking that the governments prominent in these events preferred the UN and now talk of subregional organizations as terminators of civil strife, not of a reborn OAS.

The Organization of African Unity. The simplest explanation of the massive failure of the OAU to offer collective security to its members is the lack of any consistent and reliable consensus among them. As every issue seems to be divisive, settlements can be brokered only by extraregional actors using extraregional resources.[43] Lack of consensus among shifting coalitions prevented meaningful action in Angola, Western Sahara, the Ogaden, and Chad. Other interstate disputes, such as the Shaba invasions and the Tanzanian-Ugandan wars, never reached the OAU's agenda. Two attempts at peacekeeping in Chad foundered because the warring local factions never agreed to a clear mandate for the force and because some states designated to furnish the troops were laggard in doing so. While the OAS institutions might be characterized as arteriosclerotic, those of the OAU never developed at all. Even sympathetic observers agree that the formula of "trying OAU first" in African regional disputes is a bad one, and that primary reliance on the UN is both unavoidable and good.[44] Of course, if we agree that the real purpose of OAU is not conflict management but providing the legal and rhetorical arsenal for asserting the otherwise questionable sovereignty of African states, then the organization is a success despite itself.[45] In any event, though, it provides no basis for optimism that the conflict management job in Africa can be delegated by the UN.

Other regional organizations. The major conflict management job left to the Council of Europe is the enforcement of the European Convention on Human Rights; other potential regional disputes have come under the purview of the European Community and the Conference on Security and Cooperation in Europe.[46] The shortcomings of the OAU are mirrored by the Arab League, which shows little evidence of developing the kind of lasting interstate consensus on which an institutionalized conflict management role can be based. At best, the Arab League asserts the view of a sizable majority of its members when it delegates conflict management to one of them, such as to Syria in Lebanon. ASEAN has proved useful as a negotiating forum and as a source of confidence-building measures in disputes among its members. Its supporting role in the Cambodian settlement is vital. But the Islamic Conference, the South Asian Regional Cooperation Conference, various South American and Caribbean economic associations and their counterparts in Africa (with the exception of ECOWAS), and the Asia Pacific Economic Cooperation Council have acquired no role whatever in conflict management. The Commonwealth has played a modest role in mediating democratic transitions in Africa; ECOWAS may still acquire a dominant role in West African affairs.

UN support for regional conflict management. Any conceivable future for the familiar regional organizations in local conflict management rests on the abstinence of powerful nations from regional military intervention.[47] Intrusions, even by way of proxy wars and covert support for factions in civil strife or to governments, doom hopes of conflict management by local states. Revitalization of regional organizations demands that familiar practices of major power support for weak local governments be changed as follows. The United States, France, Britain, Germany, Japan, China, Russia, and India must conclude an agreement not to furnish military assistance of any kind to insurgent groups or to governments engaged in civil strife, though civilian political aid and humanitarian relief activities remain licit. The major powers ought to claim the right to force other countries to follow the same principle of abstinence. The principle might be anchored in the regime to monitor the arms trade discussed above. Regional organizations ought to have the task of authorizing departures from this rule. Outside military aid ought to be permissible only when expressly approved by the relevant regional organization. Aid from the outside can then also be funneled through regional institutions. The UN comes into the picture because the abstinence-plus-delegation regime ought to be formally discussed and approved by the Security Council.

Reforming the Security Council
If sanctions and enforcement are to be taken as serious and permanent weapons in the arsenal of UN conflict management, procedural and substantive improvement in the machinery must be considered. More important, however, is the question of the proper composition of the Security Council because it will determine the coalition that will have to authorize future enforcement measures. The hegemony of the present Permanent Five will not suffice.

Some procedural changes in the Security Council's function as conflict manager would simply improve peacekeeping and pacific settlement; they do not reach the slippery slope to sanctions and enforcement. Others do pass that point. We discuss them separately.

There is no dearth of suggestions that aim at perfecting the peaceful settlement and simple peacekeeping function. The Security Council could hold regular closed sessions at which potential future trouble spots are discussed, operating on the basis of an early-warning/intelligence system to be made available to the UN Secretary-General. Such a system might receive information from national intelligence services, do its own research, or—more ambitiously but improbably—have its own satellite surveillance capacity. What some have called a "risk-reduction center" might be set up, a think tank that surveys any possible threat to security—migration, environmental threat, resource-related threat, ethnic and religious tensions, economic intimidation—not just interstate and civil wars. (One wonders what such a center would discover that a perusal of the major newspapers does not already disclose.) Private parties ought to be used regularly as back-channel negotiators and as sources of information. Permanent observation missions might be established in special trouble spots. NGOs ought to be associated with them officially. Systematic observation of developing tensions, before they reach the point of aggression or breaches of the peace or civil war, might be increased and appropriate UN machinery created therefore.[48] Mediation and conciliation become simpler when a special fact-finding mission does not have to be authorized in New York—when information flows in routinely and can be acted on without publicity.

Suggestions that have the potential to push the UN into the use of force are much more controversial. Both kinds of suggestions presuppose that the abstinence rule in local conflicts and civil wars discussed above be firmly accepted. UN forces could be deployed in a threatened country before the outbreak of hostilities, thus not requiring the consent of the neighboring state. The Security Council might have its own rapid deployment force in the form of standby contingents trained and equipped for the purpose; Brian Urquhart suggests reviving Article 32 for this purpose. Permission to use offensive tactics would have to be given and the capability of Blue Helmets for offensive operations be upgraded. All of this is possible; none of it is likely, however, unless the finances of the UN are regularized and the composition of the Security Council is changed.

There is a good deal of disagreement on how to alter the present enforcement machinery, or whether to alter it at all. Pérez de Cuéllar was clearly unhappy with the procedure used against Iraq. He, along with many Third World governments, regretted the coalitional nature of the Operation Desert Storm forces and the commanding role of the United States; he called for the creation of a less hegemonial mechanism and for the activation of Article 50 to assure that third countries be compensated and that force not exceed the actual need.[49] These suggestions betoken a marked lack of enthusiasm for using Chapter VII. Those who wish to upgrade and institutionalize sanctions and enforcement advocate the creation of a multinational reserve force or setting up a permanent force under the command of the Military Staff Committee.[50]

Most of these suggestions remain in the realm of fantasy as long as the resulting arrangements will be subject to a Security Council unchanged in composition and voting rules. In all likelihood the interest of the Permanent Five in dealing with breaches of the peace in some Third World areas will decline without the Cold War to stimulate concern. The threat to at least some of them must be very palpable to trigger the kind of response we saw only in Korea in 1950 and in Kuwait in 1990–1991. Small countries, especially those in the Third World, have no vested concern in being ruled by the Permanent Five and harbor a good deal of resentment toward Operation Desert Storm. Most important, however, is the envy of Germany, Japan, India, Brazil, and possibly Nigeria and Egypt. Most are major powers or aspire to be such. India, Nigeria, Egypt, and Brazil think of themselves as the rightful hegemons in their respective regions. Japan has proposed the creation of six new permanent memberships for the countries named above, without also giving them the power of veto.

This reform is inadequate to satisfy the smaller countries, and it is probably unacceptable to some, such as India, who also resent the veto held by the Permanent Five. I therefore propose a different formula likely to lend the legitimacy and authority to future enforcement operations that the last one lacked. I propose that the six nations named become permanent members and that the number of nonpermanent members be raised so as to match the new number of permanent members (probably 11). None will have the power of veto. To pass a resolution with binding force a qualified majority in favor would have to be mobilized in each group. But the exact voting strength of the permanent members should not be equal; it should follow a weighting formula similar to that used by the IMF.

Upgrading the Secretariat
Obviously, the autonomous power and prestige of the office of the Secretary-General must be not only safeguarded but expanded. The role played by Pérez de Cuéllar in Central America, personally and by means of his special representatives, is prototypical of what might be accomplished elsewhere. His successor, Boutros Boutros-Ghali, has already reorganized the top ranks of the secretariat so as to adapt them to more efficient preparation for peacekeeping and peacemaking activities. He retained the persons most instrumental in helping the UN succeed in recent years, rewarded personnel from smaller countries, and provided adequate high-level representation for the Permanent Five.[51]

Much could be done to make the Secretary-General a widely visible and highly articulate spokesperson for UN causes and a proponent of UN-legitimated solutions. This requires, of course, a person in that office possessing appropriate personality characteristics, an outcome more likely in a Security Council in which the veto no longer operates. The executive head, instead of propounding the familiar platitudes, could offer specific solutions, timetables, and formulas. He or she would have to travel and speak widely to announce a "compelling and common vision" without denying the existing pluralism of views.[52] He or she could be assisted by a greatly expanded UN volunteer corps to provide low-cost civilian peacemaking services. He or she could also enlist retired statespersons of the caliber of Jimmy Carter and Willy Brandt as local representatives in making the Secretary-General the advocate of some of the new concepts developed by the independent high-level commissions that sought to arouse the world in the 1980s.

US Policy and the New World Order:
From Hegemony to Multilateralism?

President George Bush characterized Operation Desert Storm as the beginning of a new world order; but he also exulted on March 1, 1991, "By God, we've kicked the Vietnam syndrome once and for all." He seemed to suggest that the United States ought to lead the post-Iraq world as the new hegemon, as the only surviving superpower. The UN would merely be the instrument through which this hegemony would be projected, a camouflaged leadership rather than an imperial one.

There is ample support for this vision among US opinion leaders, and much opposition as well.[53] Internationalists and accommodationists, conservative and liberal alike, seem to feel that renewed US self-assertion in the rest of the world is now feasible and legitimate. The accommodationists seem to favor the United Nations as the exclusive instrument for projecting US values, while the internationalists prefer to do so only if the US view prevails—the Bush administration's formula. Isolationists and hard-liners, however, continue to hark back to the perceived lessons of Vietnam, to demonstrate their preference for a government devoted to domestic self-perfection; they either fear the UN or harbor contempt for it.

This schism in public and elite opinion argues ill for the kind of interventionist consensus required for consistent leadership by the United States toward a new world order, whatever that hitherto undefined notion will turn out to be. I now argue that by embracing a multilateral approach toward international conflict management, this schism can be partly bridged. Washington need not choose between isolationism and an international leadership role that makes only episodic and instrumental use of the UN.

The United States has no monopoly on the power to learn, to master the intricacies of massive international interdependence in almost all realms of collective public endeavor. To learn to live in the modern world of over 170 states is to recognize that none is sovereign in any meaningful sense of that term, although some are more able to solve their problems by autonomous action than others. To learn to live in such a world is also to recognize that knowledge for action is most likely to arise from continuous consultation with others facing similar problems. And it is to realize that unilateral action, not based on a very solid international consensus, will always be widely resented and ultimately fail even if it succeeds at first.

Is it better to save the Kurds by unilateral action, or to do a somewhat less perfect job by deferring to a UN consensus that will hesitate between protecting Iraqi sovereignty and preventing genocide? Is it better to back MINURSO to the hilt (thus deferring to the UN consensus), or to remain ambivalent in the face of Moroccan efforts to hobble MINURSO (thus siding with an ally in Arab affairs)? US leaders have three choices. They can act unilaterally by sidestepping multilateral organizations; they can anticipate or engineer a hasty consensus in such organizations and then mount the operation they prefer; or they can wait for a multilateral consensus to form on the basis of a compromise that will probably fail to meet all US preferences. Internationalists of the type now in power will prefer the second alternative; hard-liners, the first; and accommodationists, the third. I am concerned with stimulating collective learning, with helping in the development of causal conceptions that recognize complex linkages among issues while allowing for the necessary partial decomposability. Hence I favor the third course of action for the United States. Learning occurs when action based on initially imperfect compromise is recognized as flawed by the member states, thus triggering an improvement in mandate and mission in the next iteration.

The shrewd practitioner of multilateralism hides the ability to be the hegemon. Multilateralism implies quiet leadership, guidance by means of continuous consultation, and patience for producing an adequately sized coalition. It means accepting compromises that fall short of the immediate goals. It also means not overloading international organizations with tasks that are likely to discredit them. The true mark of a multilaterally inclined superpower is its knowledge that there is no rule requiring it to lead all the time, and perhaps not even most of the time.

Appendix 4.1 Definition and Operationalization of Variables

I. Salience
  A. Intensity
    1. Fatalities (civil and military)
        1 = no fatalities
        2 = 1–25
        3 = 26–100
        4 = 101–1,000
        5 = 1,001–2,000
        6 = 2,001–10,000
        7 = 10,001–100,000
        8 = over 100,000

2. Duration of hostilities (years between first evidence of rival claims and settlement and/or disappearance)

    1 = less than one year
    2 = 1–2 years
    3 = 2–3 years
    4 = over 3 years

3. Likelihood of abatement for three years (examples of abatement: reducing propaganda, ending or reducing military preparation, reopening border)

    In the context in which the dispute arose, would the parties have ended hostilities and/or reduced the fervor of their claims if left to themselves by the organization?

    1 = yes, very likely
    2 = possibly
    3 = 50–50 chance
    4 = possibly no
    5 = no, very unlikely

4. Likelihood of disappearance (examples of disappearance: formal settlement, dropping claims, resuming normal diplomatic and/or commercial relations)

    In the context in which the dispute arose, when would the parties have let their claims lapse with or without a formal settlement if left to themselves by the organization?

    1 = in less than one year
    2 = in 1–5 years
    3 = in 5–10 years
    4 = in 10–20 years
    5 = in more than 20 years

5. Likelihood of isolation.

    In the context in which the dispute arose, would the parties have permitted the dispute to escalate if left to themselves by the organization by taking any of the following measures?

    1 = introducing new issues and claims, expanding the scope of fighting, or lesser measures

    2 = succeeding in obtaining the open diplomatic support of other states

    3 = succeeding in getting others to supply arms

    4 = succeeding in getting others (except the United States and USSR) to furnish irregular troops

    5 = succeeding in getting others (except the United States and USSR) to join fully in the fighting

6. Major war

    How likely was it that the Soviet Union and the United States would engage in a war over this issue, using nuclear weapons or massive conventional weapons on several fronts?

1 = impossible
2 = not impossible, but very unlikely
3 = quite possible
4 = likely

7. Intensity scale [formula for computing intensity: a χ b (c + d)(e)(f) = 6,400 maximum]

Insignificant	1–19
Very low	20–39
Low	40–99
Moderate	100–299
High	300–999
Very high	Over 1,000

B. Type of warfare
No military operations

Very limited	Military operations without fighting; casualties incidental to rioting
Support diplomacy	Military operations and fighting intended as reinforcing diplomatic moves; political moves considered primary
Defeat enemy	Military operations and fighting considered primary to defeat enemy and/or conquer its territory
C.	Extent of spread (coded at time of referral)
Bilateral	Exclusively bilateral; third parties not involved at all
Local	Third parties are giving military and/or diplomatic aid to one or both of the parties but are not preparing to fight
Regional	Third parties in the immediate geographic region enter the dispute militarily or are about to do so
Global	Third parties elsewhere in the world enter the dispute militarily or are about to do so

II. Global context
  A. Issue
    Colonial
    Interstate, Cold War (issue is communist vs. noncommunist)
    Interstate, other (non–Cold War, noncolonial)
    Internal (Cold War)
    Internal (non–Cold War)

B. Alignment with reference to Cold War (formal alliance or close diplomatic tie at time dispute was discussed by organization)

Members of same bloc

Members of opposing blocs

One member of a bloc, one nonaligned

Both nonaligned

C. Power of parties

Parties to disputes were coded in terms of the scale developed in Robert W. Cox and Harold K. Jacobson, *The Anatomy of Influence*, App. (New Haven: Yale University Press, 1973). Each state party to a dispute was coded in each five-year period.

Smallest	Cox-Jacobson score of 4 or less
Small	Cox-Jacobson score of 5–9
Middle	Cox-Jacobson score of 10–14
Large	Cox-Jacobson score of 15–20
Superpower	Cox-Jacobson score of over 20

Each conflict was then coded in terms of the following dyads (disputes involving more than two parties were coded by selecting the most powerful dyad):

Small or smallest vs. small or smallest

Middle vs. middle and all lesser powers

Large vs. large and all lesser powers

Superpower vs. middle and all lesser powers

Superpower vs. superpower and large power

III. Management

A. Decision

None: No discussion or formal discussion without decision, or formal decision to refer the dispute to another forum

Weak: Formal decision requesting compliance from parties without calling for any kind of follow-up or supervision

Strong: Formal decision requesting settlement by authorizing investigation, mediation, supervision, truce observation, peacekeeping, enforcement measures

B. Operations

None: No operation authorized.

Small: Investigation, mediation, conciliation—involving a staff of 20 persons or fewer

Large: Supervision, truce observation, peacekeeping, enforcement measures—involving more than 20 persons

C. Leadership defined as initiative plus continuing pressure to obtain organizational discussion and/or action

One superpower

Two superpowers (even if one is passive and/or abstains in vote)

One or more large powers

One or more middle, small, and smallest powers

Secretary-General (includes all situations in which the Secretary-General or the presiding officer of the Security Council, either alone or in collaboration with a member state, takes the initiative

    D. Consensus (coded on the basis of the strongest resolution that was adopted by the relevant forum; when no resolution passed, the strongest defeated resolution was coded)

The extent of agreement is scaled in terms of power:

None: The constitutional requirement for making a decision is not met in the particular organization or organ.

Weak: One superpower plus various other powers act to just meet the particular constitutional requirement; in the Security-Council, a positive vote of debatable constitutionality involving the question of whether the vote or nonvote of a permanent member was a "veto"

Security Council only; the minimum constitutional formula for adopting a resolution is just met; abstention by a permanent member is considered acquiescence

Wide:The constitutional requirement for passing a resolution is met (or exceeded) without all large, middle, and smaller powers in the organization joining the majority; in the Security Council, abstentions are considered as acquiescence

Very wide:The constitutional requirement for passing a resolution is met (or exceeded) by a wide margin; in the Security Council all unanimous votes (no abstentions or absences permitted) and all resolutions adopted without formal vote

IV. Success

Did the existence and activity of the international organization contribute to the control of the conflict? Did states behave more cooperatively than they would have in the absence of organizational action? The frame of reference is the manifest conflict-control function given to the organization in its Charter.

    A. Success in stopping hostilities

        n = no opportunity to stop through no fault of organization

        0 = failed to stop

        1 = helped to stop

        2 = stopped

    B. Success in conflict abatement for three years (examples of abatement same as in Section I.A.3)

      0 = failed to settle

      1 = helped to abate

      2 = abated

C. Success in conflict settlement (examples of settlement same as in Section I.A.4)

      0 = failed to settle

      1 = helped to settle

      2 = settled

D. Success in isolating conflict (evidence of isolation: third parties did not support disputants diplomatically or militarily when there was some chance that they might have done so)

      n = conflict had no opportunity to expand

      0 = failed to isolate

      1 = helped to isolate

      2 = isolated

Formula for computing success:

$a + b + c + d$ = raw success; maximum = 8

Success scale: None: Organizational action made no difference to outcome on any dimension (0 raw score).

           Some, limited: Organizational action made some difference on one or two dimensions (one or two 1 scores; raw score of 1 or 2).

           Great: Organizational action made some difference on three or four dimensions (three or four 1 scores; raw score of 3 or 4).

           Organizational action made a great difference on at least one dimension plus at least some difference on one other (one or more 2 scores plus one, two, or three 1 scores; one or two 2 scores plus not more than two n scores; one 2 score plus one 1 score, plus 0s or ns; raw score of 3, 4, 5, 6, 7, 8).

Appendix 4.2

Table A   United Nations: Differences in Dispute Profiles Between Past and Most Recent Eras

Variable	1945–1985	%	1986–1990	%
Intensity	high/highest	24	high/highest	33
	very low/insignificant	43	very low/insignificant	14
Type of warfare	none/rioting	80	none/rioting	69
	heavy fighting	11	heavy fighting	21
Spread	bilateral	50	bilateral	59
Type of issue	decolonization	32	decolonization	31
	other	42	other	45
Alignment of parties	opposing blocs	26	opposing blocs	31
	same bloc	18	same bloc	14
Power of parties	small vs. small	30	small vs. small	24
	super vs. others	30	super vs. others	36
Decision of IGO	no operation	22	no operation	17
Operations of IGO	large operation	16	large operation	19
Leadership	small power	62	small power	52
	Secretary-General	15	Secretary-General	24
Consensus	none/weak	26	none/weak	40

Table B   Five Regional Organizations: Differences in Dispute Profiles Between Past and Most Recent Eras

Variable	1945–1985	%	1986–1990	%
Intensity	very low/insignificant	59	very low/insignificant	47
	high	16	high	26
Type of warfare	none/rioting	86	none/rioting	60
	heavy fighting	7	heavy fighting	33
Spread	bilateral	48	bilateral	33
	local	30	local	40
Type of issue	other	87	other	87
Alignment of parties	nonaligned	51	nonaligned	47
	opposing blocs	11	opposing blocs	33
Power of parties	small vs. small	73	small vs. small	53
	large vs. small	16	large vs. small	27
	super vs. others	6	super vs. others	20
Decision of IGO	mount operation	73	mount operation	80
Operations of IGO	large operation	14	large operation	40
Leadership	small power	94	small power	80
	Secretary-General	6	Secretary-General	20
Consensus	none/weak	8	none/weak	33

Table C   United Nations: Correlates of Successful Conflict Management, 1945–1985

Successful cases:	N = 72	
All cases:	N = 149	%
Intensity	high	5
	medium	−5
	low	0
Warfare	high	−1
	medium	−2
	low	3
Spread	regional/global	7
	local	4
	bilateral	−11
Issue	Cold War	−13
	decolonization	7
	other	6
Alignment	same bloc	6
	opposing blocs	−7
	neither	1
Power of	super vs. less	−12
parties	large/middle vs. less	16
	small vs. small	−4
Decision	operation	19
	no operation	−4
	no decision	−15
Operation	large operation	15
	small operation	5
	no operation	−18
Leadership	Secretary-General and superpower	3
	Secretary-General and other	6
	one superpower	−3
	two superpowers	2
	all others	−6
Consensus	very wide	13
	wide	2
	weak	−1
	none	−14

Note: Difference in % of successful conflict management cases from all disputes referred to organization, for each variable

Table D **United Nations: Correlates of Successful Conflict Management, 1986–1990**

Successful cases:	N = 19	
All cases:	N = 42	%
Intensity	high	25
	medium	−37
	low	12
Warfare	high	16
	medium	6
	low	−22
Spread	regional/global	91
	local	18
	bilateral	−27
Issue	Cold War	18
	decolonization	−15
	other	−3
Alignment	same bloc	−4
	opposing blocs	11
	neither	−7
Power of	super vs. less	−10
parties	large/middle vs. less	−8
	small vs. small	18
Decision	operation	35
	no operation	−7
	no decision	−28
Operation	large operation	23
	small operation	6
	no operation	−29
Leadership	Secretary-General and superpower	20
	Secretary-General and other	11
	one superpower	4
	two superpowers	4
	all others	−36
Consensus	very wide	10
	wide	9
	weak	8
	none	−27

Notes: Difference in % of successful management cases from all disputes referred to organization, for each variable

Table E Four Regional Organizations: Correlates of Successful Conflict Management, 1945–1985

| Successful cases: | N = 56 | |
All cases:	N = 91	%
Intensity	high	–3
	medium	–1
	low	4
Warfare	high	–5
	medium	–3
	low	8
Spread	regional/global	–5
	local	–4
	bilateral	9
Issue	Cold War	3
	decolonization	3
	other	–6
Alignment	same bloc	5
	opposing blocs	0
	neither	–5
Power of parties	super vs. less	2
	large/middle vs. less	1
	small vs. small	–3
Decision	operation	8
	no operation	–2
	no decision	–6
Operation	large operation	5
	small operation	7
	no operation	–12
Leadership	Secretary-General and superpower	0
	Secretary-General and other	–1
	one superpower	0
	two superpowers	0
	no operation	1
Consensus	very wide	20
	wide	–5
	weak	–3
	none	–12

Note: Difference in % of successful conflict management cases from all disputes referred to organization, for each variable

Table F   Four Regional Organizations: Correlates of Successful Conflict Management, 1986–1990

Successful cases:	N = 9	
All cases:	N = 15	%
Intensity	high	–4
	medium	6
	low	–3
Warfare	high	–11
	medium	4
	low	7
Spread	regional/global	–5
	local	–7
	bilateral	12
Issue	Cold War	–2
	decolonization	0
	other	2
Alignment	same bloc	–20
	opposing blocs	0
	neither	20
Power of	super vs. less	–9
parties	large/middle vs. less	–5
	small vs. small	12
Decision	operation	–2
	no operation	2
	no decision	0
Operation	large operation	16
	small operation	–18
	no operation	2
Leadership	Secretary-General and superpower	9
	Secretary-General and other	4
	one superpower	0
	two superpowers	0
	all others	–13
Consensus	very wide	–4
	wide	4
	weak	0
	none	0

Note: Difference in % of successful conflict management cases from all disputes referred to organization, for each variable

Table G Fate of Major Disputes Adjudicated by International Court of Justice (as of December 31, 1990)

Dispute	Year of Decision	Plaintiff	Defendant	Outcome
Corfu Channel	1949	Great Britain	Albania	Judgment for Britain not implemented by Albania
Haya de la Torre (three cases)	1949–1951	Colombia	Peru	Judgment not implemented and eventually reversed on procedural grounds
Anglo-Norwegian fisheries	1951	Great Britain	Norway	Judgment for Norway implemented
Anglo-Iranian Oil Co.	1953	Great Britain	Iran	Court declines jurisdiction; Iran refuses to participate; provisional measures not implemented
Minquiers and Encrehos Islands	1953	Great Britain	France	Judgment for Britain implemented
Monetary gold	1954	Italy	US, UK, France	Court declines jurisdiction
Aerial incident of 1955	1959	Israel, US, Great Britain	Bulgaria	Court declines jurisdiction
Belgo-Dutch border delimitation	1959	Belgium	Netherlands	Judgment for Belgium implemented
Right of passage over India	1960	Portugal	India	Judgment for Portugal not implemented
Honduran border	1960	Honduras	Nicaragua	Judgment for Honduras implemented
Temple of Preah Vihear	1962	Cambodia	Thailand	Judgment for Cambodia implemented
Northern Cameroon	1963	Cameroon	UK	No judgment rendered
Status of South West Africa	1966	Ethiopia, Liberia	South Africa	Case dismissed on procedural grounds
North Sea continental shelf	1969	West Germany	Denmark, Netherlands	Judgment facilitates multilateral negotiations
Jurisdiction of ICAO Council	1972	India	Pakistan	Judgment favors Pakistan but has no effect
Pakistani prisoners of war	1973	Pakistan	India	India declines participation; case withdrawn
Fisheries jurisdiction	1974	Great Britain	Iceland, West Germany	Iceland fails to appear; no implementation of provisional measures or final award
Nuclear tests in Pacific	1974	Australia, New Zealand	France	France did not appear or implement provisional measures or final award
Aegean Sea continental shelf	1978	Greece	Turkey	Court declines jurisdiction

(continues)

Table G *(continued)*

Dispute	Year of Decision	Plaintiff	Defendant	Outcome
US Embassy in Teheran	1980	US	Iran	Iran did not appear or implement any of the rulings against it
Continental shelf	1982 1985	Tunisia	Libya	Decision facilitates bilateral negotiations
Gulf of Maine	1984	Canada	US	Ruling implemented by both
Military operations in Nicaragua	1984	Nicaragua	US	US refuses to appear or abide by adverse rulings
Continental shelf	1985	Libya	Malta	Decision facilitates bilateral negotiations
Burkina Faso/ Mali border	1986	Burkina Faso	Mali	Mali implements adverse ruling
Transborder armed actions	1987	Nicaragua	Costa Rica	Complaint withdrawn
Transborder armed actions		Nicaragua	Honduras	Decision pending
East Timor continental shelf		Portugal	Australia	Decision pending
Maritime delim- itation near Jan Mayen Island		Denmark	Norway	Decision pending
Aerial incident of 1989		Iran	US	Decision pending
Phosphate lands		Nauru	Australia	Decision pending

The following cases were not counted because they were concerned primarily with the rights of private parties and did not raise political, territorial, resource, or military issues: rights of US nationals in Morocco; Ambatielos; Nottebohm; certain Norwegian loans; guardianship of infants; Interhandel; Barcelona traction and power.

In the following advisory opinions, the de facto defendant states failed to implement the rulings addressed to them:

Admission of states to the UN	1949	All permanent members of the Security Council
Reparation for injuries suffered in UN service	1949	Jordan, Egypt
Interpretation of peace treaties with Hungary, Bulgaria, Romania	1950	Hungary, Bulgaria, Romania
Status of Southwest Africa	1950 1955 1956 1971	South Africa
Certain expenses of the UN	1962	France, USSR
Western Sahara	1975	Morocco

Source: Jonathan I. Charney, "Disputes Implicating the Institutional Credibility of the Court: Problems of Non-Appearance, Non-Participation and Non-Performance," in L. Damrosch, ed., *The International Court of Justice at the Crossroads* (Dobbs Ferry, N.Y.: Transnational, 1987), 288–319.

Table H Large United Nations Field Operations: Mandates and Missions, 1986–1991

Operation	Maximum Strength	Make One Side Withdraw	Separate Parties	Create Buffer Zone	Observe Compliance with Ceasefire and Mediate	Disarm Parties; Stop Arms Inflow	Monitor Elections and Human Rights	Administer Civilian Relief	Run Civil Administration
UNGOMAP (Afghanistan) 1988–1990	50	X							
UNIIMOG (Iran/Iraq) 1988–	400	X	X	X	X[a]	X[a]	X[a]		
UNTAG (Namibia) 1989–1990	8,000	X	X	X		X	X		X
OONUVEN (Nicaragua) 1989							X (w/OAS)		
UNAVEM (Angola) 1988–1991	70	X							
ONUCA (Central America) 1989–	1,038		X		X	X[a]			
UNAVEM 2 (Angolan War) 1991–	550					X	X		
ONUVEH (Haiti) 1991–	193						X (w/OAS)	X	
UNAMIC (advance mission in Cambodia) 1991–	380		X		X				
ONUSAL (El Salvador) 1991	170				X		X		
UNIKOM (Kuwait) 1991–	300			X	X	X			
MINURSO (Western Sahara) 1991–	2,900	X	X		X	X (w/OAU)	X	X	

a. Failed or was prevented from fulfilling mandate completely

Table I Large United Nations Field Operations: Contextual Conditions

	Stronger Party Agreed to Operation Directed Against One Party?	Withdraw Before Operation Began?	Mandate	All Parties Agree on Duration	Composition[a]
UNGOMAP	yes	yes	yes	no	no
UNIIMOG	no	no	yes	yes	yes
UNTAG	yes	yes	yes(?)	yes	no
OONUVEN	yes	—	yes	yes	no
UNAVEM	yes	yes	yes	yes	no
ONUCA	no	no	no	no	no
UNAVEM 2	no	—	yes	yes	no
ONUVEH	yes	—	no	no	no
ONUSAL	no	—	yes	yes	yes
UNIKOM	yes	yes	no	no	no
MINURSO	yes	in part	yes	yes	yes
Cambodia (UNTAC)	unclear	no	yes	no	no
Croatia	unclear	no	no	no	no

a. If no, Secretary-General determined the composition himself

Notes

I am deeply indebted to Felicia Wong for outstanding research assistance and to Charles Eckman of the University of California (Berkeley) library for important help in the retrieval of documents. The advice of Benjamin Rivlin, Gene Lyons, and Robert A. Pastor was absolutely essential. I acknowledge with gratitude the support of the University of California Institute on Global Conflict and Cooperation.

1. The scale as well as the full research design are explained in detail in Appendix 4.1. Unless otherwise noted, all statistics for the period 1945–1984 are taken from Ernst B. Haas, *Why We Still Need the United Nations* (Berkeley: Institute of International Studies, 1986). This study was also published as "The Collective Management of International Conflict, 1945-84," United Nations Institute for Training and Research, *The United Nations and the Maintenance of International Peace and Security* (Dordrecht, The Netherlands: Nijhoff, 1987), 3–72. Events data referring to the period since 1984 were collected and analyzed by myself; they are reported here for the first time. Coding was done jointly by Felicia Wong and myself. The cutoff date for events used is December 31, 1990.

2. The notion of policy science as a form of theory was pioneered by Stanley Hoffmann in *Contemporary Theory in International Relations* (Englewood Cliffs, N.J.: Prentice-Hall, 1960). My approach to a theory of international relations and my focus on explaining change are described in my *When Knowledge Is Power* (Berkeley: University of California Press, 1990); and in "Reason and Change in International Life," in Robert L. Rothstein, ed., *The Evolution of Theory in International Relations* (Columbia: University of South Carolina Press, 1991).

3. *Report of the Secretary-General on the Work of the Organisation* (September 1991), UN document A/46/1, 3.

4. See Larry Minear, *Humanitarianism Under Siege* (Trenton, N.J.: Red Sea Press, 1991); Robert A. Pastor, ed., *Democracy in the Americas* (New York: Holmes and Meier, 1989); Council of Freely-Elected Heads of Government, *Observing Nicaragua's Elections 1989–1990* (Atlanta: Carter Center of Emory University, 1990); and Jennifer McCoy, Larry Garber, and Robert A. Pastor, "Making Peace Through Mediating and Observing Elections," *Journal of Democracy* (Fall 1991), 1–13.

5. See Appendix 4.2 for the definition of all variables and subvariables.

6. See Appendix 4.2, Tables A and B, for the data on which these generalizations are based.

7. See Appendix 4.2, Tables C and D, for the data on which these generalizations are based. As a rule of thumb, I interpret any change of 10 percent or more in a subvariable in the most recent era, as contrasted with the earlier ones, as being a significant shift.

8. See Appendix 4.2, Tables E and F, for the data on which these generalizations are based. The same rule of thumb as in note 7 applies.

9. See note 6–8 for data sources regarding this section.

10. Jonathan I. Charney, "Disputes Implicating the Institutional Credibility of the Court," in L. Damrosch, ed., *The International Court of Justice at the Crossroads* (Dobbs Ferry, N.Y.: Transnational), 299–300.

11. Material in this paragraph draws on the data presented in Appendix 4.2, Table H. The evidence that the success of all peacekeeping and truce observation missions is strongly associated with the prior conclusion of a clear agreement on mandate, duration, and composition to which all the parties and the Security Council have acceded is presented by Cameron R. Hume, *Negotiations Before Peacekeeping* (New York: International Peace Academy, 1991).

12. *Report of the Secretary-General*, 2–3.

13. UNTAG is the classical operation illustrating this trend, though operations in El Salvador and Western Sahara have similar characteristics. See Johan Kaufmann and Nico Schrijver, *Changing Global Needs: Expanding Roles for the United Nations System* (Hanover, N.H.: Academic Council on the United Nations System, 1990), 77–88.

14. The General Assembly approved ONUVEH over some dissent and mandated that the Secretary-General conduct complicated consultations before similar operations can be launched, perhaps knowing that Elliott Richardson (for the UN) and Jimmy Carter (for his Council of Freely-Elected Heads of Government) had to persuade Daniel Ortega to accept the outcome of the Nicaraguan elections monitored by the UN and the OAS. ONUSAL originated in independent requests from the Salvadoran president and the FMLN, who insisted on the UN's observing human rights violations as a confidence-building measure that had to precede the elections. Therefore the FMLN insisted that Pérez de Cuéllar give wide publicity to any violation discovered. See UN Department of Public Information and Institute of Policy Studies of Singapore, *The Singapore Symposium* (United Nations, 1991), 45–49.

15. For the legal argument supporting this interpretation, see Frederick K. Lister, "Thoughts on the Use of Military Force in the Gulf Crisis," Occasional Paper Series VII (New York: CUNY, Ralph Bunche Institute on the United Nations, June 1991).

16. S/PV. 2943, 7 (September 24, 1990). Some of my information in this paragraph comes from personal interviews, some is in the *New York Times* (August 30, 1990, and March 3, 1991).

17. *UN Chronicle* (June 1991), 11.

18. I appreciate the help given by Robert Pastor and Jennifer McCoy with respect to OAS materials. The perfunctory and self-congratulatory report of the Secretary-General on election monitoring is suggestive of a more general attitude. See "La OEA en el Proceso de Observación Electoral," OEA/Ser.P, AG/Document 2672/91 (May 1, 1991). Requests were made as early as 1987 that elections in Haiti be monitored. The Interamerican Commission on Human Rights criticized Mexican electoral practices in 1990 without eliciting a request from the Mexican government for electoral monitoring.

19. This section is an abbreviated version of Haas, *When Knowledge Is Power,* chap. 4.

20. Jonathan Mann (on behalf of Doctors of the World), in *New York Times* (May 1991; exact date not available) applauding the US intervention in Kurdistan.

21. A/RES/45/101 (January 30, 1991) and A/RES/45/100 (January 29, 1991), 2. Nevertheless, the Security Council authorized armed humanitarian intervention (peacekeeping and food and medical relief) in the Somali civil war in April 1992 (UNOSOM).

22. S/21933 and S/21986.

23. For inside information on the significant role played by the UN secretariat in writing the Cambodia agreements on behalf of the Five Permanent Members and the co-chairs (France and Indonesia) of the conference of Cambodian parties, see *Singapore Symposium* (UN, 1991) 23–27, 65–79.

24. Kaufmann and Schrijver, *Changing Global Needs,* 57–73. For an exhaustive list of questions requiring clear answers before we can be sure that a consensus supporting a permanent UN conflict management role exists, see Thomas G. Weiss and Kurt M. Campbell, "American, Soviet and Third World Views about International Conflict Management," in Thomas G. Weiss, ed., *The United Nations in Conflict Management* (New York: International Peace Academy, 1990), 21–30.

25. See Weiss, *United Nations in Conflict Management*, 77–82, for a statement to this effect by former Soviet Deputy Foreign Minister (now UN Under-Secretary-General for Political Affairs) Vladimir F. Petrovsky. Soviet multilateralism is interpreted as a necessary instrument of perestroika (and limited by its survival) by Celeste Wallender in "Soviet Policy Toward the Third World in the 1990s," in Thomas G. Weiss and Meryl A. Kessler, eds., *Third World Security in the Post–Cold War Era* (Boulder: Lynne Rienner, 1991), 35–66.

26. Michael Clough, "US Policy Toward the Third World in the Twenty-First Century," in Weiss and Kessler, *Third World Security*, 67–84.

27. The phrase is Alexander George's, as quoted in US Institute of Peace, *Journal* (October 1991), 1. For a brilliant analysis of the limitations on the autonomy of the UN and its Secretary-General in the future, see Inis L. Claude, "Reflections on the Role of the Secretary-General of the United Nations," Occasional Paper Series VIII (New York: CUNY, Ralph Bunche Institute on the United Nations, September 1991).

28. *Report of the Secretary-General*, 8.

29. Ethan A. Nadelman, "Global Prohibition Regimes," *International Organization* 44, no. 4 (Autumn 1990), 479–526, shows how new norms gain general international acceptance and why the norms involved in conflict management have yet to gain such acceptance. Reorganization of the UN secretariat is discussed by Brian Urquhart in an unpublished memorandum (New York, February 1991) entitled "Reorganization of the United Nations Secretariat." The prohibition on multilateral intervention is debunked by the Secretary-General of the Institute of International Law, Nicolas Valticos, in "Non, le droit international n'interdit pas l'ingérence lors ce qu'il s'agit du droit de l'homme."

30. *New York Review of Books* (March 7, 1991), 36–37.

31. On the MTCR, see Jane E. Nolan, *Trappings of Power* (Washington, D.C.: Brookings Institute, 1991). The regime, created in 1987, consists of parallel export control regulations for missiles capable of delivering a payload of 500 kg over a range of 300 km and missile parts, on the part of seven Western governments. Russia, though not a member, agreed to abide by the same rules early in 1990, after the transfer of Scud-Bs to Iraq and Afghanistan. Unfortunately, major Third World exporters of missiles are not members and the regulations do not cover dual-use systems and parts.

32. Jack Donnelly, *Universal Human Rights in Theory and Practice* (Ithaca: Cornell University Press, 1989). The Secretary-General agrees with this qualified view. See *Report of the Secretary-General*, 9. UNDP in 1991 first published *The Human Development Report*, which contained a freedom index. This index aroused the anger of the Third World members because it showed, not surprisingly, that lack of political freedom is consistently associated with low living standards, a finding from which not even the theoretically democratic Third World states were wholly exempt. Since rich Arab states also scored poorly, the accuracy of the official UN index seems impressive. The episode underscores the extremely ambivalent attitude of Third World states toward international human rights regimes, irrespective of the rights they support in the process of convention-drafting. See the *New York Times* (June 23, 1991).

33. *UN Chronicle* (September 1991), 40–55.

34. Initiatives in the Subcommission on the Prevention of Discrimination of the UN Commission on Human Rights with respect to alleged violations are usually presented by European countries and rarely enjoy unanimous support. A comprehensive critique of China was passed by a secret ballot of 15 to 9 in 1989. Even though Resolution A/45/150 (December 18, 1990), "Enhancing the Effectiveness of

the Principle of Periodic and Genuine Elections," presents the case in terms of the kind of comprehensive argument sketched above (while directing it at the RSA), the resolution was not supported by 25 Third World countries, including China, India, Mexico, Peru, Iran, and Syria; even the democratic governments of Ecuador and Colombia failed to support the measure. On the same date the Assembly adopted Resolution A/45/151, "Respect for the Principles of National Sovereignty and Non-Interference in the Internal Affairs of States in Their Electoral Processes," which seems to take back most of the things affirmed in the above resolution (while attacking the RSA and Israel) and insists that foreign participation in national elections is intervention. Forty-four states failed to support this resolution, almost all of them European, North American, and Caribbean. For a skeptical view of USAID's efforts to link foreign aid with democratization, see Jerold Green, "USAID's Democratic Pluralism Initiative: Pragmatism or Altruism?" *Ethics and International Affairs* 5 (1991), 215–232.

35. *Singapore Symposium* (UN, 1991), 25.

36. The "concordat" idea was suggested by the Palme Commission. Further institutionalization of peacemaking is discussed by Tapio Kanninen, "The Future of Early Warning and Preventive Action in the UN," Occasional Papers V (New York: CUNY, Ralph Bunche Institute on the United Nations, May 1991).

37. *Freedom-at-Issue,* January-February 1981 and 1990. See the regular issue of *Africa Demos,* published by the Carter Center of Emory University, Atlanta, for very circumspect projections of the degree of democracy in Africa despite recent changes.

38. As advocated by Robert A. Pastor, *Perspective,* in *The Atlanta Constitution/The Atlanta Journal* (February 9, 1992).

39. See the contributions of David Laitin, Donald Rothchild, and Robert Rotberg in Robert I. Rotberg, ed., *Africa in the 1990s and Beyond* (Boston: World Peace Foundation, 1988), for analyses advocating great restraint by all outsiders with respect to intervening in African civil wars. Rotberg suggests that UN sanctions actually strengthened the RSA government, a case disputed by Robert Price in *The Apartheid Regime* (New York: Oxford University Press, 1991).

40. See, for instance, Ronnie D. Lipschutz, *When Nations Clash* (Cambridge, Mass.: Ballinger, 1989).

41. The case for the parts of the modern world that remain Hobbesian and those that do not is nicely made by James N. Rosenau, *Turbulence in World Politics* (Princeton: Princeton University Press, 1990). The theoretical basis for my argument against overaggregation comes from Herbert A. Simon. See, for instance, his *Reason in Human Affairs* (Palo Alto: Stanford University Press, 1983).

42. For present purposes I do not distinguish between activity based on the OAS Charter, the Rio Pact, or the Inter-American Peace Committee. I have relied on Richard Bloomfield and Gregory Treverton, eds., *Alternative to Intervention* (Boulder: Lynne Rienner, 1990); and L. Ronald Scheman, *The Inter-American Dilemma* (New York: Praeger, 1988), chap. 3. For a rosier assessment of the future of the OAS, see Richard J. Bloomfield and Abraham F. Lowenthal, "Inter-American Institutions in a Time of Change," *International Journal* 45, no. 4 (Autumn 1990), 867–888.

43. See Yassin El-Ayouti and I. William Zartman, eds., *The OAU After Twenty Years* (New York: Praeger, 1984), especially the essays by Olajide Aluko and Henry Wiseman.

44. *Ibid.,* essay by Berhanykun Andemicael and Davidson Nicol.

45. *Ibid.,* essay by I. William Zartman; Robert H. Jackson, and Carl G.

Rosberg, "Why Africa's Weak States Persist," *World Politics* 35, no. 1 (October 1982), 1–24.

46. *Singapore Symposium* (UN, 1991), 51–64.

47. My argument here is heavily influenced by Richard H. Ullman's in Weiss, *United Nations in Conflict Management,* 68–76.

48. For these and other suggestions, see Larry Minear, Thomas G. Weiss, and Kurt M. Campbell, *Humanitarianism and War,* Occasional Paper 8 (Providence, R.I.: Thomas J. Watson Jr. Institute for International Studies, Brown University, 1991); and James S. Sutterlin's contribution to this volume. I have also drawn gratefully on Lincoln P. Bloomfield, *International Security: The New Agenda* (Minneapolis: Hubert Humphrey Institute of Public Affairs, University of Minnesota, 1991).

49. *Report of the Secretary-General,* 6.

50. Benjamin Rivlin, "The Rediscovery of the UN Military Staff Committee," Occasional Papers Series IV (New York: CUNY, Ralph Bunche Institute on the United Nations, May 1991), discusses these alternatives. So do Meryl A. Kessler and Thomas G. Weiss, in Weiss and Kessler, *Third World Security,* 114 ff.

51. *Singapore Symposium* (UN, 1991), 42–50; *New York Times* (February 9, 1992).

52. Lawrence S. Finkelstein, "The Coordinative Function of the UN Secretary-General," Occasional Papers Series X (New York: CUNY, Ralph Bunche Institute on the United Nations, January 1992), 15, for this and other ideas here used. I have also drawn with gratitude on James N. Rosenau, *The United Nations in a Turbulent World* (New York: International Peace Academy, 1992), 69–76.

53. This typology of US foreign policy attitudes was developed by James N. Rosenau and Ole R. Holsti, who also document that the Cold War–focused US foreign policy consensus broke up during the Vietnam War and never reformed; see "The Structure of Foreign Policy Attitudes Among American Leaders," *Journal of Politics* (February 1990), 94–125; and "US Leadership in a Shrinking World," *World Politics* 35, no. 3 (April 1983), 368–392. Holsti and Rosenau report that in 1986 US elites broke down as follows: hard-liners, 25 percent; isolationists, 23 percent; accommodationists, 23 percent; and internationalists, 30 percent; see "Structure of Foreign Policy Attitudes," 130.

■ Part 2 ■
Collective Action to Deal with International Disputes

■ 5 ■

United Nations Decisionmaking: Future Initiatives for the Security Council and the Secretary-General

JAMES S. SUTTERLIN

Changes in the Effectiveness and Mandate of the Security Council

The Security Council was, with rare exceptions, largely ineffective during the first 45 years of the United Nations's existence, primarily (but not solely) because of the Cold War. Decisionmaking was often blocked by the veto, and even when decisions were made, the Council was seldom in a position to enforce them. With the practical elimination of hostility and ideological rivalry among the five Permanent Members and the notable increase in cooperation in dealing with security problems, decisionmaking in the Council has become easier, and enforcement (broadly defined to cover various forms of peacekeeping and peacemaking) has become more feasible. While the Council action in dealing with the Iraqi invasion of Kuwait has provided the most striking example of the new decision and enforcement capability, other undertakings in Angola, Central America, Cambodia, and Yugoslavia may be of greater long-range significance because the circumstances there are, mutatis mutandis, more likely to recur.

The maintenance of international peace and security is now widely perceived in far broader terms than the drafters of the Charter had in mind. While wars resulting from interstate rivalry and expansionist ambitions have not ceased (and probably will not), the large majority of conflict today is intrastate in character and stems from societal roots rather than interstate differences. The Council has long taken the position that intrastate conflict can threaten international security—as, for example, in Cyprus, southern Lebanon, Nicaragua, and, most recently, Yugoslavia. But the issue of UN "intervention"—a word still largely avoided—to resolve or alleviate internal conflict and restore stability has not been posed so clearly or insistently as is the case now and is likely to be in the future. Nor did the Council, until the Gulf War, have to face the difficult question of whether it may (or, indeed, must) intervene if a government, through its actions, threatened the lives and most basic human rights of a significant number of its population. Is there a point at which the Security Council within its mandate should decide on measures, including enforcement measures, to bring such violations to a halt for the purpose of maintaining international security?

There are two other broad problems not foreseen when the mandate of the Security Council was defined that can patently threaten international security in a profound way: (1) willful and serious destruction of the global ecosystem and (2) the acquisition by a country, in contravention to treaty obligations, of nuclear weapons or other weapons of mass destruction that constitute a threat to global security.

Taking such dangers into account, "international security" must increasingly be understood to mean protection from deadly harm for both states and populations. Such a broad definition can impose heavy responsibilities on the Security Council because it alone, among all the organs and agencies of the UN system, has enforcement authority; and member states are committed under the Charter to comply only with the decisions of the Council. The extent to which the mandate of the Security Council will be interpreted to cover threats to the security of people as well as of states is not yet clear. It is surely evolving in the case of Bosnia-Herzegovina, where, for partly political purposes, the Security Council sought to bring humanitarian assistance to the people of Sarajevo by imposing sanctions against Serbia and threatening military action.

Potential Security Council Initiatives in Preventing Conflict

The Security Council, like successive Secretaries-General, has repeatedly pointed to the importance of preventive diplomacy. Most recently, at its January 1992 Summit Meeting, the Council requested the Secretary-General to provide a report on means of enhancing the capacity of the UN for preventive diplomacy along with peacekeeping and peacemaking.[1] The Council has, in fact, had little success over the years in preventing conflict. Now, given the prevalence of intrastate conflict, the application of preventive measures can be even more complex than in the past when interstate conflict was seen as posing the main threat to international security. Yet with regard to internal conflict, too, the greater commonality of interests now apparent among the Five Permanent Members of the Council opens larger possibilities for preventive action. Through a fortunate conjunction in the political orientation of many states it has become more realistic to think of using techniques to prevent conflict in ways that until now have not been feasible.

Two tools or techniques of very considerable potential available to the Security Council for the prevention of both interstate and intrastate conflict are fact-finding and peacekeeping. Neither is new but neither has been used effectively by the Council for deterrence. The dispatch of UN fact-finders by the Security Council or the Secretary-General to assess threats of conflict (whether these derive from interstate border conflicts or resource disputes) or grave internal tensions (e.g., ethnic, religious, and human rights disputes) could have a useful effect in deterring the immediate outbreak of violence and, in addition, provide a basis for any further Council action that might seem advisable in the circumstances.

The potential of preventing conflict through the deterrent use of peacekeeping is even greater. Peacekeeping can fulfill two functions to prevent conflict from breaking out as well as to prevent its recurrence. First, as has often been suggested but not as yet implemented, if a threatening situation exists between two states (as confirmed by fact-finders or a special UN mission), a peacekeeping force can be deployed along the border even if only one party consents and deployment can only be on the territory of that party. Such a UN presence could in many potential situations serve to deter a precipitate hostile action. In considering such action it must be recognized that, as has been unhappily demonstrated, a lightly armed peacekeeping force cannot stop a heavily armed force if the government concerned is determined to proceed with an invasion notwithstanding the UN presence. Therefore, any such deterrent deployment should necessarily be accompanied by a commitment of the Security Council to take appropriate measures under Chapter VII of the Charter if the deterrent peacekeeping force is attacked.

In certain situations where domestic conflict is threatened, the Security Council could deploy a peacekeeping force at the request of the government, and with the agreement of any other organized elements involved, for purposes of stabilization and conciliation. This would require a somewhat different peacekeeping composition, although not entirely unlike that employed in Central America and in Cambodia.

Another means of preventing regional or internal conflict that can threaten an area is the timely and politically opportune provision of humanitarian and social assistance to alleviate emergency situations within societies. Somalia and The Sudan offer unpleasant examples of where this technique might have been applied but was not, or at least not at a sufficiently early stage. UN Secretary-General Boutros Boutros-Ghali, in the report that he provided in response to the January request of the Security Council, recommended both more extensive use of fact-finding and preventive deployment of peacekeeping forces for the purposes here suggested.[2]

To contemplate prevention of conflict through the timely provision of economic and social assistance raises three large questions: Does the Security Council have a mandate to deal with social threats to peace within a domestic society? Does the Council have a role in gaining the necessary cooperation of the functional UN agencies to permit timely and focused application of resources to alleviate threatening social tensions? What is the desirable relationship between the Council and the General Assembly in this aspect of maintaining international peace and security?

I will take these questions one by one (while recognizing that each could well be the subject of a separate chapter). The Security Council has authorized peacekeeping operations (broadly defined) to deal with conditions of internal tension and humanitarian need in cases where the situation has been interpreted as threatening international security. In the Congo and Namibia the action taken was preventive; in most other cases the action came after conflict had broken out. Given the prevalence of internal conflict, this is an area where future initiatives of the Council will be needed. However, while there are ample precedents, the criteria for Council action remain undefined. In the one case where the situation was not seen as threatening international security (Haiti), the Security Council did not take action but the General Assembly did. Even when the Council has acted, as in Yugoslavia, the preceding debate has revealed doubts on the part of some members as to the propriety of UN intervention. To some extent the doubts—even resistance—have reflected concern not so much of UN intervention as of intervention by an organ of the UN seen as under the control of the Five Permanent Members; in other words, there is fear that the major powers through the Security Council will gain a means of dominating smaller, poorer countries.

These developments suggest that consideration could profitably be given to two courses of action that could clarify the appropriate UN response to threatened violence within a society. First, informal and flexible guidelines should be adopted for determining when an internal crisis constitutes a threat to international security warranting intervention by the Council, not as a modification of the Charter but as an interpretation of what the Charter wording means under evolving circumstances.

Such an interpretation might be along the following lines. Within the Security Council's mandate for the maintenance of international peace and security, action by the Council is warranted if an internal crisis threatens or entails such violence, deprivation, and suffering for the population as necessarily to be of profound humanitarian concern to the international community and not be susceptible to resolution by internal efforts alone or through the assistance of the appropriate regional organization. Intervention in such instances would be taken only with the consent, and preferably at the request, of the government and parties concerned, except, as the Charter provides, for any application of enforcement measures under Chapter VII. Such guidelines could be incorporated in the precedents (repertoire) of the Council on the basis of an agreed statement by the President.

The second possible course of action relates to election-monitoring and the broader task of strengthening those democratic processes often necessary in ensuring free elections and nation-building. Taking the long view, the encouragement of free and stable societies on the basis of free elections and democratic government can reasonably be seen as an effective means of decreasing the likelihood of conflict.

Interest in this more comprehensive approach to peace has centered in the General Assembly. It earlier requested the Secretary-General to provide a report on how the United Nations could assist in holding free elections, and, at its request,[3] an Electoral Coordination Unit has been established within the Political Department of the secretariat to which member states may turn for advice on holding elections. From this it follows that UN practice in assisting in the holding of elections might be the following. The Secretary-General should be the focal point for receiving requests for electoral assistance and, if he deems it appropriate, for dispatching support missions, subject to the authorization of the General Assembly, including approving expenditures for the costs. The mission could be made up according to the needs of the situation (as has been the case in Namibia, Nicaragua, and Haiti, for example) and would not necessarily be categorized as peacekeeping.

If the mission does involve security aspects (e.g., the inclusion of military personnel, the disarmament of opposing factions, the interdiction of illegal entry), the Secretary-General could bring the situation officially to the attention of the Security Council with the recommendation that, in light of the request of the country concerned and of the views of the General Assembly, the Council authorize an appropriately structured peacekeeping operation. While decisionmaking in the General Assembly can be difficult, it would be sound policy if it, as the most democratic of the UN organs, had major responsibility in the furtherance of democracy as an element in the strengthening of international security.

An evident way of reducing the risk (and the effect) of conflict is the reduction and control of arms. The Security Council has, for the first time, taken direct action in the field as a result of the Iraqi invasion of Kuwait,[4] although the embargo on the shipment of military equipment to South Africa and more recently to Yugoslavia might also be categorized as measures of arms control. Throughout its history the Council has never formulated "plans for the regulation of armaments" as foreseen in Article 26 of the Charter. Debate and mobilization of public support has been centered in the General Assembly; servicing and the preparation of studies, in the secretariat; and negotiation, in the Committee on Disarmament.

There is no compelling evidence that any one of these functions could be better accomplished if the Security Council were involved. One rule for ensuring its maximum effectiveness is that it should concentrate on situations where direct and early action is needed and avoid subjects entailing lengthy negotiations among many states. This, however, does not exclude the possibility of preventive action by the Council relating to arms limitations. In the absence of other coercive means specifically provided in arms agreements, the Security Council, as the only UN organ with the power of enforcement, could take enforcement action in the case of noncompliance with arms treaties that threatens international security.

Taking account of this need, the Security Council, in its Summit Statement of January 1992, confirmed its intention to take appropriate measures in case of any violations of the Nonproliferation Treaty notified to it by the International Atomic Agency in accordance with the provisions of the treaty.[5] The present experience in Iraq has demonstrated the feasibility of this function even though the very special circumstances of the Gulf War may not be replicable. The Council may need to assume a similar responsibility in the event of grave threats to the environment as a result of infringement by a country of provisions of a relevant treaty or convention.

Potential Security Council Initiatives in Resolving Conflict

There are essentially two ways for the Security Council to resolve conflict: by peaceful means (Chapter VI of the Charter) or by enforcement (Chapter VII). Almost every possible peaceful means is named in Chapter VI. There is no real need to try to devise new techniques for peaceful settlement. The UN has been fortunate with the availability of skilled mediators, often the Secretary-General himself, and there is no reason to think that this will not continue to be the case.

There are two main reasons why peaceful resolution is so difficult and frequently impossible. First, in most cases each party wants to win—to come out ahead. A zero-sum game solution is not what either party wants. Second, the UN mediator lacks leverage to persuade the parties to settle for something less than their maximum objectives. Such leverage as the mediator has is usually vicarious, often the influence that member states, singly or collectively, can bring to bear in seeking a solution. There is not much to be done about the first impediment. It is doubtless here to stay. So, in thinking of future initiatives of the Security Council in the peaceful resolution of disputes, one can best look at the question of leverage. One answer that quickly emerges is that the Security Council collectively and its Permanent Members individually, for the purposes of resolving conflict, need to give early and serious attention to steps that might be taken to strengthen the position of a UN mediator or conciliator.[6]

One kind of positive leverage that can prove effective is the provision of economic or humanitarian assistance. To cite a relevant example, in former Secretary-General Javier Pérez de Cuéllar's efforts to free the hostages in Lebanon, it would have been helpful if he had been able to offer reconstruction assistance to the various communities in that fragmented country. He was unable to raise the money needed for this purpose even though the General Assembly had established a fund for the reconstruction of Lebanon. The Security Council does not have the authority to provide economic assistance; the Secretary-General, even in seeking the peaceful solution of a crisis, does not have the authority to apply resources belonging to functional offices or specialized agencies. The General Assembly can be asked by the Secretary-General to appropriate funds, but because of the severe limitations on "add-ons" to the regular budget, it is usually necessary to call for voluntary contributions, a time-consuming process of uncertain results.

So here is a lacuna in the conflict resolution equipment of the UN. It is evident that greater collaboration is desirable among the Security Council, the General Assembly, the Secretary-General, and the functional agencies of the UN system to enhance the conflict-resolution capability of the UN. The present Secretary-General has raised this objective in the Administrative Committee on Coordination, which brings together the executive heads of UN agencies and programs.[7]

Turning to enforcement as a means of ending a conflict, the two most effective forms are economic sanctions and the application of military force, both of which are available to the Security Council. Both were employed in the Gulf crisis (certainly a seminal UN experience) and within that context have been extensively discussed.

Only two conclusions need to be stated for present purposes. First, comprehensive sanctions as an instrument for collective security proved feasible and effective in the realization of at least part of the objectives agreed upon by the Security Council. While attitudes will vary in accordance with the nature of a crisis, there is no longer reason to doubt that member states in a serious case of aggression will comply with a Council decision to impose sanctions and that sanctions are a viable means to seek such compliance even if they may not always be successful. Second, the Security Council does not have the option of undertaking military enforcement with UN troops under its own direction because such troops are not presently available.

In order to enhance the enforcement capacity of the Security Council, the second conclusion should be emphasized in seeking an answer to the question of how the Security Council can best gain access to troops to enforce Council decisions. One means is that foreseen in Article 43 of the Charter, under which member states undertake "to make available to the Security Council on its call and in accordance with a special agreement or agreements, armed forces, assistance and facilities, including rights of passage, necessary for the purpose of maintaining international peace and security." It is unlikely that a UN force of sufficient size or equipment could be assembled quickly enough to meet a threat as large as that posed by the Iraqi army. It is also doubtful whether any country supplying a major component comparable to that deployed by the United States in the Gulf would be willing to place the force under the strategic direction of either the Military Staff Committee or the Council.

This does not rule out, however, the use of a multilateral force under control of the Security Council when a smaller military force will suffice or when the interests of a major power are less directly involved. Therefore, a desirable initiative for the Council to take at an early date would be to seek the agreements foreseen in Article 43 with member states. Secretary-General Boutros-Ghali has recommended this action in his June 1992 report "An Agenda for Peace." It must be recognized that the negotiation of Article 43 agreements will be a lengthy process and that some countries may be unwilling or constitutionally unable to sign such agreements despite their commitment under the Charter.

At the time the US Senate was considering ratification of the UN Charter, there was extensive discussion of Articles 42 and 43 relative to the provision of military force to the Council. Senate approval was given only after the Department of State had provided written assurance that any agreement negotiated with the United States under Article 32 would be submitted to the Congress for approval. Subsequently, the law passed by the Congress on US membership in the UN included a provision that US troops would be supplied to the UN for the purposes foreseen in Article 42 of the Charter only on the basis of an agreement or agreements that had been approved by the Congress.

Such considerations should not prevent the Council from initiating the process with as many states as possible. The Military Staff Committee explored the possibility of Article 43 agreements in the early years of the UN but under the Cold War circumstances of the time had no success. If such an effort is again undertaken, the Security Council would be well advised to appoint a senior negotiator of international stature for the task, assisted, as appropriate, by the Military Staff Committee.

The Security Council could also in the future utilize peacekeeping troops for peace enforcement, a concept that has now been endorsed by the present UN Secretary-General.[8] Sir Brian Urquhart has approached this idea by suggesting that there is a "pressing need for a third category of international military operation . . . somewhere between peacekeeping and the large-scale provisions of enforcement."[9] President François Mitterrand of France seems to have had something similar in mind when, in addressing the Security Council Summit on January 31, 1992, he said that "France is ready to make available to the United Nations Secretary-General a contingent of 1,000 men for peacekeeping operations, at any time and on 48 hours' notice. The number could be doubled within a week. The deployment would clearly mean activating the Military Staff Committee which is provided for by the Charter."[10]

Again, the need and the potential can best be clarified by a hypothetical example. In a situation such as existed in Nagorno-Karabakh, the Security Council decides to call for a cease-fire and to request the

Secretary-General to work out with the parties the procedure for implementing it. The Secretary-General (or his representative) achieves an understanding between the parties, but fighting continues. In such a circumstance a "peacekeeping" force is needed to enforce the cease-fire, of such size and equipped with such arms as may be necessary for this purpose. Such utilization of force could be justified as a provisional measure and as provided for in Article 40 of Chapter VII of the Charter.

It is not difficult to think of numerous situations in which such peace enforcement may be needed in order to avert massive loss of life and, in some cases, the possibility of interstate war. The Council will have to take account, however, of the likelihood that many member states (unlike France) would be far less willing to contribute troops for such high-risk operations than for peacekeeping operations as presently understood. The UN Charter foresees one possible solution to this problem, at least with regard to Europe. Article 53 provides that the Security Council shall, when appropriate, utilize regional arrangements or agencies for enforcement action under its authority.

NATO constitutes a unique source of well-trained, adequately armed, and logistically equipped troops that could be quickly deployed for peace enforcement purposes. Moreover, NATO members have agreed with specific reference to the Conference on Security and Cooperation in Europe (CSCE) that NATO forces may in principle be used for peacekeeping purposes. Following Article 53 of the Charter, the Security Council could request NATO to undertake peace enforcement action in its behalf in crises in Europe such as those that have arisen in Bosnia-Herzegovina and Nagorno-Karabakh. Now that Eastern European countries and the republics of the Commonwealth of Independent States (CIS) have a friendly association with NATO, there would not likely be objection to the deployment of NATO forces under a UN flag for purposes determined by the Security Council. NATO would not be legally obliged to comply with such a Council request, but having already volunteered its services for peacekeeping it would surely have to give any such request serious consideration. Its three strongest members are Permanent Members of the Security Council and of necessity would have already agreed to the proposal. A comparable "readiness" force on which the Security Council might call for peace enforcement does not exist in other regions.

These considerations indicate the broad range of potential initiatives of the Security Council in preventing conflict in the future. Much of the territory is, in a constitutional sense, still uncharted, and the practicality of possible actions is untested. That the need will arise for ground-breaking action by the Security Council can, however, hardly be contested. Indeed, a most poignant need already arose in the case of Sarajevo when the city came under siege by heavily armed Serbian elements. It might be said that what the UN needs to do is fill the role of global police officer. More aptly it can be seen as the necessary assumption by an effective Security Council of the dual role of peacekeeper and peacemaker.

Decisionmaking by the Security Council

To assess the potential effectiveness of the Security Council in such ambitious initiatives as have been suggested, it is essential to examine in some detail the Council's decisionmaking capacity. The question must be faced as to whether the Council in its present composition is competent to deal with the type of threats to international security that must now be foreseen. The present Five Permanent Members do not represent either the five most powerful countries in the world or the regions of the world where conflict is most likely to occur. At a time of expanding democracy, the Security Council thus constitutes a distinctly undemocratic institution. It is not well structured enough to enjoy the full confidence of the majority of member states.

Would decisionmaking be easier or more authoritative (two very different things) if the powers with the right of veto were more representative or a more democratic method of voting were introduced? The most sensitive element in most of the new situations for Council initiatives concerns possible infringement of sovereignty or contravention of the provision in the UN Charter prohibiting intervention "in matters which are essentially within the jurisdiction of any state."[11]

The most frequently suggested changes for the Council are the following:

- Enlargement, without change in the status of the Five Permanent Members
- The addition of further Permanent Members without the right of veto as part of an enlarged Council
- The addition of Permanent Members with the right of veto
- Replacement of France and the United Kingdom by the European Community, thus freeing a place for Japan
- Elimination of the veto

None of the above would seem to facilitate decisionmaking in the Council except the last mentioned, which must be discounted as unfeasible for the foreseeable future. The substitution of the EC for the United Kingdom and France and the addition of Japan would have the least impact on the process. It must be noted, however, that there remains a legitimate question as to whether Japan, because of constitutional considerations, could take a leadership role in collective security undertakings comparable to that taken until now by the United Kingdom and France. The recently enacted legislation authorizing the assignment of Japanese Self-Defense Forces personnel for noncombat peacekeeping duties would seem to exclude Japanese military participation in military enforcement action under Chapter VII of the Charter. The EC position would presumably have to be based on consensus within the European Community, which could result in a slower and less decisive Western voice in the Council.

Enlarging the Council through the addition of Third World countries could complicate decisionmaking on the most sensitive aspects of conflict prevention—namely, internal conflict and nation-building. The problem would become not so much the veto, which has not been exercised for some time, as achieving a positive majority in favor of action. At present the Permanent Members need to gain the support of only four other members of the Council to achieve the needed majority of 9. If the Council were enlarged to 21 with most additional members from the Third World, and the required majority were set at 12, Council decisions to take action in response to internationally threatening internal crises in Third World countries could be hard to reach—all the more so if India, Nigeria, and Brazil should become Permanent Members with the right of veto.

The Security Council in its present composition—no matter how unrepresentative it may be—has proved capable of taking the necessary decisions since the end of the Cold War. Change in its composition would not, in itself, facilitate new initiatives such as those suggested in this chapter. It follows that change in the composition of the Security Council would be justified not on the basis of decisionmaking but, if at all, on three other factors: a lack of respect that its decisions may, in the future, enjoy among the members; the degree of confidence that the majority of members will continue to place in the UN itself; and the possibility that major countries, especially Japan, will decrease their support for the UN if they continue to be denied representation commensurate with their importance and financial contributions. Japanese representatives have made clear that the last-named risk is real and demands attention.

Much of the Security Council's influence derives from the power and pressure that the Permanent Members are able to exert. As power and influence become increasingly measured in economic terms, the power and influence of the present Permanent Members will decrease, and therewith the influence of the Security Council. This suggests that to preserve its status in the future, its composition will have to be modified. If this is to be accomplished without engendering bitterness and a deterioration of the Council's decisionmaking, a careful, broadly based strategy will need to be developed that could, in the time that will certainly be required, coincide with and encourage changes in attitudes of the likely candidates for permanent membership in an enlarged Security Council.

Potential Initiatives of the Secretary-General

The role of the Secretary-General in the prevention and resolution of conflict has traditionally depended heavily on the capacity of the Security Council to perform those same functions. In the rare periods when the Council was able to act effectively, the Secretary-General became more an enabler than an initiator of action. When the Council was immobilized, both the opportunities and the need for independent action by the Secretary-General became greater.

Dag Hammarskjöld, in his authoritative Oxford speech on the international civil servant, stated that the Secretary-General should be expected to act without guidance from the Council (or the General Assembly) should "this appear to him necessary towards helping to fill any vacuum that might appear in the system which the Charter and traditional diplomacy provide for the safeguarding of peace and security."[12] He had the Congo in mind, but a more recent example is the war in Afghanistan where Secretary-General Pérez de Cuéllar was able to undertake efforts toward a solution when Council action was blocked by a veto. On the other hand, when the Council demonstrated the capacity to act in response to the Iraqi invasion of Kuwait, the Secretary-General's role became primarily that of seeing to the implementation of the Council's decisions—a task of major importance but one that left him with a certain feeling of frustration.[13]

This does not mean that a Security Council capable of decisive action, including enforcement, will deprive the Secretary-General of the possibility of important initiatives in the interest of peace. The Secretary-General's role does not need to be, and should not be, only that of implementing decisions of the Council. The persuasive power of a Secretary-General depends heavily on the support he or she has from the Council, particularly the Permanent Members. Initiatives by the Secretary-General can have greater effect if undertaken at a time, as the present, when the Council is working in relative harmony. In somewhat oversimplified terms, the Secretary-General's functions in connection with international security will center on four capacities: keeping watch in order to initiate preventive diplomacy or to alert the Council or other UN organs of situations requiring their action; carrying out the decisions of the Council; ensuring that the secretariat is capable of meeting the demands placed upon it; and encouraging cooperation among all UN functional agencies in the common purpose of strengthening international security.

More specifically, initiatives by the Secretary-General will be needed in the following three areas: early warning, democratic processes, and economic and social issues.

Early warning. In this area, potential initiatives of the Secretary-General fall into two categories: (1) structural and technological innovations to ensure the early availability of information and analysis on potential threats to security and (2) the provision of information and advice to the Security Council at an early stage on situations that may warrant action by the Council.

The electronic communication capability of the UN remains inadequate; and the communication systems in use by the various agencies and the secretariat, nonintegrated. While improvement will depend to a large extent on the appropriation of funds by the General Assembly, the Secretary-General must take the lead in persuading member states of the need. The Office for Research and Collection of Information (ORCI), established by the previous Secretary-General to facilitate early warning and preventive diplomacy, was abolished in the initial restructuring of the secretariat undertaken by Secretary-General Boutros-Ghali. The need that ORCI was established to meet remains. Therefore the Secretary-General will need to ensure that, under the new secretariat structure that is emerging, information relative to international security can be acquired, processed, and analyzed on a timely basis. In this connection, the Secretary-General could well initiate a procedure for intelligence consultation with member states and establish a system of regular consultation by senior UN representatives with governments in the various regions and with regional organizations, all with the objective of early warning of any impending threat to interstate or intrastate peace.

Now that the Security Council is able to act effectively in dealing with conflict, it is more important than ever that it be kept informed collectively of developments related to international security. The Secretary-General could usefully provide regular secretariat briefings of the Council (or perhaps of a committee of the Council established for this purpose).[14] The suggestion has been made that the Secretary-General should at the beginning of every month review the world situation with the Council. However, such a practice could be disadvantageous for the position of the Secretary-General; it could easily place him in a posture of seeming partisanship simply by raising a particular situation. This could jeopardize his later effectiveness. Moreover, by routinizing the Secretary-General's communication with the Council on security matters, the impact of his selective personal reports to the Council, including initiatives under Article 99 of the Charter, could be reduced.

Democratic processes. If past experience is a guide, states requesting UN assistance in holding free elections, or in other aspects of developing a stable government, are likely to turn to the Secretary-General as the initial point of contact. Indeed, the Secretary-General, on the basis of information available to him, could well initiate contact with governments in countries where difficulties have been reported and suggest how the UN might be of assistance. He will have to determine how requirements can best be met and judge how the UN can best provide support, deciding, as suggested earlier, whether the necessary action can appropriately be authorized by the General Assembly or whether the Security Council needs to be involved because of security aspects that may be entailed.

The composition of UN missions (whether they are called "peacekeeping" or not) whose purpose is to support democratic development within a country must be different from that of traditional peacekeeping forces, having proportionately larger civilian and police components. Models already exist in the peacekeeping operations in Namibia, Central America, and Cambodia. The Secretary-General will bear principal responsibility for ensuring that the UN is able to bring together the varied personnel required for such operations in each case as it arises, within the time limits set by the prevailing conditions. For this purpose he would be well advised to establish a working-level, interdisciplinary planning staff for peacekeeping and electoral support missions.

Finally, the Secretary-General will need in some cases to take the initiative in making the case in the General Assembly or the Security Council for UN assistance to countries facing internal difficulties. He will also have to persuade the membership of the desirability of UN involvement.

Economic and social issues. Aside from the instances of social crises that are of such intensity as to threaten international security, the Security Council has no mandate to deal with economic and social problems. The Economic and Social Council (ECOSOC) does possess such a mandate, but it has been, until now, largely ineffective. The General Assembly in 1991 agreed on reform measures that may bring improvement. ECOSOC will now meet only once a year rather than twice and will include a ministerial-level session devoted to no more than one or two subjects.

Whether ECOSOC's authority within the UN system will be appreciably increased remains to be seen. For the present, decisionmaking in the economic and social areas is widely dispersed throughout the UN system and inadequately coordinated. The Secretary-General's own mandate in this area is at best unclear and his authority outside the central UN organization essentially nonexistent. Nonetheless he will need in the future to take initiatives in these areas of several kinds, not least of all because of the increasing relevance of economic and social developments to the prevention of conflict and the maintenance of international security and to the peace-building process that is essential to both.

First, he must devise a more effective structure within the secretariat to manage UN economic and social programs. Secretary-General Boutros-Ghali's initial restructuring move, which placed all economic and social responsibilities in one mammoth department in order to reduce the number of assistant and undersecretaries-general, can be seen only as a holding action in this regard.

Second, the Secretary-General will need to recruit as a senior member of his cabinet an eminent economist who, with the support of an expert staff, will command intellectual respect throughout the UN system. This could serve to reclaim for the UN a significant influence in the formulation of global economic policy and in intellectual leadership in this area.

Third, the Secretary-General should develop plans whereby economic and social factors can systematically be introduced into the assessment of risks to international security.

Fourth, the Secretary-General should seek to persuade governments to give him greater authority to coordinate the policies of the specialized agencies in pursuit of objectives decided by ECOSOC or the General Assembly or deemed essential by the Security Council to the maintenance of international security.

Cooperation with Regional Organizations in Maintaining International Security

According to Article 52 of the UN Charter, the Security Council "shall encourage the development of pacific settlement of local disputes through . . . regional arrangements" and member states are encouraged to "make every effort to achieve pacific settlement of local disputes through . . . regional arrangements . . . before referring them to the Security Council." Given the increasing demands on the United Nations that threaten to outstrip its resources, it would be highly desirable if more of the burden of conflict prevention, peacekeeping, and peacemaking could be assumed by regional organizations. Moreover, the heavily internal nature of many regional conflicts would seem to suggest that regional organizations should have the major role in resolving them. These organizations are presumably more sensitive to the root causes of strife; their intervention might seem less like "foreign" intervention; their peacekeepers might seem more easily acceptable to the people involved, and more likely to share a similar culture and language.

On the basis of recent experience, however, none of these appears to be the case. The ability of regional organizations to either prevent or resolve local conflicts on their own has unfortunately been severely limited. Only the Organization of American States has been successful in the resolution of regional disputes without the participation of the UN, and its "solo" achievements ended some 20 years ago. As evident from the experience of the Organization of African Unity in trying to deal with the conflict in Chad in the late 1970s and, more recently, of the CSCE and the EC in seeking peace in Yugoslavia and Nagorno-Karabakh, regional organizations lack the capacity to mount peacekeeping operations that can be essential to conflict resolution. Their objectivity in a regional crisis situation is frequently suspect. Moreover, regional organizations do not have early-warning capabilities to alert them in advance to situations that may require their intervention. Only the CSCE has established a modest risk-reduction center.

The UN clearly needs at present to support and supplement regional organizations in dealing with regional crises. It can do so in the following ways, most of which have been utilized in Central America and Yugoslavia:

1. The Security Council can support and endorse the action taken by the regional organizations.
2. The Secretary-General can extend his assistance in efforts to mediate the dispute.
3. The UN, with its extensive experience and technical resources, can send peacekeeping forces to monitor a cease-fire and discourage a resumption of hostilities.
4. The UN Security Council, acting under Chapter VII of the Charter, can impose mandatory sanctions.
5. In theory, albeit probably not presently in practice, the Security Council can take military action to secure implementation of a resolution demanding a cease-fire.
6. The UN can, if needed, provide such "nation-building" assistance as supervising plebiscites, monitoring elections, and collecting arms if these are entailed in a settlement.

If the UN is to continue to provide such assistance in the case of regional conflicts, and the regional organizations are eventually to assume more of the burden, cooperation between the global and regional organizations needs to be enlarged and systematized. The common interest would be served if procedures were established under which the UN would provide technical assistance to regional organizations in such fields as peacekeeping and election monitoring, and information on developments affecting international security would be exchanged on a continuing basis.

Three specific initiatives would be useful. First, the Secretary-General could organize a meeting on peacekeeping of the principal regional organizations directed to two subjects: (1) the requirements of the organizations to develop a reliable peacekeeping capacity and (2) the assistance that the UN might render. Based on the conclusions reached at such a meeting, the Secretary-General could formulate a program for technical assistance to regional organizations on peacekeeping to be financed to the extent possible by those regional organizations able to pay and, for the rest, from the next regular UN budget in which provision for the program would be included.

Second, the Secretary-General should seek a close liaison arrangement between the CSCE conflict-reduction center in Vienna and the UN secretariat and should initiate systematic periodic consultations with other regional organizations on developments affecting regional and global security. The Security Council should be informed of the outcome of such consultations.

Third, the UN secretariat should expand its data collection and analytical function related to international security to include economic and social indicators that are at the root of many regional tensions. The Secretary-General would then be in a better position to consult with regional organizations and to bring the wider UN system into cooperative efforts with regional organizations to alleviate such tensions before they reach crisis proportions.

Conclusion

The end of the Cold War, combined with a greater commonality of interests within the international community as a whole, has opened unprecedented opportunities for the UN to take the lead in building a sounder basis for lasting peace. If this process is to succeed, major initiatives will be required of all the principal elements of the UN system and of regional and nongovernmental organizations as well.

The expanded need and greater opportunities for peacekeeping and peacemaking have already taken the Security Council and the Secretary-General into unprecedented fields of action. Both will need to go further if they are to bring about global conditions that will discourage the outbreak of conflict and ensure that international security is maintained for countries and peoples. They will be required to devise the means through which the UN can alleviate the root causes of conflict. The Security Council will have to be concerned with matters that have generally been considered outside its mandate, such as humanitarian assistance, ethnic conciliation, peace enforcement, and the strengthening of democratic processes.

This will not happen without much debate and hesitation. For this reason, the leadership of the Secretary-General will be of great importance. He will need to afford strong guidance to the Council as it faces unmapped terrain. The peace-building process will require that he exercise greater influence on the operation of the whole UN system; that he develop a stronger structure for cooperation with regional organizations and nongovernmental organizations; and that he serve as an effective spokesman in mobilizing support for the ambitious programs that the UN will need to undertake. Initiatives along the lines that have been suggested, if taken successfully by the Security Council and the Secretary-General, can do much to make multilateral cooperation in the maintenance of international security the dominant influence in the new era that has begun.

Notes

1. See UN document X/23500 (January 31, 1992).
2. Boutros Boutros-Ghali, *An Agenda for Peace* (New York: United Nations, 1992).
3. General Assembly Resolution 46/137 (March 9, 1992).
4. Security Council Resolution 687 (April 3, 1991).
5. UN document S/23500 (January 31, 1992).
6. For the comments of Secretary-General Boutros Boutros-Ghali on this subject, see Section IV, par. 34, of *An Agenda for Peace.*
7. *Ibid.,* par. 40.
8. *Ibid.,* par. 44.
9. Brian Urquhart, "A Way to Stop Civil Wars," *Providence Journal-Bulletin* (February 1, 1992).
10. Cited in *New York Times* (February 1, 1992).
11. UN Charter, Article 2, par. 7.
12. Dag Hammarskjöld, *The International Civil Servant in Law and in Fact* (Oxford: Clarendon Press, 1961).
13. Former Secretary-General Pérez de Cuéllar has suggested in an unpublished interview that when the Security Council decides to adopt a resolution requiring extensive implementing action by the Secretary-General, the Secretary-General should be included in the drafting process. This was not done in the case of Resolution 687, which set forth the conditions for the cease-fire in the Gulf War.
14. When in the early 1980s the Security Council held a series of informal meetings to consider how its effectiveness might be improved, Secretary-General Pérez de Cuéllar proposed to provide the Council with regular summaries of information relative to international security. He also provided for the installation of a television monitor outside the Council's consultation room so that during a crisis Council members would have immediate access to news from the wireless services. For reasons that are difficult to explain, several Council members at that time reacted negatively to the idea of regular information summaries, and the idea was dropped. The television monitor was installed but a number of Council members complained that the Secretary-General had acted without authorization. The monitor is still available but not in use.

■ 6 ■

The Requirement for a
Multinational Enforcement Capability

JOHN MACKINLAY

The Cold War logjam in the United Nations was moving when Mikhail Gorbachev heralded the arrival of a new era in the General Assembly in December 1988. UN negotiators had already started to release tension from the protracted violence in Namibia, Angola, and Central America.

But the UN's institutional growth had been deformed by Cold War rivalry; its highly developed facilities for negotiation had outstripped its ability to organize effective military cooperation or enforcement. The seriousness of this imbalance had escaped the UN community in New York. When members decided to combine forces to take military action against an aggressor state for the first time since Korea, they found there was no structure within the UN capable of mounting and directing an operation of this size, in spite of the political decision to reverse the Iraqi aggression.

Many factors have blocked the development of effective UN enforcement procedures, most significantly the indifference of individual member states, particularly those that had developed their own unilateral force-projection capability. Although the UN now needs an effective instrument to underwrite its decisions when addressing impending conflicts in this new era, many member states and especially their representatives in New York are reluctant to tackle this problem, and few diplomats understand the difficulties of developing military cooperation on this scale.

This chapter explains why the UN's enforcement capability has been neglected, examines the results of maintaining a low level of military capability, and suggests how this trend could be reversed.

Operation Desert Storm

On August 2, 1990, Iraqi combat troops seized Kuwait; at once the UN became the focus of international reaction. By August 25 the Security Council had passed five resolutions: a condemnation of Iraq; a call for Iraq's unconditional withdrawal; the demand for the release of hostages;

and an effective closing off of the conduits for exporting Iraq's oil and halting its supply of weapons and vital materials.

In New York the UN became the epicenter of intense international activity. In September 1991, Security Council Resolution 669 encouraged widening efforts to negotiate and canvass the military support needed to redress the Iraqi aggression. Deals were struck to persuade and encourage nations, opposed to the growing call to use force, to set aside their interests and allow the organization of an effective response to continue unimpeded.[1] At the head of an emerging lobby for enforcement action, it was the United States that coalesced a wide span of regional and national support within the aegis of the UN.[2]

It should have come as no surprise, therefore, that Resolution 678, authorizing the use of "all necessary means," which the United States had strived energetically to obtain, transferred at a stroke the initiative, focus of activity, and stage lights of attention from New York to Washington.

The wording of the resolution conferred on the United States and its coalition allies a most desirable combination of UN authority with a considerable element of operational freedom; for them it was the just result of a series of intensely negotiated agreements. But for smaller countries, hoping for an endorsement of their reliance on a UN system of collective security, it was a bitter disappointment. Many privately echoed the Cuban objections to the Security Council that Resolution 678 "was an unrestricted authorization to the United States and its allies to use their enormous and sophisticated military might."[3] At the same meeting, Yemen pointed out that the command of these forces would have nothing to do with the UN, even though their actions would be authorized by the Security Council.[4] It was in effect a carte blanche. The UN, having provided the forum for the initiative, would now play a diminishing role in the events that followed.

Prior to Resolution 678, in the diplomatic euphoria of New York as each resolution seemed to break new ground toward the manifestation of a UN enforcement action, member states had failed to see what now is obvious. The authorization of Operation Desert Storm demonstrated more clearly than any action before that there were still important reasons why the practical execution of a collective enforcement counterstroke by the UN was no more than a theory. Moreover, deep-seated resistance against the UN's taking a military initiative had, in this example, continued to prevail under the most favorable circumstances for cooperative action. In the case of Iraq, an already reconciled Security Council, further united in the face of a mounting list of rapine activities committed by a widely unpopular oppressor nation, would not seriously consider invoking the UN's military provisions for enforcement.

What had unfastened the resolve of the victorious allies who, in 1945 after the crushing defeat of an earlier tyrant, had pledged themselves to Chapter VII of the UN Charter for this very contingency?

The Failure to Develop an Enforcement Capability

When the Charter was drafted, its authors were preoccupied with conflict among states. Their vision of a returning scourge was another world war—state against state, Clausewitzian in scale, where victory would be measured by territorial gain. The language of the Charter referred to "aggression," "self-defense," and "armed attack" in which force was used by conventional armies. Two pillars were to uphold the Charter and safeguard the world against this threat: negotiated settlement of disputes under Chapter VI and, where that failed, Chapter VII enforcement.

The use of collective force relied on establishing the same level of cooperation and trust among the world powers that was achieved to defeat Hitler. To translate their collective will into a plan for action would require a degree of military coordination reminiscent of the huge multinational landings on Normandy beaches.

In the postwar era the consensus of the allies evaporated with the onset of East-West tensions. The authors of the Charter could not have anticipated the nature of global tension that developed almost immediately after the San Francisco conference in 1945 or the political structures that developed as a consequence of the rise and decline of the world powers. During the Cold War, the bipolar struggle between the Western alliance and the communist bloc drove a wedge into the Security Council that prevented the Permanent Members from developing an effective modus operandi in the UN. Under these circumstances, it became impossible to improve the untried San Francisco prototype for collective enforcement.

Instead, a lesser instrument, peacekeeping, was developed to guarantee the agreements successfully negotiated under UN auspices. Peacekeeping, therefore, was an expedient of a divided Security Council, which lacked the consensus for collective action but could agree to use a less powerful means that would not impinge on superpower interests in the zero-sum game that prevailed during the Cold War.

Consequently, peacekeeping had several characteristics that prescribed its wider use. The confidence and full support of the Security Council were essential prerequisites. A peace force could deploy only with the consent of all parties in conflict, particularly the host nation in which the force would be stationed. To achieve an international balance, participating nations would have to represent a spectrum of international interests. Permanent Members of the Security Council did not, as a rule, contribute to peacekeeping forces except with strategic movement and logistic support. Their military assets were used by the UN on a case-by-case basis—these were generally strategic facilities that were seldom stationed in the area of operations and never under the command of the UN force. Finally, peacekeepers could not use force except in self-defense.[5]

Under these conditions, peacekeeping became narrowly constrained.

Unless the zone of conflict met with the stringent preconditions for their use, UN forces could not be deployed. Unlike a combat unit, peacekeeping forces could not often create the conditions for their own success.[6] They acted rather in the role of an umpire or a referee. The referee's success relied on the consent of the players and their understanding of the rules of the game, but never on the pugilistic skills of the referee.[7]

Being lightly armed and impartially disposed was a benefit to the peacekeepers. It protected them on the battlefield and allowed them to move freely and negotiate dispassionately. Their military role was mainly reactive. They could operate only when hostilities had ceased. They could not enforce a solution or drive away an aggressor. Veteran peacekeepers stressed the value of being regarded as impartial and nonthreatening; many saw the aggressive efficiency of powerful armies as an obstacle to acceptance by local parties. By applying these rules strictly and following a consistently low-key style, the techniques of peacekeeping achieved many successes during the Cold War. In their role as referees or custodians of UN agreements, peacekeepers developed a range of useful procedures to reassure fighters, disarm violence, and stabilize the battlefield.[8]

But in the long term, the peacekeeping alternative may have acted as a brake on the development of the military responsibilities of the UN. Although peacekeeping was the only activity of the UN to involve armed forces, its organization and control was intended to bypass the Military Staff Committee (MSC). During the political confrontations of the Cold War there was no alternative, but now in a new era some of the competing interests that had prevented the development of more effective procedures toward collective action have been removed. Nevertheless, the use of lesser instruments like peacekeeping, and the continued exclusion of the staff and military forces of the Permanent Five from its development, reduced the incentive and withheld the means to search for better procedures for using collective action.

The political element of peacekeeping conferred a degree of acceptability on what was a fairly low standard of military operations. Because UN contingents in principle had no enemies in their area of operations, there was less pressure on them to be militarily effective. In the field, there was no need for total operational reliability by day and night,[9] and gaps in logistic arrangements were tolerated because they did not crucially diminish the political outcome of the peace process, as they might in an operation of war. In the UN secretariat there seemed to be no need to maintain an effective staff capability in New York; there was no sophisticated information-assessment capability, no staff system to maintain a 24-hour vigilance, and no map room where events could be plotted in detail. Contingency planning was carried out by coopted staff officers who came and went on an ad hoc basis. There was no nucleus of effective military staff to capture the doctrinal lessons that emerged from these experiences,[10] and the military functions in New York headquarters were largely conducted by a civilian secretariat whose knowledge of military operations did not extend beyond the requirements of peacekeeping.

Diplomacy Outstripping UN Military-Organizing Capability

In an institution staffed largely by diplomats and international civil servants, it is entirely understandable that much effort had been spent on extending the facility for mediation and political cooperation, particularly in the Security Council after Gorbachev's dramatic policy changes began to take effect.[11] A greater sense of collegiality had developed, and the UN's governance had grown as each new peace agreement was successfully negotiated. However, even in the late 1980s—after Iran-Iraq, Afghanistan, Namibia, Central America, and Angola—when new initiatives may have been considered with greater facility than before, the cooperative development of a procedure to mount a military force that was capable of more than the accepted rituals of peacekeeping was fatally overlooked.

Even with the exceptional use of UN forces in the Congo and the occasional violence in Lebanon, UN peacekeeping was characterized as a largely undemanding military routine. Consequently, the representatives from some member nations and the predominantly civilian staff of the UN secretariat were encouraged to underestimate the complexity and importance of developing a procedure to deliver an effective military instrument under the provisions of Chapter VII. As a result, in November 1990 when the full significance of Resolution 678 was registered on the members, many were surprised and deeply disillusioned. "It may have been the UN's most desolate hour," observed Stephen Lewis. "It certainly unnerved a lot of developing countries who were privately outraged by what was going on but felt utterly impotent to do anything."[12]

The Security Council seemed to demonstrate beyond all doubt in Resolution 678 that the UN's outstanding characteristics as a forum for international negotiation, particularly in respect to acting as a focus for the coalition in the Gulf, were not matched by a collective ability to organize and direct the necessary forces that could underwrite these agreements. The leading armies of the allied coalition preferred to fall back on the more developed structures of the NATO alliance rather than the untried prototype of Chapter VII.

The price of 40 years of unbalanced development was that not only had the responsibility for operational direction of the coalition forces been removed from the supervision of the UN, but there was no means whereby the secretariat could monitor the highly complex events in the Gulf that had been building up since August 1990. The Secretary-General was limited to regular but after-the-fact briefings by the leading nations in the coalition. They told him of plans that were already activated and interpreted for him the situation on the ground; but they did not share with him their future intentions. The impartial information consistently available was provided by the media. But even the correspondents in the Gulf were closely controlled by supervisory constraints.[13] For sound operational reasons they were not allowed to carry out investigatory reporting where their presence could become awkward.

By these means the majority of UN member states, on whose behalf the operation was ostensibly conducted, was not in a position to judge or even comment on what was happening. For example, without independent intelligence sources, the intense public debate during the fall of 1990 on the success or failure of the sanctions was a one-sided exercise. The Secretary-General had no effective surveillance capability of his own, and interested member states could know only what the coalition chose to tell them. The "outsiders'" efforts to participate in a collective process were limited, their knowledge of the situation was edited, their political decisions were reactive, and their influence was marginal. Without information, they could understand little of the allied coalition's future intentions. In retrospect, even the expurgated assessment of war damage and casualties may not be accurately revealed for several decades.[14]

Although an international organization can be only as effective as its members allow it to be, the poor monitoring capability in UN headquarters was exacerbated by an institutional disregard for the basic requirements of a military staff system. To some extent the ritual nature of peacekeeping duties in the long-standing buffer zones of the eastern Mediterranean had never required the secretariat to develop a better system. As a result, there was no monitoring capability, not even a reliable map room where members could obtain an impartial update of events.

Since 1945 the members had barely developed a sufficient level of military cooperation to allow the elementary deployment of uncontested peacekeeping forces. In December 1990 the impending requirement was for a major operation of war by land, sea, and air. The scale and swiftness of this development took the coalition partners by surprise, whatever their political motives—operationally they had no alternative except to free themselves from UN command and control.

The Characteristics of Successful Military Cooperation

By removing operational control to Washington, Resolution 678 placed on the allied coalition the unprecedented task of organizing 600,000 troops, 3,600 armored vehicles, 1,700 attack aircraft, and 150 warships provided by the 35 participating nations into a viable instrument of war. The US military staff who achieved this feat were assisted by a number of prevailing conditions. In contrast to UN operations of the past, that were hastily mounted, the US staff had a realistic preparation time of six months—from the Iraqi invasion in August 1990 to the onset of the air attack by coalition forces in January 1991. During this period, their preparations in Saudi Arabia were uninterrupted by enemy action although the threat was ever present. The Iraqi surveillance capability was ineffective, and the scale and nature of the coalition activities could be concealed. Because a nucleus of powerful forces was provided by members of the NATO alliance, it was possible to use NATO cooperative procedures by air, land, and sea. NATO military facilities were made available to enhance aspects of the coalition blockade and its air defense measures.

In addition to employing their military advantages, the US military planners showed an unusual degree of resourcefulness. They combined an acute awareness of the various political sensibilities of their allies with technical adaptability and some inspired practical organization. The essential characteristics of the coalition command function can be summarized as follows: (1) resolute political leadership to counter the Iraqi attempts to divide the coalition; (2) sophisticated command structures flexible enough to allow some allies to distance themselves from the UN war plans for humanitarian, political, and religious reasons but sufficiently cohesive to provide effective direction in battle; and (3) detailed operational planning to design a mutually agreeable military objective and then allocate suitable tasks to the 35 disparately equipped and qualified contingents.

To overcome the practical difficulties of integrating the diverse combat and logistics support units, the US military staff was required to allocate real estate to arriving contingents and determine their subordination within the force; organize cooperation at sea; allocate the use of air space; allocate the use of the electronic spectrum and control the use of electronic countermeasures; develop mutually acceptable rules of engagement; direct the buildup of logistic support; plan for handling causalities, prisoners, and refugees; and organize joint force training among nations.

The initial organizational phase of Operation Desert Storm had, in fact, been an explicit demonstration of the range of military staff planning capabilities that would be required to execute a Chapter VII action. Three conditions have become clear: (1) the military staff playing the leading role in harnessing the diverse assets of the involved contingents would, at the end of the process and de facto, be left holding the reins that controlled the force, (2) only the United States had the strategic assets to deploy a sufficiently powerful force to take on an operation of this scale; and (3) the only existing cooperative procedures that could be used to hold together contingents of this sophistication had been developed in the NATO alliance during the period of the Cold War.

In Operation Desert Storm, the importance of the military organization in the overall success should be contrasted with the Cold War–era peacekeeping missions of the UN, in which member states had assumed that if the political conditions were right, the military element would sort itself out on the ground in due course. In the past, peacekeeping forces had been seen as largely symbolic and their activities marginal to the overall peace process. For this reason, contributing nations showed little hesitation in subordinating their comparatively tiny contingents to the command and control of the UN system.

But in Kuwait, for the first time since the Korean War, UN members were being required to subordinate effective combat units to a supranational command to carry out a dangerous operation of war. The routines of peacekeeping were not intended to be adapted for collective enforcement. The levels of military involvement were obviously much greater. A nation might be prepared to abdicate control of a small contingent of troops for an uncontested peacekeeping task, but in an operation of war the political risk of defeat—let alone the loss of life, ships, and aircraft—required an effective approach to cooperative military operations that was far beyond anything in UN experience.

In the previous military expeditions of the UN, there was also a strong element of consent by the host nations in the theater of operations. This ensured that intervention was uncontested and rarely required forceful responses from the UN. However, as the element of consent was reduced, so the importance of good military organization increased until it became a crucial factor of success.

Collectively, diplomats and international civil servants in New York could hardly be characterized as having a military bias in their professional attitude and experience. Very few officials in the UN staff could have understood how technically difficult it is to achieve a sufficient degree of military cooperation among allies to conduct an operation of war. On the other hand, few of the leading participants in UN peacekeeping were powerful military nations or part of an effective alliance. They failed to see, or did not want to see, that they had reached a stage in their development when they needed a military coordinating capability in addition to their highly developed negotiating skills.

Even in NATO, undeniably the most powerful military alliance in the world, the level of integration is relatively superficial and had, in fact, taken decades to achieve. NATO nations tend to operate according to national standards within their defined areas of responsibility. At a military level they developed a robust working relationship with one another. The habit of military cooperation enables several national contingents to form and re-form their assets into variable compositions according to task. Units can be detached and reattached with relative ease. Command can be delegated so that a unit from one country can act in close support of another. Operations are fast-moving and involve aircraft, ships, and armor.

But this level of cooperation can be used only in very specifically defined circumstances, and it has taken years of staff experience, training, and field exercises to achieve. In the UN the problem of developing a similar standard of military coordination has never been seriously addressed. Although the trappings of a military staff system can be seen in New York, it is a flimsy structure that will collapse in an operation of war. The vital staff functions of operational planning and support are conducted at the lowest common factor of acceptability. Governments are reluctant to submit men and women to such a command structure if there is a likelihood of facing a contested deployment.

The principle of excluding the Permanent Members from peacekeeping activities ensured that the UN's only area of military cooperation had been developed in a very unsophisticated way. It could not benefit from the organizing experience of either the Warsaw Pact or NATO. Although the MSC continued to meet ceremonially throughout the Cold War,[15] it had ritualized its office to such an extent that by 1990 there was no apparatus, ability, or inclination to design an interim control mechanism for the Gulf. When a token meeting did take place at the insistence of the then–Soviet Union in the fall of 1990, it was already too late.

At the end of 1992, the principal obstacle still facing the world organization may not be how to start the process of developing a more sophisticated approach to coordinating military operations but how to open the eyes of a predominantly nonmilitary staff in New York that this is even a problem.

Political Control

Faced with another crisis on the scale of the invasion of Kuwait, it is unlikely that the leading nations in a future coalition will receive carte blanche in the style of Resolution 678. Most members would now support former Soviet Foreign Minister Eduard Shevardnadze's view that "no single country, not even one as powerful and rich as the United States can, or had the right to play the role of global policeman. No one country, even the smallest and weakest, would agree with the idea of restraining the violators of order in the world if the restraining was done by a single power."[16] A debate has already opened on the political control mechanisms that should operate over the field commander of a future multinational enforcement or intervention.

There is some support for the Russian proposal to resuscitate the MSC with a view to its taking on a more active role in planning and coordinating future UN military operations. Some feel that the MSC would be an ideal forum in which to consider and develop a concept for future enforcement operations. Unfortunately, the MSC members themselves—notably, the United States but also France and the United Kingdom—have at great expense maintained a capability for unilateral overseas military action. They have consequently grown accustomed to adopting a unilateralist approach to safeguarding their national interests. They may be unwilling to strengthen the MSC if this requires them to abandon that capability. They are also reluctant in principle to submit powerful military forces to a UN command system over which they have only partial political control, although in exceptional circumstances this too has been waived. Without the support of the MSC's most sophisticated military members, it is hard to see how a proposal involving a greater role for the MSC can succeed.

The proposals for a standing UN military force would on the face of it overcome the objections to control by a single nation. A permanently formed international force or field headquarters would be established as a permanent basic structure to which appropriate multinational contingents could be swiftly grafted to form a more muscular and effective military instrument. However, a force that is integrated to this degree reflects a close political alliance. Even in NATO, national contingents operate largely on a federal system within their own areas of operational responsibility, and integration can be achieved only in planning and some support functions. This degree of political harmony and trust has obviously not been reached in the UN. A standing force reflecting the real accord of the membership would not be more than a token military formation.

The proposal to organize a UN mercenary force in which (temporarily stateless) soldiers are recruited directly into a standing UN formation is less militarily practical. Its political weakness lies in that, if challenged, it would not project the conviction and weight of support of a similar force comprising of contingents of powerful military nations, particularly of Permanent Members of the Security Council. Militarily, it may be possible in this manner to form a UN corps of security watchpersons to patrol passively and report incidents, but this type of unit could not conduct an operation of war. The UN Guards Contingent, deployed as "police" in this capacity to northern Iraq in the wake of Operation Provide Comfort in 1991, relied on the previous operations and continuing presence in Turkey of a powerful and sophisticated multinational force, largely drawn from NATO.

Standing forces in the above examples would be very expensive to train and maintain. Once a military force is removed from its sustaining base, the cost of maintenance becomes exorbitant. In the UN "mercenary force" example, the capital costs of developing a system of UN bases for them would be enormous. Any military force requires constant realistic practice and retraining if it is to remain combat ready and alert. It also needs to have up-to-date weapons systems and modern supporting aircraft and vehicles if it is to be credible. Few member nations would politically and financially support a standing task force that would be capable of conducting an operation of war.

In the short term, if the UN had to face an emergency on the scale of the Gulf crisis, the members would have no military option to convening another coalition force organized under a single nation's military staff. Politically, it may not be acceptable to allow the reins of control to be held entirely by one nation. A compromise that may be acceptable in extremis would involve allowing a single nation or alliance structure to organize the military force in the field, and the UN retaining a collective overseeing responsibility through the Security Council, without delegating total operational freedom to an individual member.

As long as the operational mandate allowed tactical decisions to be made by the field commander, without lengthy political discussions to decide each move, the force should be able to carry out elementary security operations. It is unlikely in the near future that a collective action under the direction of the Security Council could achieve anything approaching the sophistication of Operation Desert Storm, but a protective operation involving light forces on the scale of Operation Safe Haven is a possibility.[17]

In the longer term the UN will have to develop a much more sophisticated approach to coordinating effective military forces under its own arrangements. This will require a larger and far more professional military staff in the secretariat, representing armies from major military powers as well as the peacekeeping contributors. An improved military staff would enable the following:

- The Secretary-General to receive state-of-the-art military advice
- The secretariat to develop an improved contingency planning capability
- The organization and assembly of effective military forces that are more than a token military presence
- The development of a UN modus operandi for the conduct of collective enforcement operations

The debate over a concept for collective operations that amount to more than peacekeeping[18] must now include nations possessing the required military sophistication. Improved communication links need to be established among staff in alliance forces, national defense ministries, and an appropriate office in the UN secretariat. There is an urgent requirement to agree upon procedures for future operations among UN members and to establish an improved structure for political direction. New concepts will have to be developed into workable procedures, and they will have to be war-gamed, practiced by staff, and exercised by troops on the ground. There is much to be learned from NATO in this area. A regional structure of UN staff colleges will soon be needed where diplomats, civil servants, and military staff officers from all nations and alliances can meet, study, and develop a workable concept for global security. A less reactive UN secretariat is urgently required, with its own impartial information-assessment staff and an enhanced and doctrinally creative military staff. All these actions would serve to strengthen the credibility of the UN as a just enforcer as well as an adept negotiator.

There are understandable reasons some diplomats, particularly from developing countries where military forces occasionally behave in a rapine and unlawful manner, will continue to resist efforts to improve the capability and effectiveness of the UN's military staff. There may also be a genuine constitutional reluctance by some nations to contribute military troops for enforcement. It is also possible that the United States, France, and the United Kingdom will stall the process of military development when the UN begins to achieve an organizing capability that threatens their own scope for unilateral action. But the great majority of member nations, particularly those whose armed forces are constitutionally subordinated to a democratically elected government, must now strive for an improved military capability in the UN. They cannot continue to express grief and dismay at the US role as coalition force leader and at the same time resist efforts to establish a better system for collective security.

Notes

The author wishes to acknowledge that this chapter is partially derived from his current research project with Jarat Chopra, in particular "Future Multinational Military Operations," *The Washington Quarterly* 15, no. 3 (Summer 1992), 113–134.

1. "China Opens Door to Sanctions," *London Telegraph* (August 7, 1990), 12.

2. "Dollar Does the Talking as US Secures Support," *London Telegraph* (December 1, 1990), 2.

3. UN Press Release, SC/5237 (November 29, 1990), take 12.

4. *Ibid.,* take 7.

5. UN document S/11052/Rev. 1 (October 27, 1973).

6. Alan James, "Painful Peacekeeping: The UN in Lebanon 1978–1982," *International Journal* 38, no. 4 (Autumn 1983), 32.

7. John Mackinlay, *The Peacekeepers: An Assessment of Peacekeeping Operations at the Arab-Israeli Interface* (London: Unwin & Hyman, 1989), 14.

8. For a discussion of these issues, see Alan James, *Peacekeeping in International Politics* (London: Macmillan, 1990); and UN Department of Public Information, *The Blue Helmets* (New York: United Nations, 1991).

9. Mackinlay, *Peacekeepers,* 150.

10. Indar Jit Rikhye, "The Problems of International Peacekeeping," Royal United Services Institute Lecture (September 29, 1976).

11. See Thomas G. Weiss and Meryl A. Kessler, "Moscow's UN Policy," *Foreign Policy* 79 (Summer 1990), 94–112.

12. Stephen Lewis, "A Promise Betrayed," *World Policy Journal* viii, no. 3 (Summer 1991), 539–550.

13. The constraint on the media in Operation Desert Storm was exercised through visa restrictions applied by the Saudi government, and accreditation conditions were exercised by coalition allies and the reliance, particularly during the air war, on the military press releases as opposed to independent reporting techniques.

14. The disparity between the assessed casualties suffered by Iraqi forces and civilians and those suffered by coalition nations is so great that there has been some reticence on the exact Iraqi casualty figures. The lack of hard facts has been exacer-

bated by the tendency to slant the statistics to support varying political assertions about the level of response, the level of carnage and dismemberment in the area of direct hits, and the system of mass burial after hostilities.

15. See Benjamin J. Rivlin, "The Rediscovery of the UN Military Staff Committee," Occasional Paper IV (New York: Ralphe Bunche Institute, 1991).

16. Eduard A. Shevardnadze, *Working Together,* Occasional Paper 7 (Providence, R. I.: Thomas J. Watson Jr. Institute for International Studies, Brown University, 1991), 13.

17. For a discussion of political-military problems of this option see *Newsweek,* World Affairs (April 29, 1991), 13–14.

18. See Jarat Chopra and John Mackinlay, "Future Multinational Military Operations," *Washington Quarterly* 15, no. 3 (Summer 1992), 124–125.

■ 7 ■

The Role of Regional
Collective Security Arrangements

TOM J. FARER

The conflicts and contradictions spilling out of the Cold War's carcass lend renewed poignancy to the old epigram that the only thing more disappointing than *not* grasping the object of a lifelong desire *is* grasping it. In pursuit of a secure global liberal regime, having struggled successfully to block the thrust of Soviet power, the West finds that its victory has uncapped new sources of violence, illiberalism, and insecurity.

For all of its tensions, the Cold War was the longest period of peace in European history. The once explosive Balkans snoozed on the margin of events. Whatever its diminished independence of action, Poland lived without fear of extinction. Germany and France, hereditary belligerents, partnered each other in the dance of European integration. The British could practice the art of war only by sailing nearly to Antarctica. To the peoples of the West, armed conflict began to appear as a pathology native to the Third World, even if sometimes stimulated, aided, and abetted by the First and Second Worlds. Today, in the cold dawn following celebration of the new age, threats to the interests of the West are revealed as more permanent and protean than the Cold War, and the search for "collective security" is renewed.

After considering briefly in this chapter the various purposes of collective security arrangements, I examine the nature and underlying assumptions of collective security and suggest the characteristics that distinguish it from other formulas for enhancing global order. Then, after reviewing the post–Cold War prospects for collective security arrangements, I sketch the theoretical advantages and disadvantages of regional and other limited-membership schemes and locate them in the mosaic of global law enforcement. Finally, I assess the law enforcement potential of existing arrangements and suggest the location and character of new ones.

Purposes and Character of Collective Security

When collective security is praised, it is usually in the name of order. The word *order* appears on the tongue unaccompanied by definition. Yet if we are to think clearly about collective security, definition is required because the character of the order that we seek will influence not only the content of substantive norms that are one aspect of order but also the shape of the processes for enforcing those norms.

Should order be conceived simply in terms of an effective ban on violent self-help by states seeking to vindicate their perceived rights and interests? If so, the search for it seems likely to fail because, in any large and heterogeneous community lacking powerful institutions equipped to enforce the community's laws, the threat of self-help is an important restraint on deviance. By allowing individual and collective self-defense against an armed attack "until the Security Council has taken measures necessary to maintain international peace and security,"[1] Article 51 of the UN Charter explicitly acknowledges this constraint on banning force from the lexicon of statecraft.

If a right to employ force defensively against an actual or imminent attack is deemed both inevitable and necessary for deterring and containing predatory violence, order could then be equated with banning violence for all other purposes. Those purposes include the prophylactic response to mere preparation for the illegal use of force, vindication of legal rights, and attempts to establish new rights. Such a ban might, moreover, inhibit action to address matters high on the special agendas of Western elites: ideological concerns (defending human rights and democratic government); concerns about the proliferation of weapons of mass destruction; and concern with nonmilitary threats to global health and welfare, such as operating unsafe nuclear power plants, devastating rain forests, and dumping toxic wastes in the global commons.

A number of Western scholars and a smaller number of statespersons contemplate unilateral armed action in defense of human rights.[2] But no one seems yet to envisage violent unilateral initiatives on behalf of trees and clean seas or even for maintaining the existing oligopoly with respect to the deployment of bacteriological, chemical, and nuclear weapons.[3] What must be alluring, given the prominence of these concerns, is the shimmering prospect of collective coercion where positive incentives fail.

Political leaders and policy analysts generally see collective security arrangements either as useful supplements to unilateral action or as the option of first choice. Literally, "collective security" could refer simply to an alliance for deterring and defending against armed attacks. As such it would be a familiar element in balance-of-power politics. In practice, it is generally employed to denote an alternative to balancing—namely, a collective institutionalized commitment not to balance but to gang up on any state that acts in defiance of collective judgments about permissible behavior.[4] Collective security arrangements are designed, in other words, for law enforcement. They are therefore premised on consensus among the participants about the limits of state discretion in the pursuit of national interest and on a collective will to enforce those limits.

It follows that for traditional realists,[5] the idea of collective security is deceptive if not delusional. According to their hypothesis, the imperative of survival in a competitive political system without central authority induces among the leaders of all states an obsession with power and hence with the interstate allocation of its constituents. Governments of leading countries strive single-mindedly to amass power and employ additional increments to acquire still more.

On these assumptions, the imperious requirements of the balance of power prohibit cooperation unless the benefits of the balance are evenly distributed. Where actions or mere conditions could cause an unequal distribution of the benefits of cooperation without significantly altering the balance of power among cooperating states—for example, arrangements to improve weather prediction or mail delivery—rules can be negotiated with confidence about compliance. But with respect to matters that can impact significantly on short-, medium-, or long-term military security, each participating state commits itself in anticipation of absolute gains for itself and no comparatively greater gains for any other consequential actor. In short, collaboration will not affect the balance of power. Whatever the supposed sanctity of formal agreements, as soon as that condition appears likely to fail, even if it be as a consequence of events beyond the control of the parties, the logic of survival in an anarchical system requires the party adversely affected to withdraw.

One must therefore assume that states will renege on a commitment to gang up on a delinquent if the delinquent, by virtue of its place in the balance, contributes to their security. Conversely, of course, if the delinquency threatens the balance, the threatened states will swarm to perform. But if the realists are right, the swarm is induced by the passion for balance rather than for the imagined long-term value to be derived by maintaining the integrity of solemn pacts.

Realists would no doubt cite US policy in the Gulf as evidence of the theory's predictive power. In 1980 Iraq invaded Iran to acquire territory and thus violated flagrantly a bedrock norm of the UN Charter. Iran, much more populous, appeared to be a potentially more powerful state, as well as one with ambitious designs on the security of its neighbors. The Iraqi attack did not induce a general call for sanctions. When, in the course of the war, it seemed that Iran might win and thereby realize its potential to become the dominant actor in the Gulf region, the United States began actively to assist the delinquent and helped to frustrate Iran's punitive goals. In 1990

Iraq invaded Kuwait to acquire territory. Had it succeeded, Iraq would have become the regional hegemon. The rest is history.

One could accept (I do not) the realist hypothesis and still conclude that institutional arrangements ostensibly dedicated to collective security, rather than being mere screens behind which the calculus of the balance of power functions, still can make an independent contribution to peace. The state of the balance is not, after all, subject to easy verification.[6] Many of the sources of power, such as national cohesion and the quality of leadership, are not subject to quantification and are easily misperceived. Even more material factors, like the quality of arms and fighting units, have in the crucible of war shown a striking capacity to surprise the most objective observers. And many critical observers are by no means objective.

The perceived state of the balance will, after all, affect the allocation of power and prestige within states. Since self-interest powerfully influences perception, groups threatened with a loss of power and prestige from the internal adjustments required by a shift are likely to resist seeing it; conversely, groups that will gain from a shift will be inclined to exaggerate the magnitude of every movement in the balance. Given the obstacles to a uniform perception, national estimates may easily lag behind or leap ahead of events to such a degree as to trigger the premature transfer of allegiance, paranoid preemption, suicidal defiance, and other pathologies that abort measured adjustment to the changing realities of power.

If they do nothing else, intergovernmental institutions encourage sustained communication among states and disseminate credible information.[7] By stimulating and structuring discourse and facilitating cognitive convergence, a collective security organization including more than one of the principal balancers (the "poles" of a bi- or multipolar international system) can reduce the risk of balance-eroding misperception by national elites.

Moreover, collective security regimes incorporating only one great power and its allies can heighten the prospect for order. Under the realist hypothesis, such regimes are in essence mutual security alliances; hence the central concern of participants is maintaining their collective power vis-à-vis other alliance systems. But given the volatile nature of power and the hypothesized imperative of treating alliance relationships as expedients, the great powers' dependencies will, within the constraints imposed by the hegemon and the larger balance, compete among themselves. By organizing themselves into a regime[8]—that is, by formalizing the norms of the alliance, increasing communication, and establishing institutions capable of producing reliable information—the participants help to clarify the limits of allowable competition and assist the hegemon in monitoring compliance and deterring deviance. Thus they enhance order and reduce the frictional costs of maintaining it pending their inevitable separation when partners change.

Suppose, for instance, that the United Kingdom were a member of the

Organization of American States. In that case, Argentina would presumably have pressed its claim to sovereignty over the Falkland/Malvinas Islands within the Organization's political organs. Raising it there would probably have given the issue a higher profile within the US State Department than it acquired as the result of desultory bilateral negotiations between London and Buenos Aires.[9] And through the medium of the OAS, Washington would have been drawn into the process of negotiation.

As a participant, Washington would probably have sent out signals to both parties underlining its opposition to conflict among its allies over the issue. Washington's interest would have heightened British sensitivity to the Argentine mood and thus increased the likelihood of Whitehall's pursuing a diplomatic settlement or signaling its intention to fight. US pressure for a solution might have lent decisive weight to the argument within the British political establishment for transferring sovereignty to Argentina. Coincidentally, Washington's declared antipathy to any acts disturbing the peace of the anticommunist alliance, a declaration bristling with the threat of punitive sanctions, would probably have deterred the Argentinian military.

Of course many observers of international relations, and most proponents of collective security, believe that realism exposes an important but not the only source of state behavior.[10] In his influential study of relations among the countries of Western Europe as they evolved after World War II, Karl Deutsch concluded that peoples in different political units could achieve a depth and velocity of communication and interdependence and a sense of shared social values that overrode their historical perceptions of each other as potential enemies.[11] Thus they came to form, in his phrase, a "security community." Within such a community, the members ceased to view with alarm unequal increments of national power.

If Deutsch is right in his judgment that nations can experience a stable transformation of mutual perception, then collective security arrangements that do more than lubricate the balancing of power are plausible. For instance, if a rogue elite seizes power within one member of a security community and threatens another, other states can gang up to discipline the rogue without reference to its place in a national power balance among community members.

It is unnecessary to hypothesize a cognitive revolution in North American and European states (i.e., a radical transformation in the way their populations perceived themselves and each other) in order to explain the postwar intimacy and cordiality of former competitors and even murderous foes. As John Mearsheimer has recently argued, both peaceful order within the Western and Eastern alliances and the Cold War peace between the blocs complied with realist expectations.[12] A bipolar distribution of power produced tight alliances with subsidiary actors clustering around the polar states subject to rigorous discipline. Nuclear weapons in the form of invulnerable second-strike forces and frighteningly plausible escalation scenarios gave the balance an air of permanence, in part by inhibiting the West from actively encouraging apostacy in the East.

Security communities are not the only alternative to the realist paradigm. On the basis of empirical inquiry and rational-choice theories refined in the study of microeconomics, analysts have claimed that states form looser, contractarian communities premised on a certain subordination of immediate advantage to the estimated longer-term benefits of cooperation. The resulting "regimes"[13]—consisting of norms, principles, rules, and associated institutions that stabilize expectations in a given issue area—are seen as acquiring an independent capability to refract the application of power, in part by influencing the flow of information to decisionmakers and by facilitating transnational alliances among elites with common values and cognitions.[14]

An apparent majority of analysts agrees that state behavior on various issues with operational regimes cannot be explained purely in terms of a compulsion to exploit asymmetry of power and maximize the relative benefit of every interaction. It also seems broadly agreed that powerful states may accept considerable short-term sacrifices in order to realize the larger and longer-term gains of broadly based cooperation within the framework of such regimes.[15] More contentious, however, is the question of whether regimes can soften the unilateral search for advantage and correspondingly lower the barriers to sustained cooperation in the security area.

Enthusiasts for collective security from Woodrow Wilson to the drafters of the UN Charter, have answered that question in the affirmative. Some contemporary analysts, like Robert Jervis, cautiously concur.[16] Jervis reads great power behavior within the Concert of Europe as an early instance of leading states, operating within a contractual framework, restraining themselves from the exploitation of transient opportunities to enhance their power at the expense of other parties to the contract. Restraint flowed from relative satisfaction with the territorial status quo, exhaustion after two decades of general war, the experience of sustained strategic cooperation, and a common appreciation that war endangered internal order.

Cooperation despite the security dilemma may also have reflected tactical doctrine and military technology that appeared to preclude attainment of decisive strategic advantage from a first strike against a state with roughly equivalent military power. That condition may be analogous to the nuclear deterrence of contemporary times. Finally, cooperation was eased by the initial absence of pronounced ideological differences among the great powers. As those differences intensified, they eroded consensus about what each was entitled to do in defense of its national interests. Without shared norms, cooperation faded.

Prospects for Collective Security After the Cold War

The principal determinants of whether effective global or localized collective security arrangements can be built and maintained include the following: congruent worldviews; a recent or ongoing experience of cooperation in some field; satisfaction with the territorial status quo; and the cost-benefit ratio of military action as a means for achieving greater national power. On the whole the trajectory of these determinants is favorable.

Congruent worldviews do not mean coincident worldviews. Liberal democracy is not the political lodestar of China's present leadership;[17] in his recent preview of political reform for Saudi Arabia, the Saudia Arabian King frankly rejected democracy as incompatible with Islamic norms;[18] and the Malaysian Prime Minister has this year spoken disparagingly of efforts to hold all states to the liberal democratic standard.[19] Judging by behavior, if not explicit claim, these leaders have plenty of sympathizers in other Third World capitals. While rejecting democracy, the Chinese also reaffirmed their commitment to economic reform; it translates into progressively deeper involvement in the international capitalist economy, an economy in which Saudi Arabia and Malaysia are even more deeply enmeshed. Because that economy functions well only where borders are not barriers and expectations of violence are low, those elites who come to depend on it for the maintenance of employment and the growth of national income have good reason to see illicit force as a potentially very expensive and dangerous instrument.

Moderately rational leaders pursuing traditional interests in domestic order and enhanced position in the power hierarchy of states have additional reasons for anticipating, in the generality of cases, costs disproportionate to the potential gains from violence. One reason is the changing nature of national wealth and the sources of power.[20] When a country's wealth consisted largely of mineral resources, fertile land, and fixed plant and equipment relatively simple to operate and not subject to rapid obsolescence, it was susceptible to seizure and exploitation for the aggressor's benefit. As wealth increasingly assumes the form of knowledge, technical imagination, and book-entry capital, it tends to elude violent appropriation. And the human resources that are appropriated tend to function far less efficiently in the coercive environment that an occupier must maintain in an era of mass communication and populations mobilized around the myths and symbols of an imagined national community.[21] Furthermore, the appropriation of untrained people available for conscription into the armed forces probably adds less today to an aggressor's military capabilities than at any previous time in human history. Particularly over the past 40 years, the military value of mere numbers of personnel has deteriorated radically in relation to their skills (including managerial ones) and technology.

As an instrument of statecraft, force also suffers from the growth in the number and diversity of interconnected national interests and in the extent to which cooperation with many states is a conspicuously more efficient, if not absolutely necessary, means for addressing them. Military intervention enables a more powerful state to seize a single, well-defined material benefit. But it may so injure the capacity and authority of the target state's elite as to indefinitely preclude its subsequent cooperation with the aggressor on any matter. In addition, the use of force against one state tends to have an adverse impact on other states. In heightening expectations of violence, it is bad for world business; and it will jeopardize foreigners and their property in the target state as well as the target state's capacity to meet financial and other obligations owed to third parties.

Among those states able to shield themselves from a disarming attack, nuclear weapons by themselves may have disabled force as a serious option for any purpose short of survival. Mearsheimer, still a believer in the structural inevitability of balance-of-power politics, appears to see a second-strike capability virtually as a per se balancer.[22] Proliferation thus becomes, in his view, a potential antidote to the comparative instability of a multipolar compared with a bipolar structure of power. To mine that potential, however, proliferation must be managed in order to avoid (1) nuclear weapons acquisition by states without the will, resources, and orderly command and control required to safely deploy a credible second-strike force and (2) preemptive attacks on a state as it is transiting to privileged nuclear status.

While professing to believe that these risks are manageable, Mearsheimer fails to explain how the management system would function. Explanation is necessary because it is hard to see how any group of states, much less those obsessed with relative gains and losses in all their interactions, could by means of constant improvisation coordinate requisite discriminations, sanctions, and incentives. Hence, some sort of regime is essential. But a proliferation regime would seem to require a greater degree of cooperation than the realist assumptions about state behavior make plausible. By themselves, weapons of mass destruction offer one of the strongest arguments for attempting, in the face of realist skepticism, to construct collective security systems.

Regional Collective Security in the Mosaic of International Law Enforcement

However it may deceive us as to its real lessons (which may of course teach that it has none), history leaves a deposit of models and assessments directing and limiting the sense of what can and what should be done. In deference to its inertial force, I begin this inquiry into collective security alternatives for the coming decades with a sketch and a brief operational history of the regnant paradigm. Thereafter I consider possible enhancements and alterations of functioning collective security arrangements.

If a consensus about those arrangements existed among the drafters of the UN Charter, it did not survive the onset of the Cold War. Thus one cannot describe them without crossing contested ground. What follows is a mixture of the conventional and the controversial.

The UN Charter implies that the primary security problem is armed conflict and identifies three sets of actors available to assist in deflecting, deterring, or terminating it: the Security Council and the General Assembly; regional organizations; and individual states. Article 51 of the Charter recognizes an "inherent right of individual and collective self-defense" in case of an armed attack until the Security Council has taken appropriate measures. The Council may of course act prophylactically to avert the breach of the peace. Where it perceives a situation that could escalate into an armed conflict, it can intercede and encourage the parties to pursue peaceful settlement.[23] If the situation continues to unravel and hostilities seem imminent, the Council can require the two belligerents to halt their march toward war.[24] Should one or both ignore the Council's order, it can recommend action by regional organizations[25] or individual states.[26] And if the latter do not respond to the Council's urgings, it has the authority to demand their participation in a scheme of collective sanctions.

While the Council alone can compel coercive action, it shares authority with the General Assembly to authorize "peacekeeping" operations.[27] The label has generally been attached to the UN's dispatch of multinational forces with the consent of the government on whose territory they deploy. Where, as in Cyprus, the territory is divided between a recognized and a de facto political authority, the UN has obtained the consent of both. Troops are sent not to fight but to preserve a shaky state of nonbelligerence by interposing themselves physically between antagonists. They can serve as a tripwire for further collective action, as fact-finders, and as mediators in cases where unauthorized delinquency or mutual misperception threaten to catalyze initiation or renewal of armed conflict. Able to defend themselves only against minor assaults, they can at best ward off or isolate a mere probe or unauthorized action by small rogue elements among the latent belligerents.

Pursuant to Chapter VIII of the Charter, the Security Council may use regional arrangements of one sort or another to facilitate the peaceful settlement of disputes or to carry out enforcement measures. And regional organizations acting independently (but "consistently with the Purposes and Principles of the United Nations") may deal "with such matters relating to the maintenance of international peace and security as are appropriate for regional action."[28]

The Charter does not define the terms "regional arrangements or agencies." Its language implies that their defining characteristic is the geographic propinquity of participants. It also implies some sort of voluntary institutionalized relationship, which in turn suggests commonality of interest. What the Charter does not seem to anticipate is a peace and security-oriented association of states from different parts of the globe, an association like the British Commonwealth in the first half of the century or like the alliance that won World War II and founded the UN.

Presumably, the drafters did not anticipate the revolution that would occur over the next 40-odd years in the technology of transportation and communication, a revolution that would radically alter the significance of geography as a force shaping identity and interests. Moreover, they may not have anticipated the transgeographic political arrangements that would spring both from the revolution and from the multiplication of categories of states sharply differentiated by wealth, technology, and economic structure rather than location.

So much can be said without much fear of contradiction, but beyond this point controversy swirls. At its heart lie two broad questions. Can regional organizations, without prior Security Council authorization, legitimate the use of force by some member states against a deviant member or even nonmembers for purposes beyond self-defense against an armed attack? In other words, do such organizations have an independent authority to authorize military action whenever they conclude that force is necessary to avert or terminate a threat to the peace or to other collective regional interests?[29]

The second question is whether states acting alone or in combination (but without the authorization of either the Security Council or the political organs of a regional organization) are entitled to use force for purposes other than self-defense against an armed attack.[30] Can they preempt when threatened with attack? If so, how imminent must be the anticipated attack? Can they use force to protect interests other than political independence and territorial integrity?

Questions concerning the proper limits of self-help are relevant to the task of imagining collective security regimes, because an effective regime involves more than coordinated "ganging up." Expensive in material and political terms, its operations inevitably attended by substantial frictional costs, authentic collective security operations must be selective and hence episodic.

Self-help in the enforcement of legal rights is normal, if limited, in virtually all legal systems and is inevitable in those lacking strong central institutions. In determining the occasions on which to act, the community of states must decide where self-help becomes so grave a threat to common interests that the aggrieved state must submit its complaint to the collective for evaluation and appropriate action, including inaction. Conversely, the collective may protect the general interest by legitimating fairly wide-ranging self-help measures subject to review by community institutions.

In playing its superpower role, the United States has offered a distinctive set of views about the authority of regional organizations and the proper scope of self-help. Collectively, these views constitute what we might label the "Cold War paradigm of authorized coercion." With respect to the relationship between regional organizations and the UN Security Council, Washington's position evolved in the context of its early postwar dominance of the OAS and its desire to insulate the Western Hemisphere from Soviet influence. It achieved full elaboration in the course of the Cuban missile crisis of 1962.

Before then the United States had simply insisted that regional organizations had exclusive primary jurisdiction over alleged threats to the peace within the region. On this basis in 1954 it had opposed Security Council consideration[31] of an appeal from Guatemala for protection against the CIA-trained force that would shortly overthrow it.[32] The Security Council, Washington argued (with the support of a number of friendly Latin governments), could, or at least as a matter of prudence should, take up a matter only after regional remedies had been exhausted.

Moscow's incipient emplacement of nuclear-armed missiles in Cuba raised an additional issue about the OAS–Security Council relationship. Regardless of the number of missiles, the Kremlin could not threaten the capacity of the United States to deliver a devastating nuclear response against Cuba and the Soviet Union. Therefore, President Kennedy and his colleagues did not believe that the missiles augured an armed attack.[33] While determined for a variety of reasons, domestic politics among them, to compel removal of the missiles,[34] they were reluctant to invoke the right of self-defense under circumstances that might encourage other states to adopt a flexible view of limits on the use of force. So they relied on authorization by the OAS.

While the Charter contemplates regional institutions organizing or authorizing coercion to maintain and restore peace, Article 53 states that "no enforcement action shall be taken under regional arrangements or by regional agencies without the authorization of the Security Council." Officials and scholars have proposed two reasons for concluding that the OAS acting on its own could authorize the coercive measures employed by the United States to compel removal of the missiles. One was that Article 53 can fairly be read to allow authorization before or after the fact; and if after, it could be implicit.[35] The other is that the term *enforcement measures* refers only to coercive action that is ordered rather than merely recommended.[36] For this latter claim they rely on the World Court's advisory opinion in the case involving "Certain Expenses of the United Nations." There the Court drew a distinction between peacekeeping operations and coercive acts, which the Security Council alone was entitled under the Charter to direct. Only the latter, it declared, were "enforcement measures."[37]

It follows from the consensual character of peacekeeping operations that the Court was dealing with a simple dichotomy between measures that force the will of a sovereign state and those that do not. If consent is the crucial distinction, and if there are only two alternatives, then the limited blockade imposed by the United States around Cuba was enforcement action. In effect, the United States insists that there is a third alternative (to be sure, one not before the World Court in the "expenses" case), in which the UN or a regional organization merely recommends—and by recommending legitimates—coercive measures, including the threatened use of force. Being something other than "enforcement action," the resulting military operations, when authorized by a regional organization, escape the Article 53 requirement of Security Council authorization.

How the proposed distinction between recommended and required measures advances the purposes and principles of the UN has always been unclear. Security Council review is peculiarly desirable when a regional organization, rather than assuming direct responsibility for military operations against one or more UN members, delegates to individual states a broad discretion to use force on behalf of regional peace and security in circumstances where the authorized action is not designed to deter or halt aggression. However, unlike the UN, regional organizations could be dominated by a single state or an ideological bloc; they could, in other words, be coterminous with a great power and its closest allies. In such cases, the distinction between action by the organization and action taken by certain member states with the blessing of the organization makes no difference. Under the US view, the regional organization, although no more than a thinly disguised power bloc, could legitimate military action against a geographically proximate member of another major faction in global politics and, indeed, against extraregional states that sought to bolster the local pariah by sending aid.

As the Cold War has drawn to a close, the United States seems to have revised its approach to regional organizations to allow UN assistance in cleaning up the residue of East-West conflict in the Americas. With the OAS as a junior partner, the UN monitored the 1988 Nicaraguan election and the transition to a post-Sandinista regime, while coincidentally handling the disarmament of the contras.[38] Then, at the request of the Central American heads of state, the Secretary-General set about mediating the civil conflicts in El Salvador and Guatemala. With the full support of the United States, the UN catalyzed an agreement in El Salvador and will assume for an indefinite period of time the role of benevolent third party in the postwar political system. Beyond simply monitoring compliance with the terms of the settlement, it will actually assist in absorbing the guerrillas into the political and administrative institutions of the society, shrinking the armed forces, and effecting dramatic institutional reform.[39]

The Cold War paradigm of legitimate self-help extends well beyond defense against an imminent or ongoing armed attack. Whatever its concerns at the time of the Cuban Missile Crisis about too supple a conception of self-defense, Washington came gradually to transcend them. By the end of the Cold War, it had implicitly or explicitly claimed a right to use force (subject to the principles of necessity and proportionality) to rescue citizens threatened by anarchy or a hostile government; seize persons guilty of terrorist acts against its citizens or of conspiracies against the country's security and welfare; punish governments for violent acts directed against official personnel and property as well as ordinary citizens; and terminate military assistance to insurgents.[40] Moreover, following the oil boycott, through the medium of its Secretary of State it had envisioned the use of force to abort a boycott that threatened irreparable damage to the civic order of target states.[41]

The Cold War paradigm thus combines the following elements: (1) individual and collective self-help going far beyond common defense against a conventional armed attack and (2) regional organizations' enjoying exclusive initial jurisdiction and the discretion to recommend and legitimate the use of force by one member state against another or against organs or agencies of nonmembers operating in the region in ways determined by the regional organization to threaten the area's peace and security. The first element remains controversial. Censure of interventions in Grenada and Panama—by the UN General Assembly[42] and the Permanent Council of the OAS, respectively[43]—evidenced widespread opposition to the broad right of self-help claimed by Washington. Probably a majority of international legal scholars outside the United States[44] and a substantial number of their US counterparts[45] support the view that the Charter limits self-help to self-defense against an actual or imminent armed attack, possibly including an armed attack against nationals when they are abroad. As for the paradigm's second element, the United States itself now seems dubious about the claim of exclusive primary jurisdiction, a claim insistently rejected by the Soviet Union during the Cold War.

By the late 1960s, the United States could no longer command the weighted majority in the OAS required for authorizing coercive action by its members. In the 1970s it had to fight a rear-guard action to maintain collective economic sanctions against Cuba, a battle from which Washington eventually withdrew.[46] And in the 1980s, the United States found most of the Latin American countries among the main opponents of its anti-Sandinista campaign.[47] So after successfully if narrowly securing post facto ratification by the OAS of its invasion of the Dominican Republic in 1965,[48] the United States did not again seek legitimation for its coercive initiatives in the hemisphere.

The other intergovernmental arrangements generally recognized as regional organizations within the meaning of the UN Charter—the Arab League and the Organization of African Unity (OAU)—have not been active in the security field. While inactivity by regional organizations over the past 25 years has inhibited articulation of a well-defined alternative to the Cold War paradigm, implicit in criticism of OAS action and inaction in the 1950s and 1960s is an alternative in which such arrangements would function very much as arms of the Security Council.

Organizations generally referred to as "subregional" have occasionally asserted competence to take or authorize action in the security field for purposes other than collective self-defense against armed attack. The Economic Community of West African States (ECOWAS), led by Nigeria, dispatched an expedition to Liberia to restore order after organized government, such as it was, had collapsed into the maelstrom of a three-sided and murderous civil conflict.[49] And the Organization of Eastern Caribbean States (OECS) issued the call for intervention invoked by the United States as one of the justifications for its occupation of Grenada.[50] The ECOWAS intervention escaped formal censure and, to the extent it was noted in the West, seems to have been welcomed. OECS fared less well. The United States was censured by the General Assembly, including the United Kingdom, which broke from its normal solidarity with the Reagan administration. The General Assembly thus rejected the OECS claim of entitlement to intervene through an external proxy when confronted with a violent displacement of the widely recognized head of state in a member country.

ECOWAS and OECS are generally described as "subregional" organizations. The acts and omissions that have marked the international community's response to the behavior and the claims of these two associations raise two important questions. Does contemporary international law allow geographically contiguous states to create an institution and endow it with irrevocable authority to impose agreed norms of behavior on the participants even to the extent of securing military assistance from nonmembers? Do associations of noncontiguous states bound by some other sort of tie— ideology, for example—enjoy comparable freedom to institutionalize collectively authorized intervention?

The Case for Nonregional Organizations

Insofar as associations of states, whatever the basis for their decision to contract among themselves, decide to lower the barrier of sovereignty in their mutual relations, is there any basis in international law and policy to conclude that they cannot? Suppose the Anglophone states of the Caribbean, virtually all of them indisputably democratic, were to enter into a pact with the United States, Canada, the United Kingdom, France, and The Netherlands, pursuant to which the latter agree to intervene and restore democratic government in the event of an unconstitutional seizure of power in any of the former.[51] Any state can withdraw from the arrangement on one year's notice. In a literal sense the pact would create a multilateral protectorate. But unlike the nineteenth-century variety, it would not result from coercion or the bribery of a tiny elite.

It could be argued that the single most important incident of sovereignty is the authority to exclude foreign forces from the national territory and that no government can mortgage the nation's sovereignty. However, there seems little doubt that it can if in doing so it does not violate the right of self-determination enjoyed by the ultimate source of sovereignty, the people. In the context of decolonization, the UN has maintained the principle that an act of self-determination that alters sovereignty is decisive. Once the Eritreans, for example, were held to have accepted local autonomy under the umbrella of Ethiopian sovereignty, the UN would not hear claims of a right to sever the tie.[52] If a people, acting through democratically chosen representatives, can dissolve its sovereignty by merging into another sovereign, surely any mere dilution of sovereignty is compatible with the basic expectations of the international community.

Thus I see no normative objection to groups of states contracting to authorize mutual intervention pursuant to some collective mechanism operating on behalf of shared interests. Such arrangements would remain subject to the jurisdiction of the Security Council, which could intervene if a pact became an instrument of oppression by more powerful members. Nor do I see any reason why such contractual arrangements may not be employed like regional organizations by the UN to carry out peacekeeping tasks in or to implement enforcement measures against countries that are not members of the pact. If the individual pact members are subject to the Security Council's call, so is the instrument that they have created to facilitate collective action. Contractual arrangements might be employed on an ad hoc basis, or they might have a mandate for specified prophylactic activities. What follows from this analysis is that regional arrangements should be seen simply as one species of the genus.

Virtues and Prospects of Regional and Other Subglobal Collective Security Arrangements: Judging Comparative Advantage

Overlapping jurisdiction among the UN, regional and other subglobal arrangements, and individual states characterizes the international system's present security structure. Inertia and the asymmetry of national power, as well as diversity of national interests and values, would seem to dictate continuation of the tripartite structure. However, it will no doubt undergo continuing modification through collective efforts and the force of events.

Rational participation in the effort to shape the character of the security system requires, among other things, some appreciation of the comparative advantages and disadvantages of subglobal contractual arrangements. One evident advantage is the felt complementarity of interest and value that animates the participants to formalize their relationship. A second is size. At some point the number of members begins to effect a sharp disparity in social values, cognitive tendencies, diplomatic style, and national interests. Size alone would seem to obstruct that interpenetration of civil societies and that velocity of communication among governing elites, which, by building material and affective interdependence, progressively blunts the horns of the security dilemma. Even if the particular contractual arrangement does not require consensus, size also affects the capacity for expeditious and decisive action. The dimensions of these difficulties vary dramatically with the homogeneity and openness of the national units.

At the theoretical apogee of their development, contractual security arrangements arrive at a stage at which the range, depth, velocity, and generally positive character of interpersonal and interinstitutional relationships across national frontiers have made war virtually unthinkable to elites and the general publics. Whether as cause, effect, or concomitant, common values and relatively high levels of cooperation along a wide band of concerns mark such security communities.

One shared value and structural characteristic is a liberal capitalist sociopolitical order.[53] Authoritarian and totalitarian neighbors might espouse identical models of the ideal society, but they would not tolerate the dense pattern of private transnational relationships and interdependencies and the associated mutual transparency that obstruct recourse by governing elites to force as a means of resolving differences. Mutual transparency arises as well from the freedom of speech and media. In addition, only the governments of liberal democracies undermine the ideological source of their own authority when they attempt to coerce each other, since in so doing they challenge the principle of respect for the exercise only of voluntarily delegated power.[54] Furthermore, authentic democracies alone have political institutions surrounded by an aura of legitimacy and shaped to the purpose of accommodating the competing demands of heterogeneous social interests. Hence they normally have fewer incentives than do authoritarian regimes to promote a belligerent nationalism and to demonize other states, the desperate measures sometimes employed by authoritarian states to deflect internal pressures for change.

The results of empirical studies at least coincide with the conclusion stemming from deductive methods of inquiry that war between democratic states is highly unlikely.[55] They do not absolutely confirm the hypothesis, however, because by historical standards the sample is very small and even within that sample the data is a bit problematic. Democratic governments did not become the norm even in Western Europe and the Western Hemisphere until very recently. As late as 1914, two of the five great powers in Europe were autocracies, and a third, Germany, was at best partially democratic. But even if the data were deemed worthless, one would still have to concede that the logic of democratic polities makes them by far the most plausible builders of lasting security communities.

From the perspective of the global security system, homogeneity has its risks. If participants are homogeneous, a contractual security arrangement should be able to define ends and implement decisions with relative coherence and expedition. Participants will tend to see issues and options for addressing them in much the same way. By virtue of the broad range of their common interests, the members will have fewer incentives to demand payoffs for cooperation in a particular case. And to the extent that homogeneity supplements the arrangement's contribution to flattening mutual fears, it facilitates cooperation in ventures that benefit all participants, albeit unequally.

Possession of common values means that the participants can include defense and promotion of those values among their security interests. Of course that is a virtue only if one likes the values being advanced. The Holy Alliance in the early nineteenth century, like Latin American military regimes in the late twentieth, demonstrated that authoritarian states may cooperate in defense of their preferred political project.[56]

Since human rights and democratic government now enjoy a privileged status in the global system, the risk is perhaps minimal that intervention by democratic states to protect or reestablish democracy in a pact member might inspire analogous conduct by contractually linked authoritarian governments. But, Fukuyama to the contrary,[57] the liberal paradigm is not uncontested. As noted above,[58] the Chinese Prime Minister explicitly rejected its relevance, and Saudi Arabia's monarch ruled out representative democracy for its alleged inconsistency with Islam. The Association of Southeast Asian Nations (ASEAN) states as a group have stubbornly resisted calls for the application of sanctions against Myanmar.[59] Close monitoring of contractual associations by a restructured Security Council in which democratic states predominate and no state has a veto would sharply reduce the risk that certain regimes would contract among themselves in part to maintain order at the expense of human rights and democratic government.

Homogeneity facilitates the formation and operation of institutions designed to further the security of the participants in their mutual relations. It also facilitates cooperation for purposes of deterring or mastering threats to security originating outside the group. In this second respect, its contribution is problematic: A world fragmented into homogeneous security organizations would not be tranquil. Building security regimes out of homogeneous units is ironic. These are the units least in need of solemn pacts and formal institutions to avoid colliding with one other. As their regime decreases the security dilemma for the members in their mutual relations, it may correspondingly intensify the dilemma in their relations with other states. Data and deduction confirm the propensity of democratic states to regard authoritarian ones with furious suspicion.[60] The latter are certain to reciprocate, particularly when the former are in an evangelical mood.

The dangers to international peace and cooperation inherent in the extant and, I believe, enduring tendency toward clustering on the basis of ideological and cultural affinities constitute a second reason for placing the Security Council or some successor association of leading states at the center of the global security system. But given the diversity of interests, cultures, and values, its performance is likely to be uneven. Exclusive reliance on a global organization to contain the interbloc security dilemma would be imprudent. In designing the global security system, as in designing a bridge or a plane, redundancy is a virtue. The subglobal organizations themselves need to participate in minimizing their potential conflicts.

In diagrammatic terms, we have principally three alternative relationships among subglobal regimes and the UN. One could be expressed by means of a central circle of authority and power surrounded by satellites connected directly to it but not directly to one other. In a second diagram, lines only somewhat thinner than those that run to the center would run between treaty organizations. And in the third, the organizations would not only be linked, they would overlap.

One possible type of connection between security organizations would be economic, as where security regimes coincide with trade blocs and the blocs negotiate mutual concessions concerning barriers to the movement of capital, goods, and people.[61] To maintain peace, the most important connections would be measures for arms control and disarmament, plus measures—such as open skies, mutual inspection of military installations and observation of military maneuvers, and regular exchange of visits and personnel among security establishments—to increase transparency.

Overlap would occur if two or more associations of states operated as one for certain purposes. For example, the OAS might enter into a pact with hypothetical security agencies in northern and Southeast Asia to adopt collective measures against violators of agreements limiting the transfer of weapons of mass destruction or to establish a jointly owned company for extracting manganese nodules from the deep-sea bed of the Pacific.

Subglobal Security Arrangements:
UN Tour d'Horizon

How do these speculations about the possible evolution of subglobal organizations compare with the pattern of development implied by the present incidence of regional and other arrangements with latent or actual security missions? Planners of a new world order do not write on a blank slate. Subglobal contractual arrangements with latent or actual security missions dot the global landscape. Institutions, like people, display a will to survive. By their existence, they generate belief in their necessity and inevitability and constrict efforts to imagine a future without them. It certainly will be easier to design them in than to exclude them.

In inventorying and assessing the potential of subglobal security arrangements, we might begin with those that claim a security mandate other than or in addition to coordinating collective self-defense against armed attack. The great variety of security-related activities may usefully be clustered into six broad categories: providing a framework for negotiating and implementing confidence-building measures; promoting the peaceful settlement of disputes; appraising the claims of members that they are entitled to vindicate by force legal rights violated by other member states (i.e., a claimed right to engage in self-help); authorizing and coordinating peacekeeping measures; authorizing and coordinating the application of coercive measures against members or nonmembers that threaten collective security interests whether by armed attack or otherwise; and encouraging latent belligerents to alter the ricocheting mutual perceptions of interest and identity that underlie their hostility.

Western Hemisphere

Of the three generally recognized regional arrangements—the OAS,[62] the Arab League,[63] and the OAU[64]—the first has in the course of its life performed all of the aforementioned six functions, the second has occasionally performed several of them, while the OAU has done little beyond the promotion of peaceful settlement. Looking to the future, the OAS is the regional organization that has by far the most favorable prospect of serving as one pillar of a refurbished global order. It enjoys the leadership of a hegemonic state comfortable with the territorial status quo and committed by ideology and interest to barring the use of force among members. (With the passing of the Cold War, the United States is more likely than in the past to impose this commitment on itself.) It enjoys ideological coherence, liberal capitalism having become privileged in the discourse of national elites.[65] The growing Hispanicization of the United States[66] increases the cultural coherence of the member states and the shared sense of common destiny, a sense that has deep historical roots. Economic complementarity seems likely to overcome mercantilist opposition to free trade initiatives. The security regime may soon coincide with an economic one.

Recent action by the OAS signals acquisition by member states of the will to use some collective measures for the pursuit of common political values. Article 2(b) of the OAS Charter declares that one of its essential purposes is to "promote and consolidate representative democracy, with due respect for the principle of nonintervention." Washington's Cold War-induced activism added to the legacy of US intervention in the hemisphere and drove most Latin members to emphasize nonintervention at the expense of democracy.

Now the emphasis is shifting. In their 1991 Declaration of Santiago,[67]

OAS foreign ministers, after recognizing need for renewal in the light of new international challenges and demands, announced their "decision to adopt efficacious, timely and expeditious procedures to ensure the promotion and defense of representative democracy." To that end, they instructed the OAS Secretary-General

> to call for the immediate convocation of a meeting of the Permanent Council in the event of any occurrences giving rise to the sudden or irregular interruption of the democratic political institutional process or of the legitimate exercise of power by the democratically elected government in any of the Organization's member states, in order . . . to examine the situation, decide on and convene an ad hoc meeting of the Ministers of Foreign Affairs, or a special session of the General Assembly, all of which must take place within a ten-day period.

And, they added, the ad hoc meeting or the special session would be convened in order to "adopt any decisions deemed appropriate, in accordance with the Charter and international law."

It was under these provisions that the OAS adopted economic sanctions against Haiti following the coup against President Jean-Bertrand Aristide.[68] While sanctions against Haiti evidence a significant increase in ideological cohesion, the failure to back economic measures with military ones when the former seemed to fail suggests that, at least for the time being, the diversity of the members make the organization a weak guarantor of representative democracy. Certain members have democratically elected governments without the requisite culture and institutions; hence defending governments will not, in every case, amount to the defense of real democracy. Moreover, the size and complexity of some members make the prospect of intervention seem intolerably expensive. Their de facto invulnerability cannot be squared with the principle of legal equality among member states. Contractual guarantees, if made at all, are likely to run between small, homogeneous, and indisputably democratic states on the one hand and between the largest states on the other. As suggested above,[69] the most plausible arrangement would involve several European states; thus it would fall outside the OAS framework.

Middle East

The Arab League[70] possesses few of the qualities that make the OAS a likely security vehicle for the new international order. Rather than containing one state incontestably able to enforce peace, the League encloses several with the means and incentives to fracture it. Where the OAS contains virtually all of the states that tend to regard each other as an actual or potential security problem, the Arab League incorporates only some of the more relevant actors and omits three of the most consequential: Iran, Israel, and Turkey. OAS members other than Argentina have no major quarrel with nonmembers, but important League members and three of the states adjacent to the League's perimeter view each other with hostility.

Despite a nominal commonality of faith and ethnicity among its members, in fact the Arab League encloses heterogeneous elements—heterogeneous in collective self-image, in material interest, in ideology, and in social and political organization. It calls to mind Karl Deutsch's definition of a nation as "a group of people united by a common dislike of their neighbors and a common misperception about their ethnic origins."[71] Important differences among Arab League states—for example, along the fault line between the secular and the religious fundamentalist—are replicated within states, thus inviting mutual intervention and promoting mutual mistrust. Since the principal markets for League member exports and the sources of key imports lie outside the region, economic interdependence is not available to offset the repulsive effects of political and philosophical differences.

Through the middle decades of this century, pan-Arabism competed hard with state-centered nationalism and Islam for the loyalty of the educated classes.[72] To the extent that transnational communal feeling survives, it provide majorities of the Arab League with a certain measure of authority to enforce norms. That authority proved insufficient to restrain Iraq from seizing Kuwait. Indeed, pan-Arabism sends contradictory signals about the inviolability of frontiers. All Arabs are brothers, and brothers do not steal from each other, but all borders are arbitrary and should yield to the higher interests of the extended family.

Every plausible scheme for reducing the risk of war within the region requires the deep involvement of leading actors outside it, particularly the United States. Mirror-image perceptions among many indigenous states of relentless enmity and irreconcilable conflicts of interest discourage efforts to imagine, much less pursue, regional collective security strategies. Given the importance of the area's one great natural resource, a peace consisting of armies on hair-trigger alert glaring across contested frontiers insufficiently guards the interests both of the rich northern states of the globe and of the developing and impoverished southern ones. Furthermore, such a peace guarantees a huge continuing diversion of global capital into weapons systems, the further proliferation of weapons of mass destruction and their deployment under problematic safeguards against unauthorized and inadvertent use. At existing levels of hostility, insecurity, and paranoia, concern over proliferation and, after it occurs, over a disarming first strike will function as the hair triggers of renewed conflict. So will the acts of local antigovernment groups with transnational links and increasingly powerful weapons.

Reliance on the mechanism of global collective security is problematical. The mere risk of UN enforcement measures against first users seems unlikely to offset indefinitely the temptations to preventive war. A formal commitment from the United States to side with victims might be more effective. But is such a commitment likely in an environment where, because of the level of armament and tension and the transnational links of antigovernment groups, distinguishing between the offensive and defensive use of force will often be difficult?

Until expectations of violence are lowered, regional actors will remain bound to a security dilemma of classical proportions. The regionwide interlock of threats, rivalries, and material interests will plague efforts to build confidence and mediate disputes on a very limited front. Hence the case for an inclusive regional framework. Building one, however, will be hard to reconcile with the balance-of-power approach that dominates policy discourse in Washington in part because no such framework yet exists. As it tries to fabricate power balances among Middle Eastern states, the United States inevitably positions itself as a committed player rather than an honest broker of the conflicts that make a regional organization so desirable in concept and elusive in fact.

The conflicts of identity and interest that rend the Middle East encourage one to dismiss the idea of regional collective security, but the potential costs of a major conflict in the area do the reverse. The very effort to construct an inclusive regional organization would compel structured and sustained discourse about norms of peaceful coexistence. Once constructed, it would perforce induce regular communication and some measure of cooperative activity among its members. Its bureaucracy and more informal fact-finding mechanisms could generate a steady flow of credible information. In these ways, even a rudimentary organization could contribute to a gradual change in the members' perceptions of their interests and of each other.

Imagining the shape of and routes to an inclusive regional arrangement would carry us well beyond the compass of this chapter, but no such arrangement now seems possible unless and until two things happen. However they may be liked or disliked by other Arabs, the Palestinians endure as the irreducible symbol of Arab humiliation at the perceived hands of the West. So one thing that must happen is achievement by the Palestinians of political and economic arrangements that a majority of them will deem consistent with a dignified communal life. The other is the West's finding a mutually agreeable idiom and areas of practical cooperation with Islam as an ideology and a political force (although not necessarily with all its particular manifestations). Meanwhile, improvisation is the name of the game.

Africa

Despite gross asymmetries between power and wealth, with the exception of Iraq's descent on Kuwait, the life of the Arab League has coincided with the absence of open war between any of its member states.[73] The active presence of the superpowers and their competitive alliance relationships with regional antagonists, compounded with the availability of an easily demonized enemy (Israel) on which to focus hostility and to blame domestic disappointments, adequately explain the armed peace that prevailed until the Gulf War.

In Africa peace among member states, with one exception, has coincided with the life of the OAU. But it can be explained in terms of the symmetry between power and wealth; the marginal capacity of African security forces to police their own populations much less to project force across frontiers without an invitation; and the presence of powerful extraregional actors.

As the Holy Roman Empire was once described as being neither holy, Roman, nor an empire, one could fairly note that the OAU, in terms of its ability to do anything, hardly amounts to an organization, and that by including the Arab states on the continent's northern rim, it is not really African, and its unity is paper thin. As is still true of the Arab League, a central strand of the rope binding together the OAU's disparate parts in an association of symbols and rhetoric was a bête noir (South Africa) linked with a collectively recalled experience of humiliating domination by Europe's imperial states. Poverty and military weakness were other elements of African commonality. They bound in the sense that they encouraged a common position at global fora in favor of nonintervention and transfers of wealth from the developed to the developing states. But they divided in that they encouraged dependence on external actors rather than each other.

Whether the OAU's relentless political pressure accelerated Portuguese decolonization, the defeat of white-supremacist government in Rhodesia, and the crumbling of apartheid in South Africa is unclear. Other forces had altered the cost-benefit ratio of alien-minority government before there was an OAU.[74] Indeed it was the operation of those forces that produced the organization's founders.

To the end of promoting order, the OAU has acted primarily by declaring norms—essentially the compound norm of nonintervention, respect for colonial boundaries, and no right of secession—and promoting peaceful settlement through mediation and good offices. We have few instruments for gauging success or failure. Within the narrow limits of its collective goal of preserving peacefully the existing state structure and promoting national cohesion, the Somali-Ethiopian war of 1978 was a conspicuous failure. The OAU's intransigent attitude toward secessionist claims and indifference to minority rights have disabled it as a potential mediator of internal struggles in places like Ethiopia, Nigeria, and The Sudan.

The significant peacekeeping ventures in Africa have come from other sources—the UN in the case of the Belgian Congo and Namibia, ECOWAS in the case of Liberia. The OAU's feeble attempt in Chad in the early 1980s unraveled because of internal political tensions and a lack of financing. Nor has the OAU shown any capacity to respond to humanitarian disasters. Drought and starvation in Africa have been the province of Western governmental and nongovernmental institutions and of UN agencies. On the human rights front, until recently the OAU did not function at all. Finally, at the end of the last decade, it provided a framework for the establishment of institutions with a mandate to promote respect and expose violations. The machinery has just begun to operate.

If the symbols and memories of a common subordination to the West still have a certain affective power, then the OAU may have a small residual role in reinforcing norms against aggression. But given the weakness of most African states and their preoccupation with internal problems, interstate peace will very largely maintain itself for the next decade or two. For collective action on behalf of other items on the modern security agenda, African states will have to strengthen existing subregional organizations like ECOWAS and create new ones. If South Africa manages the transition to some form of majority rule without tearing itself apart, then it will inevitably become the fulcrum of a southern African security regime.

Europe

Africa, for all its agonies, is in the extreme background of contemporary discourse on global order.[75] Such is the price of weakness. First prize for serving as the focus of interest and concern goes to Europe (including the former Soviet republics); and the second, to Asia.

For Europe, both the risks and opportunities on the one hand and the institutional alternatives on the other are fairly clear. In Western Europe the gravest risk, albeit a remote one, is disintegration of the security community constructed during the Cold War. There are no states with discernible impulses to territorial expansion. All have democratic political systems. The generation on the threshold of political power may lack a personal memory of World War II, but it has been educated to imagine cooperation among West European states as the norm and exposed to none of the jingoistic bombast that, during the half century or more before the last world war, was passed off as history in Europe's schools.[76] Corporate ownership and management are incomparably more integrated transnationally now than at any time during the balance-of-power era in European history. The rigors of global competition demand close economic cooperation as never before. The full list of integrative forces is long. As for disintegrative ones, they seem no stronger than those differences in culture and short-term economic interests that fuel divergent policy preferences in different regions of the United States.

If either democracy within or political amity among the states of Western Europe seemed problematical, there would then be a strong case for rejecting proposals for institutional change that might impede the deepening of integration among present members of the European community. "Deepening" integration means two sorts of development: (1) removal of virtually all barriers to movement of goods and people and (2) increased centralization of decision concerning fundamental issues of economic and foreign policy. Together, these developments would require a considerable delegation of national sovereignty and a coincident strengthening of democratic control over executive power.

Adverse political reaction to the Maastricht agreement,[77] which called for less than fully centralized control over basic economic policies, revealed the barriers of national feeling to movement beyond incremental harmonization in that area. The subsequent difficulties experienced by community governments as they have tried to formulate a single and effective response to the conflict within Yugoslavia[78] suggest the height of the obstacles barring harmonization in foreign policy. However, the apparent consensus reached in mid-June 1992 to support use of military means if absolutely necessary to provide humanitarian relief for Sarajevo,[79] like the earlier one to impose sanctions on Serbia,[80] suggest, albeit tentatively, that the barriers may not be insuperable.

Deepening of integration seems to be a formidable task for 12 states with well-established, fully operational democratic systems, half of which have been collaborating within an integrative framework for almost four decades, and a strong majority of which is on roughly the same level in per capita income, educational achievement, and technological endowment. Adding states hitherto professing neutrality in their foreign relations—Austria, Sweden, and Switzerland—is calculated to make the task more formidable still. Adding states with fragile or suspect democratic governments, high unemployment, and dubious economic prospects should transmute the merely difficult into the impossible. This explains the sustained dispute between advocates of deepening integration before adding states and those who favor rapid incorporation of the Eastern European states—at least of Poland, Czechoslovakia, and Hungary—in order to enhance their chances for consolidating democracy and beginning sustainable economic growth.

The priority assigned to deepening integration particularly among Germany, France, Italy, and the United Kingdom also spills over onto the question of what place the United States should occupy in Europe's future. In guaranteeing Western Europe's continental security and oil supplies, the United States preempted what would otherwise have been a powerful incentive for the members of the EC to integrate their foreign and defense policies. Since the Cold War, it has discouraged proposals for a European defense force that would operate outside NATO.[81]

I endorse the proposition that a strong US commitment to the European continent as a whole will help deter interstate violence east of the Elbe and provide useful insurance against any possible reversion toward old-fashioned balance-of-power politics within the EC stemming from unease about the exercise of German power. But I think that the institutional implications of that proposition are still unclear.

Important items on the US and Western European security agendas include defense and promotion of democracy; protection of human and minority rights; preemption or containment of civil conflicts; reasonable control of population flows; suppression of national and transnational terrorism; and preemption of latent environmental disasters. NATO and the Conference on Security and Cooperation in Europe (CSCE) are the two active institutions—in contrast with the born but barely quickened Western European Union (WEU)—with collective security as their principal purpose. The former, still limited in membership to the old North Atlantic anti-Soviet coalition, has now established the constitutional basis for employing its powerful forces in the service of the latter.[82] The CSCE includes all arguably relevant actors and has a mandate and precedent for confidence-building measures. But its consensus decisionmaking system is ill suited to collective security. Nevertheless, without constitutional change it can elaborate norms of good behavior, insert itself as a mediator, and find facts on which other institutions, including the Security Council or an enlarged NATO, could act if action were required.

Richard Ullman has argued that at "the core of any collective security organization . . . is not a voting mechanism but rather agreement upon what constitutes danger and a shared willingness to use military power to resist a major challenge to the status quo."[83] Consistent with his claim, the coalition that drove Iraq from Kuwait demonstrated that where consensus exists (and leading states are entangled for reasons of material, symbolic, or institutional interest), rogue elephants can be caged by improvised measures.

But in the years ahead, the eastern part of Europe is likely to be plagued not by gross violations of fundamental norms capable of activating a collective response, but rather by less dramatic and more numerous delinquencies: persecution of minorities; creeping coups against democratic government; jousts over borders; and violations of arms control agreements. Through many small delinquencies, the historic opportunity to build democratic polities in all of Europe and to forge a continental security community could be lost. What is needed, therefore, is the transformation of the CSCE into a security organization capable of acting decisively to identify threats to security and to activate appropriate responses ranging from good offices through all severities of economic sanction to force.

Asia

Unlike Europe, Asia is not a candidate for an overarching security regime. It appears, rather, as a conceptual envelope loosely enclosing several geographically distinct "clusters" of states, or "subregions." Actions by any one country tend to affect others within a cluster to a greater degree than they generally affect states outside the cluster.

One such cluster consists of the present members of ASEAN, plus Burma, Cambodia, and Vietnam. Japan and China no doubt also fall within this cluster; however, they are so implicated in other security systems that it seems more useful analytically to see them as transcending all of them, like another great Asian power, the United States, and, arguably, Russia. Moreover, for all their interest in Southeast Asia, China and Japan are so involved with each and with North and South Korea and Taiwan that they may also be seen usefully as forming with those three countries a second Asian cluster. Pakistan, India, Bangladesh, and Sri Lanka are the main components of yet a third cluster.

None of the three has a security regime, although as an organ of regular consultation among governing elites, ASEAN could be a point of departure for creating one.[84] All three contain two or more states that regard each other as serious threats to fundamental security interests. The first goal of a security arrangement in each case, then, would be to build confidence and mutual respect for political independence and territorial integrity. That goal translates into arms control and various measures—open skies, short-notice challenge inspections, mutual secondment of officers, limits on troop and aircraft movements, weapons reduction, and weapons-free zones—that increase the transparency of security policy and minimize the opportunity for a decisive first strike.

Since key subsystem actors have security problems with states outside the cluster—India with China, China with Russia, Vietnam with China, perhaps in the Indonesian elite's mind their country with both Japan and China—arms limitations in particular may be difficult to negotiate without the participation of outside states. A second problem is uncertainty about the commitment of all parties to the territorial status quo. Pakistan has never accepted the proposition that Kashmir is Indian. China regards Taiwan as a part of the national body. Brunei's oil and its fragile, ideologically obsolete, and ostentatiously self-indulgent ruler are a standing temptation to neighbors.

Both the depth of distrust within each subregion and the implication of extraregional states in the security concerns of members argue for a larger framework, one including all consequential Asian states plus Russia and the United States, within which more localized arrangements might gradually be organized. Despite their diversity, its members would probably endorse and agree to act collectively to restrain the use of force for purposes other than self-defense. If united by that broad principle, they might well be able to agree on mechanisms for appraising claimed rights to self-help, for fact-finding, and for third-party assistance in seeking the peaceful settlement of disputes.

It is in Asia, not Europe, that traditional balance-of-power politics is programmed to operate in the coming decades. Politics, compounded with historic antagonisms and relatively high levels of technology, encourages the further proliferation and deployment of weapons of mass destruction. As in the case of the Middle East, that is sufficient reason for the United States to lead the search in this unpromising territory for collective security arrangements, however rudimentary. When the Soviet Union still existed, President Gorbachev proposed establishment of an Asia-wide security organization.[85] Washington was unsympathetic.[86]

Now, its assumptions presumably shaken by the disappearance of so many familiar landmarks of the past half century, Washington may reconsider the virtues of unilateral or largely extemporized law enforcement. For those, after all, are the only alternatives to some sort of collective security regime. And improvisation will be far more difficult in an area where European allies will have few incentives to participate in any substantial way. The sole surviving superpower should begin consulting with the leading Asian powers on the rules of the game and alternative arrangements for enforcing them. Even before then, however, Washington should place collective security at the forefront of its discourse with Japan. A refined, stable, and unambiguous partnership between Washington and Tokyo is the basis from which an effective Asian security system, interfacing comfortably with Europe, might grow.

Conclusion

This discussion of limited-membership organizations as instruments of collective security could draw more or less friendly fire from two directions. Some readers may shell it for unreasonable optimism implicit in the very act of conjecturing about regional organizations in places like the Middle East and Asia where important actors seem almost to define themselves in terms of their mutual hostility. Despite caveats, I may sound like certain figures in the peace and dispute-resolution field who, being themselves in possession of a broad and amiable tolerance, seem unable to imagine people who care enough about their values and enmities to kill for them.

Having spent a portion of my professional life investigating and exposing terrorist regimes, I need no imagination to summon such figures; memory suffices. But although they often employed sadistic thugs for whom the imposition of pain was its own reward, the principals in such governments not infrequently thought of themselves as people driven by extraordinary circumstances to extraordinary means for the defense of grand ideals. Their violence was not a matter of taste. It was not an end in itself. It sprang from contingent perceptions of their own and other peoples' identities and interests. And those perceptions were hopelessly frozen because neither domestic nor foreign actors were available for initiating and structuring a discourse about alternatives to the dialogue of terror.

El Salvador demonstrates that even after years of bloodletting between parties with seemingly irreconcilable ideals and infinite distrust, discourse can change when conditions are favorable. One of those conditions was the interest of influential external forces (the United States, a majority of Latin heads of state, several European states, and Moscow) in fostering settlement. Another was the availability of a prestigious figure institutionally committed to impartiality (i.e., the UN Secretary-General) and animated by personal desire and institutional position to press for, to shelter, and to shape direct negotiations, as well as to provide certain guarantees to the more vulnerable party.

I am unable to see much risk to international order in trying to bring traditional antagonists together inside a collective security mechanism. Exclusive reliance on balance-of-power strategies appears to me far more dangerous.

A temperamentally very different set of readers may attack along the lines of what Nick Onuf and others call postmodernist thought, which moves the central focus of analysis and imagination away from the state. Of course I too appreciate that today vast social forces elude state control, that even powerful contemporary governments experience great difficulty in monitoring, much less controlling, the movement across frontiers of capital, goods, and people. A substantial shift of effective power away from national governing elites to private and transnational institutions is no doubt taking place.

But to argue that the state is a less effective actor than classical realists assume is very different from proposing that it has virtually left the stage. Saddam Hussein reminded us that states still can become animated by grand strategies of predation. In so doing, however, he discovered that an immediate threat of armed attack is not the only challenge that can concentrate the energies of even so plural a polity as the United States.

While they may be slowly rotting from within, states retain an unrivaled power to mobilize people and resources for the purpose of killing us.

Notes

1. UN Charter, Article 51.

2. See, for example, Anthony D'Amato, "Agora: US Forces in Panama," *American Journal of International Law* 84 (1990); and W. Michael Riesman, "Coercion and Self-Determination: Construing Charter Article 2(4)," *American Journal of International Law* 74 (1984). See also Fernando Teson, *Humanitarian Intervention: An Inquiry into Law and Morality* (Dobbs Ferry, N.Y.: Transnational, 1988).

3. See Richard Falk, "Democratizing, Internationalizing, and Globalizing: A Collage of Blurred Images" (unpublished manuscript, March 1992); or Lincoln P. Bloomfield, *International Security: The New Agenda* (Minneapolis: Hubert Humphrey Institute of Public Affairs, 1991).

4. See, for example, Stephen M. Walt, *The Origins of Alliances* (Ithaca:

Cornell University Press, 1987); and Thomas J. Christensen and Jack Snyder, "Chain Gangs and Passed Bucks: Predicting Alliance Patterns in Multipolarity," *International Organization* 44 (Spring 1990).

5. See Hans J. Morgenthau, *Politics Among Nations: The Struggle for Power and Peace,* 5th ed. (New York: Knopf, 1973).

6. Even Morgenthau acknowledges as much. See *Ibid.,* 145–158. See also Barry Buzan et al., *The European Security Order Recast* (New York: Pinter Publishers, 1990); and Aaron L. Friedberg, *The Weary Titan* (Princeton: Princeton University Press, 1988).

7. See, for example, Ernst B. Haas, *When Knowledge Is Power: Three Models of Change in International Organizations* (Berkeley: University of California Press, 1990).

8. See Stephen Krasner, ed., *International Regimes* (Ithaca: Cornell University Press, 1983).

9. For a recent account of the Falklands/Malvinas War, see Lawrence Freedman and Virginia Gamba-Stonehouse, *Signals of War: The Falklands Conflict of 1982* (Princeton: Princeton University Press, 1991).

10. See Robert O. Keohane and Joseph S. Nye, Jr., *Power and Interdependence,* 2d ed. (Boston: Scott, Foresman and Co., 1989); and Robert O. Keohane, ed., *Neorealism and Its Critics* (New York: Columbia University Press, 1986).

11. Karl Deutsch et al., *Political Community and the North Atlantic Area* (Princeton: Princeton University Press, 1957).

12. John J. Mearsheimer, "Back to the Future: Instability in Europe After the Cold War, " *International Security* vol. 15, no. 1 (Summer 1990).

13. See Krasner, *International Regimes,* 8, 2.

14. See Peter M. Haas, "Do Regimes Matter? Epistemic Communities and Mediterranean Pollution Control," *International Organization* 43 (Summer 1989).

15. See, for example, Helen Milner's review essay of Joseph Grieco's *Cooperation Among Nations,* in *World Politics* 44 (April 1992), esp. 475–478.

16. Robert Jervis, "Cooperation Under the Security Dilemma," *World Politics* 30, no. 2 (January 1978), 187.

17. Statement of Chinese Premier Li Peng to the Heads-of-State Meeting of the Security Council (January 31, 1992). UN document S/DV.3046, 92–93.

18. *New York Times* (March 2, 1992), A1, col. 4, and A5, col. 1. Royal Decree no. A/90 (*Sha'ban* 27, 1412 A.H.) and Royal Decree No. A/91 (*Sha'ban* 27, 1412 A.H.). A third decree stipulates that a provincial government system be formally established for the 14 provinces within a year.

19. *Washington Post* (January 28, 1992).

20. See Carl Kaysen, "Is War Obsolete?" *International Security* 14, no. 4 (Spring 1990), 42–64; also, cf. John E. Mueller, *Retreat from Doomsday: The Obsolescence of Major War* (New York: Basic Books, 1989).

21. Benedict R. Anderson, *Imagined Communities: Reflections on the Origins and Spread of Nationalism* (New York: Verso, 1991).

22. Mearsheimer, "Back to the Future," 19–20, 27–29.

23. UN Charter, Chapter VI, Articles 33–38.

24. UN Charter, Article 40.

25. UN Charter, Article 53.

26. UN Charter, Article 41 and Article 48.

27. See Bruce Russett and James S. Sutterlin, "The UN in a New World Order," *Foreign Affairs* 70, no. 2 (Spring 1991).

28. UN Charter, Article 52(1).

29. See Tom J. Farer, "Law and War," in Cyril E. Black and Richard A. Falk, eds., *The Future of the International Legal Order* III (Princeton: Princeton University Press, 1971), 56–62.

30. *Ibid.* For a range of not readily reconciliable views, see, for example, Myres McDougal and Florentino Feliciano, *Law and Minimum World Order* (New Haven: Yale University Press, 1961); Myres McDougal, Harold Lasswell, and W. Michael Reisman, "Theories About International Law: Prologue to a Configurative Jurisprudence," *Virginia Journal of International Law* 8 (April 1968); Julius Stone, *Legal Controls of International Conflicts* (New York: Rinehart, 1954); Ian Brownlie, *International Law and the Use of Force by States* (Oxford: Oxford University Press, 1963); Derek Bowett, *Self-Defense in International Law* (Manchester, 1958); Oscar Schachter, "The Right of States to Use Armed Force," *Michigan Law Review* 82 (1984); Anthony D'Amato, *International Law: Prospect and Process* (Dobbs Ferry, N.Y.: Transnational, 1987); and Hans Kelsen, *The Law of the United Nations* (New York: Praeger, 1950).

31. See the Declaration of the Caracas Inter-American Conference of 1954, *Documents in American Foreign Relations 1954* (1955), 412.

32. For an account, see Stephen Kinzer and Stephen Schlesinger, *Bitter Fruit: The Untold Story of the American Coup in Guatemala* (Garden City, N.Y.: Doubleday, 1982); Piero Gleijeses, *Shattered Hope: The Guatemalan Revolution and the United States, 1944–1954* (Princeton: Princeton University Press, 1991); and Richard Immerman, *The CIA in Guatemala: The Foreign Policy of Intervention* (Austin: University of Texas Press, 1982).

33. See Abram Chayes, "Law and the Quarantine of Cuba," *Foreign Affairs*, April 1963, and his *Cuban Missile Crisis* (New York: Oxford University Press, 1974). Also, see James G. Blight and David Welch, *On the Brink: Americans and Soviets Re-examine the Cuban Missile Crisis* (New York: Hill and Wang, 1989); and Raymond Garthoff, *Reflections on the Cuban Missile Crisis,* rev. ed. (Washington, D.C.: Brookings Institute, 1989).

34. See Theodore C. Sorensen, *Kennedy* (New York: Harper and Row, 1965), 667–718.

35. See Chayes, "Law and the Quarantine of Cuba."

36. Leonard Meeker, "The Dominican Situation in the Perspective of International Law," *Department of State Bulletin* LIII (July 12, 1965), 60, 62.

37. See "Certain Expenses of the United Nations" (1962), ICJ 151.

38. See Robert A. Pastor, "Nicaragua's Choice: The Making of a Free Election," *Journal of Democracy* 1, no. 3 (summer 1990).

39. *New York Times* (January 2, 1992), A1, A12. Also, cf. Terry Lynn Karl, "El Salvador's Negotiated Revolution," *Foreign Affairs* 71, no. 2 (Spring 1992).

40. Tom J. Farer and Christopher C. Joyner, "The United States and the Use of Force: Looking Back to See Ahead," *Transnational Law and Contemporary Problems* 1 (Spring 1991).

41. *New York Times* (February 4, 1975) and *New York Times* (February 16, 1975).

42. UN General Assembly Resolution (December 29, 1989), UN document A/RES/44/240. The intervention was described as a "flagrant violation of international law and of the independence, sovereignty and territorial integrity of States." The vote was 75 in favor of the resolution, 20 against, and 40 abstentions.

43. OAS CP/Res. 534 (800/89) (December 22, 1989). The resolution passed by a vote of 20 to 1, with 5 abstentions.

44. See the exchange among European and US international lawyers: "The Future of International Law Enforcement: New Scenarios—New Law?" forthcom-

ing publication under the auspices of the Kiel Institute for International Law in January 1993.

45. Oscar Schachter's article, "In Defense of International Rules on the Use of Force," *University of Chicago Law Review* 53 (1986), is an exemplary expression of this view. See also, "The Use of Armed Force in International Affairs: The Case of Panama," *Report of the Association of the Bar of New York City* (June 1992).

46. OAS, Sixteenth Meeting of Consultation of Ministers of Foreign Affairs (San Jose, Costa Rica, July 29, 1975), Resolution 1.

47. The Contadora Peace Proposal, which offered an approach contrary to the policies of the Reagan administration, was put forward by Mexico, Panama, Colombia, and Venezuela. Four additional states—Brazil, Argentina, Peru, and Uruguay—joined the efforts of the initial four as the Contadora Support Group.

48. See Abraham F. Lowenthal, *The Dominican Intervention* (Cambridge, Mass.: Harvard University Press, 1972); and Piero Gleijeses, *The Dominican Crisis: The Constitutionalist Revolt and American Intervention* (Baltimore: Johns Hopkins, 1978).

49. *New York Times* (August 11, 1990), A3; and *New York Times* (August 29, 1990), A1.

50. See Christopher Joyner, "The United States Action in Grenada: Reflections on the Lawfulness of Invasion," *American Journal of International Law* 78, no. 131 (1984). See also Scott Davidson, *Grenada: A Study in Politics and the Limits of International Law* (Brookfield, Vt.: Gower, 1986); and William C. Gilmore, *The Grenada Intervention: Analysis and Documentation* (New York: Mansell, 1984).

51. Tom J. Farer, "The United States as Guarantor of Democracy in the Caribbean Basin: Is There a Legal Way?" *Human Rights Quarterly* 10 (Spring 1988).

52. See Tom J. Farer, *War Clouds on the Horn of Africa,* 2d rev. ed. (New York: Carnegie Endowment for International Peace, 1979), 25–40.

53. See Michael W. Doyle's trilogy: "Kant, Liberal Legacies and Foreign Affairs: Parts I and II," *Philosophy and Public Affairs* 12, nos. 3 and 4 (Summer and Fall 1983); and "Liberalism and World Politics," *American Political Science Review* 80, no. 4 (December 1986).

54. See, for example, Randall L. Schweller, "Domestic Structure and Preventive War: Are Democracies More Pacific?" *World Politics* 44, no. 2 (January 1992). See also Gregory F. Treverton, *Covert Action: The Limits of Intervention in the Postwar World* (New York: Basic Books, 1987); and Loch Johnson, *America's Secret Power: The CIA in a Democratic Society* (New York: Oxford University Press, 1989).

55. See, for example, Steve Chan, "Mirror, Mirror on the Wall . . . Are the Freer Countries More Pacific?" *Journal of Conflict Resolution* 28, no. 4 (December 1984), 617–648.

56. See Robert Jervis, "Cooperation Under the Security Dilemma," *World Politics* 30, no. 2 (January 1978).

57. Francis Fukuyama, *The End of History and the Last Man* (New York: Free Press, 1992).

58. See nn. 17 and 18.

59. *Los Angeles Times* (January 28, 1992), A8.

60. See Doyle, "Kant, Liberal Legacies and Foreign Affaris"; Schweller, "Domestic Structure"; and Chan, "Mirror, Mirror."

61. Of course, if these concessions are not generalized through a most-favored bloc principle, if mercantilism replaces free trade as the most powerful economic paradigm, the threat to collective security stemming from ideological clustering should intensify.

62. See Tom J. Farer, "The OAS at the Crossroads: Human Rights," *Iowa Law Review* 72 (1987).

63. See, for example, Fawfig Y. Hasou, *The Struggle for the Arab World* (Boston: KPI, 1985); Muhammed Khalil, *The Arab States and the Arab League* (Beirut: Khayats, 1962); and Boutros Boutros-Ghali, *The Arab League, 1945–1955* (New York: Carnegie Endowment for International Peace, 1954).

64. See R. I. Onwuka and A. Sesay, eds., *The Future of Regionalism in Africa* (London: Macmillan, 1985); and Dominic Mazzeo, *African Regional Organizations* (New York: Cambridge University Press, 1984).

65. See *New York Times* (April 11, 1991), A14.

66. See Andrew Hurrell, "Latin America in the New World Order: A Regional Bloc of the Americas?" *International Affairs* 68, no. 1 (January 1992); and Robert Pastor and Richard Fletcher, "The Caribbean in the 21st Century," *Foreign Affairs* 70, no. 3 (Summer 1991); with M. Delal Baer, "North American Free Trade," *Foreign Affairs* 70 (Fall 1991); and Sidney Weintraub and M. Delal Baer, "The Interplay Between Economic and Political Opening: The Sequence in Mexico," *The Washington Quarterly* (Spring 1992).

67. Resolution on Representative Democracy adopted June 5, 1991, OAS AG/RES. 1080 (XXI-0/91).

68. OAS, Ad Hoc Meeting of Ministers of Foreign Affairs, "Support to the Democratic Government of Haiti," OEA/Ser.F/V.1 - MRE/RES, 1/91 corr. 1 (October 3, 1991).

69. Doyle, "Kant, Liberal Legacies and Foreign Affairs."

70. Hasou, *Struggle for the Arab World;* Khalil, *Arab States and the Arab League;* and Boutros-Ghali, *Arab League.*

71. Karl W. Deutsch, *Nationalism and Social Communication* (Cambridge, Mass.: MIT Press, 1966).

72. Albert H. Hourani, *A History of the Arab Peoples* (Cambridge, Mass.: Harvard University Press, 1991).

73. There has been frequent covert intervention—for example, Egypt's intervention in the Yemeni civil war conflict in the 1950s. Moreover, during the 1971 conflict between the Jordanian army and the Palestinian Liberation Organization, Syria was poised to intervene before being deterred by Israeli threats.

74. See John Strachey, *The End of Empire* (London: V. Gollancz, 1961); and Eric Hobsbawm, *Nations and Nationalism Since 1780: Programme, Myth, Reality* (New York: Cambridge University Press, 1990).

75. Compare Stephen Van Evera, "Why Europe Matters, Why the Third World Doesn't: American Grand Strategy After the Cold War," *Journal of Strategic Studies* 13, no. 2 (June 1990); with Fantu Cheru, *The Silent Revolution in Africa* (New Jersey: Zed, 1989); and Michael Chege, "Remembering Africa," *Foreign Affairs* 71, no. 1, 1992.

76. Stephen Van Evera, "Primed for Peace: Europe After the Cold War," *International Security* 15, no. 3 (Winter 1990/91), esp. 23–25.

77. See Nicole Gnesotto, "European Union After Minsk and Maastricht," *International Affairs* 68, no. 2 (April 1992).

78. See, for example, Gregory F. Treverton, "The New Europe," *Foreign Affairs* 71, no. 1 (1992).

79. *New York Times* (June 28, 1992); and *Washington Post* (June 27, 1992), A13. See also Charles Krauthammer, "Too Soon for Intervention," *Washington Post* (June 5, 1992); and Jim Hoagland, "It's All or Nothing in the New World Order," *Washington Post* (June 23, 1992).

80. *New York Times* (May 31, 1992), A1, A8.

81. See David Robertson, "NATO's Future Role: A European View"; and

Robert L. Pfaltzgraff, Jr., "NATO's Future Role: An American View," in Nils H. Wessell, ed., *The New Europe, Proceedings of the Academy of Political Science* 38, no. 1 (1991).

82. *Los Angeles Times* (March 11, 1992), A4; and *Los Angeles Times* (April 2, 1992), A4.

83. Richard Ullman, "Enlarging the Zone of Peace," *Foreign Policy* 80 (Fall 1990), 112.

84. See Karl D. Jackson et al, eds., *ASEAN in Regional and Global Context* (Berkeley: Institute of East Asia Studies, University of California, 1989).

85. *Los Angeles Times* (April 18, 1991), A9.

86. *New York Times* (May 7, 1991), A3.

■ Part 3 ■
Conclusions and Recommendations

■ 8 ■

Collective Security and US Interests

LINCOLN P. BLOOMFIELD

Matthew Arnold once wrote of "wandering between two worlds, one dead, the other powerless to be born." A century later, a year after the triumph of collective security in the Gulf and the epiphany of George Bush's "new world order," the question had already turned to management of the spreading global disorder. In the limbo between the Cold War and an indecipherable future, UN peacekeeping was the quick fix of choice. US leaders still spoke of a new commitment to collective security to keep the larger peace. But few Americans[1] seemed sure exactly what collective security meant in the new global environment.

On three fateful occasions—December 1941, June 1950, and August 1990—there was no doubt what "collective security" meant. Uniformed military forces of one country attacked across a recognized international boundary in an unambiguous act of armed conquest in which US interests were unmistakably at risk.

Yet all three events—Pearl Harbor, Korea, and the Gulf—were aberrations in a long history of going it either alone or with a few good friends. Even 1941's great leap out of a century and a half of isolation was ambiguous when it came to shared decisionmaking. And the US-led UN coalition that undid North Korea's 1950 aggression lacked Security Council unanimity, never claimed to be "enforcement" under Chapter VII of the UN Charter, and represented a brief hiatus in the almost half century of UN paralysis.

Three major changes—the implosion of the Muscovite empire, the spread of political democracy, and the decline of US-bashing in the UN—encouraged Americans once again to talk seriously about collective rather than unilateral responses to external disorders. George Bush's "new world order"[2] postulated a new consensus about maintaining peace and security. At the Security Council's first Summit of heads of state in early 1992, those worthies reaffirmed "their commitment to the collective security system of the Charter to deal with threats to peace and to reverse acts of aggression."[3]

The first test of the revitalized system had been Iraq's mugging, trashing, and political extinction of Kuwait in August 1990. However incoherent Washington's policy explanations and however exceptional the oil stake, Iraq violated the one rule of international conduct everyone supports. Success in expelling Saddam Hussein from Kuwait, if not from power, finally consummated the marriage between the UN and the one power whose backing is a precondition for any collective security system.

But an Iraq-type war is the least likely contingency. It may be an age of economic interdependence and integration, but the conflict agenda perversely features a near-epidemic breakup of larger political units reflecting ancient quarrels. The explosive power of religion, language, and race combine to generate brutal civil mayhem and ethnic "cleansing." Responses to the savaging of Bosnia and the crushing of democracy in Haiti tested not the primordial principle on which everyone agreed in Iraq but the unexplored issue of forceful intervention on humanitarian grounds. From Yugoslavia and Nagorno-Karabakh to Cambodia and Haiti, what stirred the major powers were humanitarian rather than security concerns.

Hence, the new meaning of "collective security" begs for clarification. Some redefine "security" as predominantly economic/environmental.[4] But military security remains all too real. My working definition of collective security is an advance commitment by the community of nations, preferably as a whole, to enforce the UN's strictures against aggression and genocide by force if necessary.[5]

An advance commitment to oppose aggression—subject to the veto— has been a US treaty commitment since 1945. But if the lesson of the 1930s was that collective security is essential to deter and, if necessary, counter aggression, the lesson of the 1920s was that peaceful change with justice is essential to prevent it. It was never credible that the United States and other major powers would commit in advance to go to war against "aggression" regardless of circumstances.[6]

From 1945 to 1989 universal collective security was replaced in the real world by alliances and UN peacekeeping. But following the stunning transformation in Eurasia, the Security Council ambitiously expanded peacekeeping missions, and UN Secretary-General Boutros-Ghali called for a species of what might be called "peacekeeping plus," whereby states would make available substantially armed volunteer units for what he termed "peace enforcement."[7] A new model of collective armed preemptive intervention was emerging that was situated somewhere between peacekeeping and outright community warfare against aggressors, enforcement.

Once again Americans will have to decide how collective or unilateral they want their security responses to be. Unlike in the early 1940s, both mainline Republicans and Democrats now vote for the UN rather than

Uncle Sam as the world's police officer. Yet there are significant differences regarding the role America should play.

For Republicans, "the U.N. cannot foster peace without American military might clearly backing up its activities."[8] Democrats were less sanguine about a repeat of Operation Desert Storm: "On occasion our stake in [a regional conflict] may call for our forceful intervention. But whenever possible [it] should be multilateral. . . . Otherwise we will find ourselves policing the world."[9] The political right echoed the "Fortress America" of the 1950s in portraying a perilous future but rejecting either an active US role abroad or "leaving it to the UN."[10] Other isolationists blasted Bush for "using collective security [as] an excuse for gratuitous meddling in matters that are none of our business" where absence of US interests should evoke a "so what?"[11]

Washington's ultimate choices will be burdened with unique historical baggage. That singular history comes in five phases. First was a pre–World War II United States that could not stop the world but got off anyway. Phase two began when the United States was propelled by Pearl Harbor into not just involvement but unchallenged leadership. The third phase came when a badly disillusioned United States created its own limited model of collective security within military alliances under self-defense Article 51 of the UN Charter. Four was a phase of sudden miracles: Soviet communism in bankruptcy and the United States astonishingly leading a broad majority UN coalition, including Russia.

Stage five is still problematic and takes the form of a question: To what extent is the United States prepared as a matter of settled policy to share decisionmaking with a UN Security Council majority on security matters that directly affect US interests or, for that matter, the American conscience?

Phase One: The United States' Discovery— and Rejection—of Collective Security

For most Americans, the notion of security as "collective" was historically not only alien but downright anathema. In the nineteenth century, security was provided by munificent nature in tacit alliance with the British Navy. In the first three decades of the twentieth century, forays into empire and then war in Europe produced inner conflict between the self-image of a proudly autonomous America and the multilateral vision of a fast-growing peace movement.

World War I was Europe's war until traditional US freedom of the seas was jeopardized by unrestricted German submarine warfare. Once America was in Europe's war, US war aims, with equal historical authenticity, infused realpolitik with the ideals of cooperative and humanistic internationalism. President Woodrow Wilson's 14 Points faithfully echoed the Jeffersonian impulse to frame foreign policy in lofty altruistic terms.

During the war Wilson became intrigued with the idea of world order in a moral framework of "legal wars" laid down by Grotius and other philosophers of just war. In July 1918 he charged his confidant, Colonel House, to prepare a draft on world security on the model of British scholar Alfred Zimmern's popular "fire brigade," which went beyond conventional pieties of war prevention to explicit rights of intervention by a league of peace-loving countries employing real sanctions against real war-makers.[12]

Wilson presented House's draft, supplemented with British and French notions, to the 1919 Paris Peace Conference.[13] In the heady atmosphere of victory, Wilson's dream of a League of Nations overcame the deep skepticism of both Lloyd George, Britain's popular white-maned Welsh Prime Minister, and Georges Clemenceau, the fiercely nationalistic "Tiger" of French politics and journalism. (Wilson's third interlocutor, Premier Orlando of Italy, seems to have distinguished himself mainly by occasional fits of weeping.)[14]

In the Covenant of the League of Nations that finally emerged, Article 16 asserted a new norm defining aggression as an "act of war" against all. But instead of fighting, member states would enforce an embargo. Wilson placed his faith in the embargo concept, enthusiastically describing it as "automatic. There is no 'but' or 'if' about that. . . . There should be no communication of any kind. . . . It is the most complete boycott ever conceived."[15]

If such an embargo failed, the theoretical possibility existed of collective military action. But it was left to individual states to decide when Article 16 was applicable, and Wilson foreshadowed more decades of ambivalence by rejecting the bold plan advanced by Léon Bourgeois for "airtight collective security" (which would win Bourgeois the Nobel Peace Prize). Article 16 became a dead letter apart from a brief moment of political courage when Mussolini invaded Ethiopia in 1935, quickly squelched by the craven Hoare-Laval sellout.

Was the League's failure America's fault? British Prime Minister Stanley Baldwin insisted that no one else would act while America remained in self-imposed isolation: "Never . . . would I sanction the British Navy being used for a naval blockade until I knew what the United States of America is going to do."[16] France, as usual irritatingly correct, consistently rejected all disarmament proposals unless the United States would become a party to the security system.

Wilson painted a glowing picture of the United States as the champion of the new internationalism and its operational offspring collective security. But the Senate's rejection of both Treaty and Covenant reflected a truer picture of national interest in the minds of US citizens. The depth of

America's historic allergy was mirrored in the statement to the 1932 Disarmament Conference that "the United States will not . . . make any commitment whatever to use its armed forces for the settlement of any dispute anywhere." As late as 1937 Secretary of State Cordell Hull articulated the policy's paralyzing ambivalence: "This country constantly and consistently advocates maintenance of peace. . . . We avoid entering into alliances or entangling commitments but we believe in cooperative efforts."[17]

Phase Two: The US Embrace of Collective Security

By the late 1930s President Franklin Roosevelt was becoming persuaded that the evils of Nazism, Fascism, and Japanese militarism had to be checked. But his countrymen were not ready even for his 1937 hint that collective action was needed to "quarantine" aggressors. On the outbreak of war in Europe in September 1939, Roosevelt could imply an active American role when he spoke in general terms of achieving "for humanity a final peace which will eliminate . . . the continued use of force between nations." By January 1940 he felt able to speak to a sharply divided Congress of "the leadership which this Nation can take when the time comes for a renewal of world peace."[18]

As the defense buildup expanded, President Roosevelt advanced further. In his Four Freedoms speech to Congress in January 1941, he called for preventing aggression through "world-wide reduction of armaments ['freedom from fear'] pending establishment of a wider and permanent system of general security."[19] Seven months later, in the Atlantic Charter declaration, British Prime Minister Winston Churchill signed on to this formula. But fearing criticism at home, Roosevelt watered down Churchill's draft, which identified "effective international organization" as the key to security,[20] which would have surely pressed isolationism's hottest button.

Only weeks before Pearl Harbor, even as Congress unmuzzled American sea-lane defenses by further amendments to the Neutrality Laws, polls still showed three-fourths of the US population to be averse to active involvement. Most of them also sympathized with Britain. But the isolationist tradition defined the majority American view up to the Sunday morning in December when Japanese carrier aircraft bombed Pearl Harbor.

For the first time since the British torched the national capital in 1814, all Americans agreed that national security was unambiguously imperiled. Coming on top of France's shocking collapse the year before, Japan's attack achieved the transformation from isolationism to proactive involvement, which Roosevelt and his pro-British supporters had never succeeded in implanting in the body politic. Americans were now keen to shape a new global order that would never again tolerate aggression from which they would once more have to rescue Europe.

Within weeks of the attack, Roosevelt proposed to his 26 new allies meeting in Washington—a group casually labeled "the United Nations"—the priorities that would define US postwar planning. First, disarm the enemy. Second, concentrate on the goals of economic stability and political justice that history teaches are the keys to a durable peace. Third, develop in the hands of the "responsible" (i.e., "powerful") few a "police power." This could only mean a system of collective security to quarantine aggressors, foreshadowed in Roosevelt's Chicago speech, and, if necessary, move to force.[21] The last item would be some kind of international organization, still the most politically neuralgic thought of all.

When Roosevelt had proposed Lend-Lease to the Congress in early 1941, he put disarmament on the fast track as the key to security, in parallel with efforts to achieve economic justice.[22] Wartime plans for a successor to the League continued to envisage disarmament first, then commitments to protect everyone's security, and only then creation of appropriate institutional mechanisms.

This conceptual sequence dominated American thinking about collective security. But in retrospect there was a deep logical flaw in first disarming both good and bad guys, then putting the cops on the street, and finally setting up police headquarters complete with rule book and hierarchy—it was a serious misreading of history and even common sense. But skittishness from the isolationist past about international organization remained a potent subtext to the rhetoric of the peacemakers. It was not until 1944 that postwar planners felt free to acknowledge that no country disarms unless it feels unthreatened, and that abstract commitments require formal structures if they are to become operational.

The planners deserve our sympathy. Like all history, this episode can be understood only in its context, which in the words of the official chronicler was a "fundamental departure from traditional American positions . . . [posing] new and strange problems" for America.[23] And unlike 1919–1920, "America" meant not just the Wilsonian internationalists but the nation as a whole.

But the nation was changing even as Americans greatly preferred to cheer from the sidelines. In the 1942 presidential campaign, the administration stayed in close touch with Republican candidate Thomas E. Dewey (via John Foster Dulles). In 1940 Republican presidential candidate Wendell Willkie had become a crusader for internationalism, to the undisguised disgust of GOP isolationists. On his return from an extraordinary 1942 round-the-world trip touching the Middle East, the Soviet Union, and China, he proclaimed that "America must play an active, constructive part in . . . keeping the peace."[24]

An Advisory Committee on Postwar Foreign Policy was created within three weeks of Pearl Harbor. It remained inhibited about concrete details but nevertheless gave clear paramountcy to the collective security puzzle. By early 1942 there were references to an unspecified "United Nations

Authority," with Secretary Hull arguing that ". . . some international agency must be created which can—by force, if necessary—keep the peace among nations in the future."[25]

The new American stance was basically nonpartisan and, unlike in 1919, this time also bridged the gulf between Capitol Hill and 1600 Pennsylvania Avenue. Article II of the Constitution spells out the powers of the Executive, but it is no historic accident that Article I concerns the powers of the Congress. In this foreign policy revolution the Congressional role was critical.

The Fulbright Resolution of September 21, 1943, favored "the creation of appropriate international machinery with power adequate to establish and to maintain a just and lasting peace." In the Senate the Connally Resolution, passed on November 5, 1943, by the extraordinary vote of 85–5, called on the United States, acting under the Constitution, to join in support of an "international authority with power to prevent aggression." The so-called B[2]H[2] (Ball, Burton, Hatch, Hill) House resolution went even further, recommending "maintenance of a United Nations military force . . . to suppress by immediate use of such force any future attempt at military aggression by any nation."[26]

The pivotal figure in making the policy bipartisan was Michigan Republican Senator Arthur H. Vandenberg. Vandenberg's metamorphosis from leading isolationist to leading multilateralist began, like many for Americans, on December 7, 1941. By 1944 Vandenberg was urging that "we should go ahead and perfect a plan for collective security." But with his Polish-American constituents in mind, he added that "we should make [this plan] wholly contingent upon a just peace."[27]

Still, even during the war not all Americans were on board. The influential columnist Walter Lippmann was writing that the victors, rather than some international organization, should enforce peace treaties against the Axis powers.[28] And in June 1944 Roosevelt had to reassure Congressional leaders that "we are not thinking of a superstate with its own police force and other paraphernalia of coercive power." Instead, states were to maintain their own power for joint agreed action—the formula that was to prevail at Dumbarton Oaks and San Francisco.[29]

A new and menacing shadow of mounting concern about strains in the Soviet wartime alliance was falling over the unfolding American venture. Contentious issues included Allied postponement of a second front in 1942 and 1943; Moscow's incessant complaints about insufficient US help; stalemated British-Soviet negotiations over Poland; and the old American moral aversion to discussions during wartime about postwar territorial arrangements. Suppressed fears about Soviet postwar cooperation ran as a worrisome parallel track alongside optimistic assumptions about organizing the postwar world.

"Peace with justice" had already become code for opposing reported

Soviet misbehavior in Poland and the Baltic states, as well as for thwarting Churchillian dreams of restored empire. As Vandenberg put it in his diary, the United States couldn't subscribe to defending a new status quo "unless and until we know what [it] will be." In his key speech to the Senate, on January 10, 1945, Vandenberg brought the threads together. The USSR was unilaterally acting to secure its future. So "the alternative," Vandenberg contended, "is collective security."[30]

By 1944, with victory a real prospect and the Dumbarton Oaks talks under way, US planners had to get specific about the powers of a collective security agency. Various formulas were tried, all of them politically sensitive. In April, Secretary Hull called for "maintenance of adequate forces to preserve peace and . . . institutions and procedures for calling this force into action to preserve peace."[31] Two months later the Republican platform unprecedentedly favored "responsible participation by the United States [in an organization] to prevent military aggression and to attain permanent peace."

The war in Europe ended on May 8, 1945, two weeks after the Charter-drafting process began in San Francisco. Chapter VII of the final document spelled out the solemn new obligation to oppose aggression through organized security arrangements, up to and including holding hands and collectively jumping over the cliff of military enforcement action. The international community had finally, if retroactively, acted to correct the willful blindness of the 1920s and the catastrophic blunders of the 1930s.

Phase Three: Collective Security the Morning After

Even before World War II ended it was obvious that the alliance with the Soviets was under severe strain. Shortly before his death, Roosevelt wrote to Stalin of his "bitter resentment . . . for such vile misrepresentations of my actions," which were being met with "such distrust and lack of faith."[32] Even as the Charter was being crafted, the conditions for an effective universal collective security system were again being eroded.

It can be argued that even under the most tranquil of circumstances, neither the United States nor certainly the Soviet Union was prepared to surrender a high degree of sovereignty to a binding collective security system. Senate ratification of the UN Charter took place against the background of America's historic singularity, and US assent was conditional on retaining a veto power over any commitment of US armed forces, however overwhelming the majority voting for the same.

The boundaries of the US commitment were codified in the implementing legislation, the "United Nations Participation Act of 1945." Section 5(a) empowers the President to apply blockade-type collective measures when asked to do so by the UN Security Council. UN Charter Article 43 provides for states to negotiate agreements making national forces available to the Security Council for enforcement purposes. Section 6 of the Act authorizes the President to negotiate Article 43 agreements subject to Congressional approval, although without authority to commit any other forces, facilities, or assistance.[33] In the fast deteriorating political climate in the two years following, the demise of Article 43 seemed the very symbol of failure.[34]

The first test came not in a Cold War context, but with the always neuralgic Palestine question. The United Kingdom had deposited on the lap of the UN Britain's explosive Palestine mandate. The United States then took the lead in negotiations resulting in the partition resolution passed by the General Assembly on November 27, 1947. When the UN Palestine Commission informed the Security Council that the partition plan could be carried out only if the Council acted with force, if necessary, Washington agonized over the implications of implementing its own policy.[35]

One historian writes of the "adoption by all presidents since Roosevelt of his policy of collective security."[36] American leaders would continue to pay rhetorical tribute to the abstract principle of universal collective security. But at US (and Latin American) insistence, the Charter provided in Chapter VIII for regional organizations to act on breaches of the peace in the first instance, until the Security Council could take over.

Senator Vandenberg had insisted at San Francisco that regions be linked to the global commitment: "We are no less faithful to . . . the dominant supremacy of the United Nations in the maintenance of peace and security. No, we are the more faithful."[37] Unfortunately the UN-sanctioned regional bodies—the OAS, OAU, and Arab League—failed to do much better than the UN in enforcing the peace. Collective security would take actual shape in US-led alliances ranging from NATO (North Atlantic Treaty Organization) to NORAD (North American Air Defense Command), CENTO (Central Treaty Organization), SEATO (Southeast Asia Treaty Organization), and ANZUS (Pacific Security Treaty).

NATO was created in 1949 and effectively marked the change back to traditional coalition diplomacy in the name of collective security.[38] Few pretended that NATO was a UN regional organization in the original sense. But Article 51 of the Charter presciently allowed for individual and collective self-defense against aggression until the Security Council acted as it was supposed to. It was Senator Vandenberg who interrupted the NATO treaty negotiations to insist, in the landmark Senate resolution bearing his name, on explicit reference to the Charter. That extraordinary politician-turned-statesman told the Senate on June 11, 1948, that "the first necessity is [to recognize] the indispensability of the United Nations as the key to collective security. . . . [The Resolution] encourages individual and collective self-defense against armed aggression within the Charter and outside the veto." The Resolution was passed 64–6.[39]

As the Cold War unfolded, other crises tested the collective security principle. When the Netherlands launched its first "police action" in the Indonesian War of Independence, Australia called for UN action under Chapter VII. The Soviets, ever ready to drive wedges into the Western alliance, enthusiastically backed the call. Paris and London said no, and Washington (which would subsequently be chosen as neutral chair of the UN Conciliation Commission) was willing to bring pressure but go no further.[40]

The North Korean attack on South Korea in June 1950 was the first clear-cut act of aggression in the UN era, and widely recognized as such. When US representative Ernest Gross woke UN Secretary-General Trygve Lie with the news, that bluff Norwegian's first outraged words were, "Why, that's a violation of the UN Charter!" The UN's "police action" was of course only possible because the United States had substantial forces in Japan and the Western Pacific (the United Kingdom and other ground forces did not arrive until the end of August), and the Soviets were boycotting the Security Council over communist China's exclusion from the Chinese seat at the United Nations.

The United States acted in the Korean War as the Council's "Executive Agent," as it also did de facto 40 years later in the Gulf. That combination of majority consensus and preponderant American raw power may not have been what the founding fathers had in mind. But it was and continues to be the only practical way to make collective military enforcement operational. For the United States to carry the major load reflected the real distribution of power in the collective systems of both 1950 and 1991.

When it was temporarily winning in Korea, Washington pressed the 1950 General Assembly to adopt the "Uniting for Peace Resolution" to avoid future paralysis by giving enforcement powers to the Assembly. Since the Assembly may legally only recommend, that act was doubtless "unconstitutional" and, in retrospect, unwise. Yugoslavia seized on it six years later to embarrass the United States and its aggressing Western allies in Suez. At the time it represented a sincere, if somewhat panicky, attempt to adapt the collective security principle to uncongenial geopolitical circumstances.

Crushing the dream of universal collective security was one of Stalin's many crimes. But in fact coordinated enforcement against aggression was also rejected by many of the nearly 100 new states, which did not always share and often bitterly opposed US policy premises. Moreover, in most of the conflicts brought before the UN, no aggressor could be agreed upon or even identified.

The UN's underlying problem was not a defective Charter or inadequate institutional structure. It was the absence of a genuine political community sharing fundamental values. The UN Charter limits membership to "peace-loving" states, but that turned out to mean anyone except the Axis powers. The post–Cold War UN may finally fulfill its high promise. But during that turbulent period there was simply insufficient commonality to support the familiar attributes of a political community, such as a police or taxing power. Even today the UN simulates government but cannot act like one.

Some smaller states were prepared to accept limited "governmental" functions. Australia led the fight at San Francisco to eliminate the great power veto on enforcement. But as international relations came to resemble a religious war with basic values at stake, the United States and other great powers had no real incentive and many disincentives to accept the sovereign legitimacy of this minimally coherent "committee of sovereigns," in Harlan Cleveland's phrase.

During that period Washington acted unilaterally when it perceived a threat—for example, to overthrow governments in Guatemala and Iran; to abort the 1956 British-French-Israeli aggression against Egypt; and in 1958 to land the marines in parallel with a UN operation in Lebanon. Vietnam was the ultimate expression of the "do-it-yourself" American version of collective security. A little-appreciated consequence of Vietnam was the reluctance of the professional American military to be sent to war again for ambiguous and publicly divisive purposes. Nevertheless, in the 1980s Washington chose to "enforce the law" all by itself against regimes in Grenada, Libya, and Panama.

Phase Four: The New International Landscape

Someone said that it is easy to predict the future; what is hard is trying to figure out what is going on now. The backdrop for reconsideration of American approaches to collective security is the altered security agenda itself.

Historically, collective security implies the extreme case where a Hitler, Mussolini, Tojo, or Saddam Hussein engages in nonnegotiable military conquest. Another unambiguous border-crossing that imperils a global jugular vein could again elicit collective action with strong US support. But all-out cross-border aggression that threatens vital interests may well require the least fresh attention. The most needful "threat responses" imply considerably more—that is to say, less—than a repeat of Operation Desert Storm.

On the plus side, the familiar litany of territorial and border conflicts is being dealt with, always belatedly, by UN peacekeeping forces.[41] These symbolic presences, invented in 1956 as a kind of Charter "Chapter VI 1/2," have typically been quasi-military, nonfighting, mutually agreed upon, and injected after hostilities cease. Truce-maintaining peacekeepers such as those in Lebanon, Cyprus, Central America, Cambodia, and Yugoslavia have acquired a growing legitimacy that comes close to being habit-forming. They will be needed as long as diplomacy fails to apply more purposeful preventive diplomacy to settle legitimate grievances through peaceful change procedures.

There is also growing awareness of the need to counter the spread into a widening circle of potentially genocidal nuclear, chemical, biological, and radiological weaponeering that tyrants and war-makers see as an "equalizer." (But over the horizon lie less noticed threats to fragile electronic networks on which global financial stability depends, and perhaps illegal assaults on the environment via illicit shipments of nuclear waste.)

What is least clear is how the community should deal with our age's bizarre mix of nation-building and nation-breaking. Murderous civil war in the Balkans, the overthrow of democracy in Haiti, and spreading battles in parts of central Eurasia long smothered under the stabilizing blanket of Soviet imperial rule have all exposed a dangerous vacuum in Western decision centers.

The most pressing need turns out to be a politically acceptable international force of national fighting units with a mandate to force the way to relief for civilians being slaughtered or abused in internal power struggles. What the system confronts is an unexpected blurring of the line separating the traditional three Ps of peace observation, peacekeeping, and peacemaking from the big E of enforcement.[42] What was tested by recent collective interventions in Cambodia, Yugoslavia, and Haiti was not the primordial principle on which everyone agreed in Iraq but the far stickier issue of intervention on humanitarian or moral grounds.

The time has come to update the collective security model from the nineteenth to the twenty-first century and to rethink the compartments into which the Charter segregates various categories of security threat and response. It helps to consider instead a continuum along which security menaces will arise in the coming years. Roughly speaking, at the minimalist end is a state-launched bomb-thrower or electronic terrorist. Next is civil strife that turns into internal mayhem upsetting regional peace or afflicting the global conscience. Next come violations of rules limiting building of nuclear, chemical, or biological missilery. Then come cross-border military provocations. At the far end are the rare open invasions of someone else's country.

A graduated continuum of remedial measures can be imagined to cope with that order of ascending threats to peace and security. First of all, Article 33 of the Charter still enjoins states to negotiate and, it is hoped, settle their disputes before calling upon the UN, which typically receives conflicts when they are close to hopeless. Collective responses range from the diplomat with the briefcase and the observer with the binoculars and electronic sensors; to the technical teams with bodyguards; to nonfighting peacekeepers; to deterrence via UN-flagged national ships, tanks, and assault helicopters; to the still uninvented model of armed humanitarian intervention; to the extreme case of, as it were, a repeat of Operation Desert Storm.

An egregious violation stumbled on by an inspector or peace observer would elicit a Security Council call for compliance, followed by a small group of technicians—the equivalent of a posse or SWAT team in the form of blue-bereted UN, International Atomic Energy Agency (IAEA), or other inspectors accompanied by UN guards in civilian gear, monitoring and reporting with backup from national intelligence as was done for the UN in Iraq by the CIA and MI-5. Failing compliance, the Security Council, in a glare of global publicity, would invoke economic sanctions under Article 41. Only if sanctions failed would international military forces be employed.

The emerging collective security system should thus look more like law enforcement than war-fighting. Credible and politically acceptable collective security scenarios will thus initially feature not armies, navies, and air forces but a step-by-step police process that mimics familiar domestic law enforcement, even though ultimate decisions will continue to be made by member states and not some supranational agency. As the Gulf operation demonstrated, a UN framework makes it easier for others to accept intrusive security policing that the international community's interest requires. And calling it "policing" might take the curse off the American allergy to advance commitments and foreign command of US forces.

The process will require a substantial buildup of the IAEA inspection and UN guard corps, both of which could have other useful employment between crises. There should also be national earmarking, not of vast armies but of trained technicians and US marshal-type "peace officers." A training center should be offered by a member state or region (such as the Nordics have done for years in training peacekeepers for the UN). National units would be rotated regularly, with training through simulation and field exercises.

Various proposals have been made to fill the new "Chapter six-and-three-quarters" gap in the collective measures spectrum. Secretary-General Boutros-Ghali's vision combines benign peacekeeping with more muscular "peace enforcement." At the Security Council Summit, French President Mitterrand offered to make collective security concrete with a contingent of 1,000 soldiers "for peacekeeping operations, at any time, and on 48 hours notice," an offer renewed in August 1992 in Yugoslavia.[43] Joseph Nye suggests a 12-nation rapid deployment force to deal with aggressions in which the United States has no direct interest.[44] All these combine to create a new mix we might label "peacekeeping plus/collective security minus."

Collective security, incidentally, does not always have to mean the UN Security Council, though that is where everyone is now turning. Indeed "not every conflict in the world has to be taken on by multilateral organizations," according to National Security Adviser Brent Scowcroft.[45] Regional, subregional, and transregional arrangements are also becoming more relevant to the peacekeeping end of the spectrum.

NATO will now undertake European peacekeeping operations if asked by the 52-member Conference on Security and Cooperation in Europe. The Economic Community of West African States has sought to keep the peace in Liberia, and the Organization for African Unity is discussing regional peacekeeping. Even Russian leader Boris Yeltsin told the Commonwealth of Independent States that its defense pact represented "collective security" toward which "the entire world is moving."[46]

On the negative side, the Organization of American States (OAS) failed to back up its words in Haiti, while the European Community, rich in funds and armed forces, displayed an appalling poverty of will toward near-genocide on its borders in Yugoslavia. These point up the problem of armed intervention against one of one's own, noticed earlier when NATO boggled at intervening in Cyprus and the OAS likewise in Cuba. The UN proves in many instances to be more acceptable for armed peacekeeping, doubtless because of its universal legitimacy.

Phase Five: Collective Security and US Policy—Incantation or Interest?

US policy in Operations Desert Shield and Desert Storm in fact followed the Cold War playbook: US political initiative, skillfully telemarketed coalition-building, and unstinting American military power for the common purpose. What was startlingly new was the assignment to the reformed UN Security Council a primacy not seen since 1950. Also new was an unprecedented US hat-passing to pay the bills. As Fred Bergsten put it, "Collective leadership . . . meant that the United States leads and the United States collects."[47]

In the Gulf War the realities of global power diffusion and US financial stringency modulated US unilateralist impulses, and Washington behaved as if its political, moral, and financial interests were best served within a collective framework. President Bush told the Security Council Summit in January 1992 that "our triumph in the gulf is testimony to the UN's mission—that security is a shared responsibility."[48] In the words of one columnist, Bush has "made collective security his rhetorical trademark."[49]

The vision became slightly myopic when the Pentagon's draft of its Defense Planning Guidance for the Fiscal Years 1994–1999 was leaked to the media. This manifesto about future US global leadership rested on the premise of "integration of Germany and Japan into the U.S.-led system of collective security." It rather breathtakingly asserted that the United States "will retain the preeminent responsibility for addressing selectively those wrongs which threaten not only our interests, but those of our allies or friends, or which could seriously unsettle international relations." It was hard to think of any security function left for either those allies or the UN to perform.[50]

In the absence of a coherent presidential strategic vision, military planners had dutifully filled the vacuum with standard, if somewhat lurid, war college doctrine. Their more sophisticated boss, General Colin Powell, quickly corrected the formula: "The wave of the future is the United States taking the leadership within the United Nations and the Organization of American States."[51] A month later Secretary of State Baker definitively spelled it out: A "policy of American leadership called 'collective engagement' [will] increasingly rely on world institutions and broad coalitions to do together what the U.S. might once have done alone."[52]

But how much confidence are American political leaders at times of crisis likely to place in multilateral instruments for the most sensitive national decisions? How likely are politicians in office to favor long-term community-building against short-term allied or domestic payoffs? And is the United States still unique in enjoying the option of embracing or not embracing the constraints of multilateralism? Or do the multiplying webs of interdependence and the new primacy of economic power make obsolete the old American sense of particularity?

Answers require an analysis of three linked propositions: (1) the likelihood that US power will remain decisive to the success or failure of a collective security system; (2) the continuation of national interest as the operational criterion for state behavior; and (3) the elasticity of that criterion to encompass collective action.

That an effective international security system depends on active US participation is a generally accepted proposition. As two UN supporters write: "Without U.S. leadership in forging a new collective security system based on the U.N. Charter . . . the only alternatives when the next bully comes along will be another large-scale commitment of U.S. troops or letting an aggression go unpunished."[53] The logic is impeccable and appealing to the internationalist-minded.

But suppose the United States does adopt a cooperative model of collective security, foregoes some freedom to act unilaterally, and decides to turn to the UN in the event of armed aggression or other grave international security threat. Will others always find the US position congenial to their own interests? The same UN supporters report that "even some American allies, who once complained that the United States failed to use the U.N., now fret that it may use the world body too much, turning it into a mere instrument of U.S. foreign policy."[54]

This raises the question of whether any collective security enterprise can function when one military-economic superpower plays a hegemonic role. In limited security groupings such as NATO, US hegemony was, in fact, the alliance's condition sine qua non. It is also the case that realistically the new order's "promissory notes," as a recent author put it, can be redeemed only by a single hegemonic power.[55] Many agree, however sotto voce, with the position of Yugoslav dissident Milovan Djilas that "if the power of the United States declines, then the way is open to everything bad. It will be a tragedy . . . if you lose your capacity to lead."[56] The United States cannot become smaller than it actually is, and its power will inevitably be resented by the weak, except those at the receiving end of aggression.

As for the second proposition, some dismiss the "national interest" criterion as obsolete and, by definition, self-serving. The first is incorrect; the second is true but incomplete. Not only big but small and medium-size powers have always consulted their own, as opposed to everyone's, interest as a canon of decisionmaking.

The real issue is how enlightened that definition of interests turns out to be, in terms of giving weight to the interests of the community as a whole. Smaller powers usually construe their interests as best served by collective frameworks that do not leave them to the mercy of big powers. But the United States in the 1950s acted on the premise that every place on the globe where a noncommunist government appeared represented a "vital" US interest, to be defended alone if necessary. Again in the 1980s, Washington went it alone in Grenada, Panama, and Libya. From a tactical standpoint, Operation Desert Storm could theoretically have been run as a wholly US operation, although at enormous political and financial costs.

Henry Kissinger once wrote that "the doctrine of collective security is irrelevant to all but the most overpowering challenges to international order," because its assumptions about common interest and risk-taking rarely apply.[57] But in the changed international landscape the list of "vital" US interests is selective rather than global.

After 45 years of a costly uphill slog with full pack, Americans want the rest of the community to share the load. But they show little desire to repeat the error of their grandparents and drop out of a world in which the United States is deeply immersed. A 1992 poll showed a rise from 49 to 55 percent since 1989 among Americans who prefer to rely on UN forces even in conflicts where the United States has an interest, including an extraordinary rightward shift in domestic support for the UN's performance.[58] President Bush spoke for most when he allowed that "we're not the world's policeman."[59]

Most Americans would probably agree that, as a recent American Assembly concluded, "the United States and others must help manage the transformation from the cold war to a new order based on a modern notion of collective security."[60] The old allergy to pooling sovereign powers is eroding in the age of nationalism without autonomy, and Americans are more confident that they will benefit from more durable community institutions, even if occasionally outvoted. Even then there will be occasions when US vital interests are at stake and no multilateral organization will act. Such rare gaps in the collective security pattern can be filled only by the democracies combining in what should be labeled "coalitions of the willing."

When Hans Morgenthau and Arnold Wolfers defined national interest four decades ago, universal collective security seemed visionary and even dangerous. But Morgenthau at the same time defined *influence* as "the reputation for power." In the period ahead, US interests would be well served by interpreting *influence* as the "reputation for leadership" in processes of collective action that this time rest on a broad international consensus and a deeply rooted American commitment.

A redefined collective security system will work if the United States interprets its interests more broadly than during the bizarre and fearful last half century—and if the rest of the community accepts the reality of unequal power symbolized by American military strength and other people's money.

Notes

1. The author uses the term *Americans* to indicate those who are, in fact, citizens of the United States. It would have been stilted to use circumlocutions to avoid this usual parlance. Canadians, Mexicans, and Central Americans should not be offended by this geographically incorrect but clear and commonplace expression.

2. For a critique of the so-called new world order, see the author's "The Battle of the 'Neo's'," *World Monitor* (February 1992).

3. *New York Times* (February 1, 1992).

4. For example: "National security is a meaningless concept if it does not include the preservation of livable conditions. . . . [It has] become increasingly evident that a militaristic definition of national security is outmoded." Michael Renner, "Introduction," in *National Security: The Economic and Environmental Dimensions* (Worldwatch Paper 89, May 1989). See also the author's *International Security: The New Agenda* (Hubert H. Humphrey Institute of Public Affairs, University of Minnesota, 1991), 5–9.

5. According to the *Dictionary of Political Science*, collective security is "the guarantee of the territorial integrity and independence of each state by all states; [it] requires agreement on the particular status quo to be defended, acceptance of the sacrifices entailed, and sufficient power to cope with any combination of states likely to challenge the system" (New York: Philosophical Library, 1964), 102–103. Collective security is usually defined as universal and sometimes as representative as well: "No nation . . . can be allowed to dominate it," in *Collective Security and the United Nations* (Muscatine, Iowa: Stanley Foundation, June 1991), 10. Others do not always define it as *universal*. Hans Morgenthau saw its "organizing principle [as] a moral and legal obligation to consider an attack by any nation upon any member of the alliance as an attack upon all members," in *Politics Among Nations*, 6th ed., with Kenneth W. Thompson (New York: Knopf, 1985), 213. Inis L. Claude construes collective security as a replacement of balance of power in *Swords into Plowshares* (New York: Random House, 1971). Others conclude that neither con-

cept has any agreed meaning—for example, Ruth B. Russell, *The United Nations and United States Security Policy* (Washington, D.C.: Brookings Institute, 1968), 52.

6. The inherent contradictions in the concept were recently summed up this way: "The rigid legalism that informs the idea of collective security is at odds with the . . . political process," in Robert W. Tucker and David C. Hendrickson, *The Imperial Temptation: The New World Order and America's Purposes* (New York: Council on Foreign Relations, 1992), 51.

7. "The ready availability of armed forces on call could serve . . . as a means of deterring breaches of the peace . . . [and] would be useful in meeting any threat posed by a lesser military force," in "Report to the UN Security Council," *New York Times* (June 20, 1992).

8. Richard G. Lugar, "The Republican Course," *Foreign Policy* (Spring 1992), 94.

9. Harris Wofford, "The Democratic Challenge," *Foreign Policy* (Spring 1992), 111–112; "The World Does Not Need the U.S. To Be a Global Policeman," in *Defense Monitor* XXI, no. 4 (Washington, D.C.: Center for Defense Information, 1992).

10. Republican candidate Pat Buchanan throughout his 1992 campaign derided President Bush's "new world order" and fanned the embers of isolationism. At the edge the John Birch Society lamented that "the American people are being sold one bill of goods and the chief architect of the sale is . . . Bush, the new-world-order advocate," in *International Herald-Tribune* (September 1, 1991).

11. Christopher Layne, "Tragedy in the Balkans—So What?" *New York Times* (May 29, 1992).

12. Daniel S. Cheever and H. Field Haviland, *Organizing for Peace* (Boston: Houghton-Mifflin, 1954), 48–49.

13. *Ibid.*, 51.

14. William K. Klingaman, *1919: The Year Our World Began* (New York: St. Martin, 1987), 269–270.

15. Quoted in Claude, *Swords into Plowshares*, 262.

16. *Ibid.*, 273.

17. Harley Notter, *Postwar Foreign Policy Preparation 1939–1945*, Department of State Publication 3580 (Washington, D.C.: Government Printing Office, 1950), 12.

18. *Ibid.*, 18, 23.

19. *Ibid.*, 43.

20. Ruth B. Russell, *A History of the United Nations Charter: The Role of the United States 1940–1945* (Washington, D.C.: Brookings Institute, 1958), 35–37.

21. *Ibid.*, 97. She also reports "a consensus within the United States government that if the wartime alliance was to be made into a permanent collective security organization," the United States must cooperate in the fight, *Ibid.*, 3.

22. *Ibid.*, 31.

23. Notter, *Postwar Foreign Policy*, 103, 127.

24. Wendell L. Willkie, *One World* (New York: Simon and Schuster, 1943), 203.

25. Notter, *Postwar Foreign Policy*, 88, 94.

26. Russell, *History of United Nations Charter*, 127–128.

27. Arthur H. Vandenberg, Jr., ed., *The Private Papers of Senator Vandenberg* (Boston: Houghton-Mifflin, 1952), 39.

28. Walter Lippmann, *US War Aims* (Boston: Atlantic Monthly Press, 1944) 157–169.

29. Notter, *Postwar Foreign Policy*, 269.

30. Vandenberg, *Private Papers*, 96, 136.

31. Notter, *Postwar Foreign Policy*, 252, 261.

32. Reported by C. L. Sulzberger, *New York Times* (April 12, 1970).

33. 59 Stat, 617; 22 U.S.C. 287–287c.

34. See, for example, Leland Goodrich and Anne Simons, *The United Nations and the Maintenance of International Peace and Security* (Washington, D.C.: Brookings Institute, 1955), 43.

35. I recall that a group of retired Charter drafters were called in to advise the State Department, and there was palpable bureaucratic relief when the group rejected enforcement. I recall also the subsequent charges of American hypocrisy from states that had faithfully followed our lead and now saw us chickening out. The US official line was a masterpiece of diplomatic fudgery: "If the Council should decide . . . to use armed force . . . the United States would be ready to consult under the Charter. . . . Such consultation would be required in view of the fact that agreement has not been reached making armed forces available . . . under Article 43, etc." Cited in Leland Goodrich and Edward Hambro, *The Charter of the United Nations* (Boston: World Peace Foundation, 1949), 280.

36. Stephen E. Ambrose, "The Presidency and Foreign Policy," *Foreign Affairs* 70, no. 5 (Winter 1991–1992), 137.

37. Quoted in *The United Nations Conference on International Organization: Selected Documents* (Washington, D.C.: Government Printing Office, 1946), 785.

38. Strobe Talbott argues with eloquence that in the Gulf, "while fighting with the most modern weapons imaginable, the allies were united behind a concept of collective security that had changed little in seventy years. The coalition was dedicated . . . to preserving the sanctity of international boundaries established after World War I and the notion of national sovereignty that went back at least 400 years," in "Post-Victory Blues," in *Foreign Affairs, America and the World 1991/92* 71, no. 1, 59.

39. Vandenberg, *Private Papers*, 410–411.

40. Goodrich and Simons, *United Nations and Maintenance*, 440.

41. See the author's "Coping with Conflict in the Late Twentieth Century," *International Journal* XLIV, no. 4 (Autumn 1989).

42. My own detailed analysis is contained in *International Security*, 31–37.

43. *New York Times* (February 1, 1992).

44. Joseph S. Nye, Jr., "Create a UN Fire Brigade," *New York Times* (February 1, 1992).

45. National Security adviser Brent Scowcroft, quoted in *Boston Globe* (June 23, 1992).

46. Quoted in *Boston Globe* (May 16, 1992).

47. "The Primacy of Economics," *Foreign Policy* 87 (Summer 1992), 11.

48. *New York Times* (February 1, 1992).

49. Leslie H. Gelb, *New York Times* (July 28, 1991).

50. *New York Times* (March 8, 1992).

51. Interviewed on "The McNeil-Lehrer News Hour" (Public Broadcasting System, March 27, 1992). Two months later, revised language was reported to read, "Our preference [is] for a collective response to preclude threats or . . . deal with them," in *New York Times* (May 24, 1992).

52. Speech to Chicago Council on Foreign Relations, reported in *New York Times* (April 22, 1992).

53. Edward C. Luck and Toby Trister Gati, "Whose Collective Security?" *Washington Quarterly* 15, no. 2 (Spring 1992), 46.

54. *Ibid.,* 56.

55. But the author goes on to say that this scenario is hard to justify. David C. Hendrickson, "The Renovation of American Foreign Policy," *Foreign Affairs* 71, no. 2 (Spring 1992), 55. Inis Claude argued that collective security "calls for a world of diffusion of power," *Swords into Ploughshares,* 256. Robert Jervis stated that the United States is "likely to demand primacy in setting the policy," but others won't tolerate loss of influence. According to another report: "No nation, region or group . . . can be allowed to dominate . . . a workable collective security system. . . . This rules out a Pax Americana," in *Collective Security and the United Nations.*

56. Interviewed in *New York Times* (March 27, 1992).

57. Quoted in an excellent analysis by Alan K. Henrikson, "Collective Security and Future Enforcement Actions," discussion paper (Fletcher School of Law and Diplomacy, January 1992).

58. March 1992 survey by Roper Organization commissioned by United Nations Association, under grant from Hitachi Foundation. Jeffrey Laurenti, "American Public Opinion and the United Nations, 1992," *UNA-USA Occasional Papers* 6 (New York, May 1992).

59. *New York Times* (June 1, 1992).

60. "After the Soviet Union: Implications for US Policy," 81st American Assembly (New York: Columbia University, April 23–25, 1992).

■ 9 ■

Whither Collective Security? An Unsettled Idea in a Changing World

LEON GORDENKER & THOMAS G. WEISS

What is meant by collective security? We end this book where we began, preoccupied by the elusiveness of the idea. Each chapter in the book discloses a concern about the precise definition. Although some of the authors detail their own definitions, generally they accept the historical core of the concept of collective security: coercion by an international community against any government that transgresses the peace.

A theoretical or practical elaboration of the idea that wins agreement among those who have explored collective security, either here or earlier, is more difficult to find. While world politics in 1992 indeed differ remarkably from such a few years ago, analysts may be expected to dispute which clusters of continuity and which clusters of change have a direct impact on the potential for more cooperative approaches to maintaining international peace and security. Consequently, the questions dealt with in this book have included the following: How should collective security be organized? What triggers for collective security are, or what decisional processes for such a system need to be, in place? To what degree could such a system be adapted to particular political situations and to a rapidly changing world political context? What would it take to mount a deterrent capacity that would control the behavior of putative aggressors by persuading them that military action is out of the question? What is the nature of the organized military basis for the system? Who must participate in an effective collective security system? Can there be more than one "universal" system in the world? What do experiments with collective security tell us? What reforms should be made in the United Nations to heighten its capacity as an agent for collective security? To what extent would governments, especially that of the United States, frame their foreign policies to comply with such a system?

The explorations in this book do not, of course, reach definitive answers to these questions. Rather, such explorations indicate that collective security provides a useful starting point for thinking about one crucial issue of governance in a world without a central authority. The object of this governance is mainly the state itself, and the relevant context is that of the regulation of the use of force. Collective security can then be understood as a device for directing the behavior of each government away from using war and military force for its sole benefit.

As in 1918–1919 and 1945–1946, the balance of power today has been transformed dramatically as a result of the end of a war, this time the Cold War. As in the earlier periods, there is a new concern for possibilities of collective security; unlike the earlier periods, however, the present flux has not resulted from an armed conflagration among major powers. Collective security—unlike such other outmoded labels as "North," "South," "East," "West," "superpower," and "Third World"—has at least in rhetorical terms come back to the center of policy debate, even if, as Mohammed Ayoob points out, "statehood is a more popular commodity today than ever."

The organizational devices to give collective security practical effect have been, in fact, taken quite seriously by political leaders during the last 75 years. It was adapted as an organizational keystone of the League of Nations and, in a modified form, of the UN. It deeply influenced several substantial regional organizations and military alliances. Yet no author in this book claims that a collective security system has ever been installed or used according to the prescriptions of the League Covenant or of the UN Charter, let alone in some yet purer form; and few see its establishment in the near term.

At a time of change, some contextual aspects of collective security seem constant. All of the chapters here assume that the state remains the single most important participant in global and regional politics. The idea of sovereignty, despite or because of mutations and the appearance of nonsovereignty-bound transnational actors (especially intergovernmental and nongovernmental organizations as well as transnational corporations) that are neither states nor their instruments, continues to provide a reference point for foreign policies and a conceptual basis for international legal and political analyses.

Consequently, collective security, as employed by all of the authors in this collection, implies neither the disappearance of states nor the transfer of a wide range of decisionmaking from them to another institution. It does, however, imply an added tempering element in a world of decentralized authority. While the terms *state* and *sovereignty* are unlikely to disappear from the lexicon of world politics, the possible resort to sanctions and military coercion nonetheless can serve to circumscribe and to moderate some of the most despicable behavior of governments.

The Heuristic Value of Collective Security

Discussing collective security then has to do with specific and controversial fundamentals of international politics and governance. Yet it does not describe in any recognizable way the nature or organization of world politics. Moreover, it does not set out the precise institutional features of the UN or of regional organizations that are charged with acting in the field of international security. It does not, in fact, make it possible to predict the behavior of governments. It relies on the dubious reductionist proposition that unregulated international violence always produces both universal opprobrium and willingness to act accordingly.

Nevertheless, the idea has endured. Its durability suggests that its principal benefits may be more heuristic than practical. The collective security idea helps analysts and policymakers to incrementally explore ways to maintain international peace and security that approach, but never quite replicate, the ideal type. As such, it serves to clarify and demonstrate the potential costs and benefits of actions that could be used by the international community as a whole or some part of it.

Short of the stunning response to international violence implied by collective security, a number of approaches to maintaining security with tinges of coercion have emerged. These partial measures are indeed worth considering in light of the widespread devastation and continuing turmoil that have resulted from the collective pursuit of the war that developed from the invasion of Kuwait by Iraq.

Underlying these related approaches is the assumption that disputes can be settled before they lead to breakdown and violence. The approaches include the following: peacekeeping, that curious combination of military organization and unforceful behavior that has figured so prominently in UN history and in every chapter in this book; international attention to human rights violations that are taken as forecasts of aggression; a long series of pacific settlement techniques—such as fact-finding, mediation and conciliation, steady diplomacy, and more—that are found in Chapter VI of the Charter and are intended to forestall the use of coercion but do not obviate its eventual use; humanitarian relief, which has emerged as a growing subject of concern with each additional report emanating from such places as Sarajevo and Mogadishu; the promotion of civil, democratic government; and the involvement of extragovernmental groups and persons.

As the result of the inherent logic of the UN Charter, all of these have an implied link to coercion in that enforcement is available should lesser methods be tried and fail. In fact, the entire question of using appropriate force is extremely thorny, especially as analysts of international organization—like the Charter they cite—seek to avoid or minimize violence and the use of force. Of course, collective coercion through international military enforcement action is generally treated as an ultimate exception; but recently other possible exceptional cases have also begun to emerge. For example, the principle of nonuse of force except in self-defense is central to traditional peacekeeping, as in Cyprus and Palestine; but a growing number of observers are questioning this principle. As for so many policy issues in this book, Yugoslavia in the summer of 1992 epitomized the reasons to question the wisdom of hopelessly modest weaponry and symbolic soldiers in the face of a determined rogue regime. So did fears of a breakdown of the delicate plans for revising Cambodia. Moreover, it is with difficulty that one can argue that nonviolent enforcement through extended sanctions in a country like Haiti involves less suffering for the population than a more dramatic use of military force to change a regime.

Thus, collective security summons up the need for governance of many kinds of international relationships. These are more complex than the relatively simple idea of impermissible violence among states and what amounts to an apocalyptic collective response in favor of a victim. The grossness of the response to a breakdown that literal collective security involves was obvious in Iraq and Kuwait. Experience and logic suggest that it is an instrument for a large-scale breakdown and that less forceful politico-military approaches ought, if possible, to come first. The wholesale reaction to violations of international law implied by a collective security system, moreover, has led some observers to uneasiness and the search for alternative or dampened organizational modes; the chapters by James Sutterlin, Tom Farer, and Lincoln Bloomfield set out some of them. In fact, John Mackinlay's chapter details a variety of military contingencies and a spectrum of forceful intervention between the invention of "Chapter VI 1/2" (peacekeeping) and Chapter VII (enforcement).

Practical Contemporary Applications of Collective Security

Using collective security as a heuristic guide to determine the feasibility of diverse practical applications necessarily challenges the basic assumptions of sovereignty and the state in international relations. Yet, as Oscar Schachter's chapter makes clear, the idea of sovereignty has never been absolute; it has been adapted over the decades and reflects the cumulative impact of underlying changes in global politics and society and the exigencies of governance.

Furthermore, the conception of international organizations as strictly passive instruments of governments, which is a view that has surprising resilience among so-called realists and neorealists, certainly is brought into question by the experience of the UN in handling issues of peace and security. James Sutterlin's exploration of future initiatives by the Secretary-General and the Security Council opens up perspectives that, while limited, are anything but a description of passivity. Ernst Haas's research demonstrates, moreover, that on occasion international organizations become important participants in efforts to cope with disturbances to peace; and recently the UN role has clearly been in the ascendancy. Beyond that, the conception of security, as Tom Farer indicates, has also taken new dimensions and a broader scope within non-UN organizations. Even Mohammed Ayoob, the most skeptical analyst of collective action in this book, recognizes the independent impact of universal and regional organizations on governmental decisionmakers and on makers of public opinion.

That broadening conception of security has put pressure on the original idea of collective security, which had to do primarily with the prevention of classical land grabs by expansionist governments or with long-standing disputes, usually about territory, that suddenly festered into war. In the contemporary world, bound together with rapid communications and replete with governments and other groups that dispose of heavy firepower to deter each other, it is conceivable that aggression by grabbing land is less likely.

In fact, one of the dominant themes in all the chapters of this book is what might be called the "atomization" of international relations as internal wars and ethnic particularism increasingly appear as the main challenges to peace. The logical extreme of disintegration, this new breed of challenge for collective security theorists is in Somalia, where no central government exists and where well-armed clans of the same tribe prevent even the delivery of humanitarian assistance. Similar challenges can be found in Yugoslavia and in Nagorno-Karabakh. Yet as the Iraqi attack on Kuwait and the Iran-Iraq war suggest, the classical threat to international peace still can occur. In any event, the post–Cold War era to date has been hardly characterized by an uninterrupted courtship of doves.

Beyond that, however, lie other, newer ways in which peace could be threatened. These include, as several of the chapters here suggest, threats to security by environmental destruction or pollution in which one government's actions endanger the people of other states. Economic existence, too, could be threatened in numerous ways. A part of such economic existence is provision of food, the lack of which could threaten international security. The persistent, large-scale denial of human rights, especially civil and political rights, can lead to international disturbances. It is not altogether fanciful to imagine focused psychological threats.

Hence, "security" means many things to many people; but many of the newer sources of instability would be even more difficult, both conceptually and practically, than large-scale military violence in a collective security system. The analysts in this book endeavor to be sensitive to what might be termed "nontraditional" threats, but they focus their energies on large-scale violence, both intrastate and interstate.

In this regard, the dissolution of existing states, as in the case of the Soviet Union, may produce waves of disturbance and fighting. The implosion of the former Soviet Union is quite unsettling in that large-scale civil war produces wide transnational effects; consequently, the case of the breakdown of Yugoslavia during 1991–1992 has been increasingly treated as an international issue in some ways, as the colonial breakdown and its remnant in Namibia were earlier. As for Yugoslavia, the UN emerged in the spring of 1992 as the only hope, with Europeans dithering and Washington pointedly on the sidelines. While the rhetoric has changed after the Cold War, the standard operating procedures for UN forces have remained in place: a cease-fire followed by a token military presence with weaponry inadequate to ensure that fragile negotiations remained intact. "Making the peace" in Bosnia and Herzegovena—surely a crying need and a function of collective security—seemed still beyond the reach of the international community in mid-1992. Helping to deliver humanitarian assistance there—also a desperate requirement and verging on collective security—seemed plausible to the authors here and was borne out by events when the Security Council threatened the Serbs and then took over the Sarajevo airport.

If the maintenance of the peace resulting from any of these new forms of instability and insecurity is to be an object of international action, the original notions of collective security clearly need modification. That suggests the development of novel forms of collective responses, akin to collective security but not easily contained in the original approach. As John Mackinlay argues, the emphasis may shift markedly from rapid, heavy military coercion toward earlier action. Coercion would be applied, if at all, in carefully graduated measures and by organized groupings that could be universal or regional, or by what Lincoln Bloomfield has called ad hoc "coalitions of the willing."

Organizational Issues

Whether a collective use of force or a collective effort to forestall the use of force is envisaged, practicality raises the eternal international discomfort with centralized decisionmaking in a decentralized set of relationships among governments. It is the core issue of governance of the behavior of states. It is a root cause of tension in international organization and has never been absent from the League of Nations or the UN when they undertook to maintain the peace. Devices used to gain compliance with general policies adopted by members of the so-called international community include binding legal commitments on governments; international deliberative bodies, such as the Security Council; voting systems, including the "veto"; and organization agents, such as the Secretary-General. While these approaches have so far not been reliable, neither have they been totally futile, as a long series of cases that began with the Soviet withdrawal from Iranian Azerbaijan in 1940 testifies.

An assumption at the heart of the collective security concept postulates that governments of the world can be brought to agree in advance and actually take common action to preserve the peace. The argument that this is an unlikely or even a fatuous assumption is easy to maintain. Experiences with efforts to use collective coercion—as in the Italo-Abyssinian case of 1935, in the attack by North Korea on the Republic of Korea in 1950, and in the Iraqi invasion of Kuwait in 1991—all witnessed a considerable initial rush to the collective colors. But what is more significant, some important states either opposed or only coolly acquiesced in the actions. Rather than universal support, these partly collective efforts relied on coalitions of governments, constructed for the purpose at hand within existing organizational structures.

Organizing a broad coalition, then, would most likely be required for any future use or adaptation of collective security. In essence, this approach constitutes abandoning two principles of collective security, for aggression may trigger neither an automatic response nor universal participation. It also suggests that some government, or perhaps a leading international official such as the UN Secretary-General, would have to take up leadership in getting commitments from others. In both the Korea and Iraq/Kuwait cases, the United States assumed this role, although 40 years and the end of the Cold War had intervened between the two. In the Kuwait case, all the Permanent Members of the Security Council reacted positively. So did most other governments. At the same time, some of those who had no veto, members of the Security Council or not, showed obvious discontent with the strength of major power leadership and their own lack of participation in decisions and in continued monitoring after the original decision to authorize "all necessary means."

Military aggression has the merit of a certain clarity, as compared with the newer and nontraditional threats to security mentioned earlier. Even that clarity did not lead to the perfect universal support assumed in the original idea of collective security. Consequently, the newer and less familiar sources of instability, such as the environment or humanitarian emergencies, probably would require even more diligent coalition-building than the response to clear military aggression. In other words, the breadth of the coalitions may not need to be so great as that required by collective military coercion.

If a coalition can be organized for a response to a threat to security, then decisions could be made in international organs (especially the Security Council as matters stand now) to provide legitimacy to the use of coercion. That would satisfy one of the requirements of a collective security system. It would also provide a solid basis for further international participation in what develops after coercion succeeds in changing the behavior of the offenders.

What happens after the successful use of collective security or some approach akin to it remains rather puzzling. Presumably the supporting coalition would continue to lead the decisionmaking in relevant international organs. But the coalition also could easily fall apart as a continuing mechanism to pursue action against the now-compliant offender. Considerable financial support could be required. Long-term supervision might be proposed. Conditions about negotiations of the underlying dispute would have to be set out. These and many more issues, as the aftermath of the Iraq case suggests, could sap the original supporting coalition and would require constant political diligence and leadership.

Any active coalition would at the present time have to depend largely on itself for military counsel and advance information, as the chapter by John Mackinlay makes clear. The existing international military advisory and planning facilities in the UN system fall far short of the minimum desirable professionalism. Whether other international instruments (e.g., the regional organizations analyzed by Tom Farer) could be employed remains unclear. The UN found out long ago in the Congo that most African troops were not optimal for use on their own continent. The unacceptable nonprofessionalism of the initial efforts by countries of ECOWAS to intervene in Liberia is a further illustration, as was earlier ineptitude by the OAU in Chad. For all the rhetoric about a new Europe, by mid-1992 neither the European Community, NATO, the WEU, nor the CSCE was of much use in Yugoslavia.

Were UN organs, especially the Security Council and the secretariat, to be given management tasks by a collective security coalition, as matters stood in mid-1992, a great deal of improvisation would be necessary. Without the staff establishment suggested by Mackinlay, some military advisory function would have to be patched together, as it was, for example, in the Congo. It would lack salient experience as an organization. Even if the UN Military Staff Committee were brought to life again, it has no operating procedures or body of doctrine and would no doubt need many months or even years to form them. Moreover, its past ineptitude and non-representative composition may have already discredited it.

The UN secretariat, moreover, is now too lightly staffed even for the assignments given to it; some of these, such as the operation in Cambodia or the successful but perilous venture in Namibia, are very substantial indeed. Furthermore, to make full use of the UN system, which has relevant experience in such matters as humanitarian relief and dealing with displaced persons, an unprecedented degree of coordination would be needed.

In fact, for accelerated demand for UN help to meet the challenges of peace and security, even through its traditional peacekeeping operations, is becoming quite unsettling to many observers. As these chapters were being finalized, five major operations had been mounted in the preceding 12 months, whereas the first five UN operations took 12 years; some 30,000 soldiers had to be added to the payroll in three months; and the budget had quintupled. The existing system, let alone any more ambitious one aimed to satisfy the requirements of collective security, might well now be on the brink of being overwhelmed.

Whatever the management requirements, the financial system for supporting the policies of a collective security coalition or of the UN organs is woefully deficient. Emergency allocations quickly exhaust reserve funds. Contributions to both the reserve funds and the normal operating costs funds for peacekeeping lag far behind obligations. Parliamentary decision-making calendars rarely coincide with UN mandates; even when there is total agreement about mandates, UN coffers have only 50 percent of assessments six months after an authorization, which creates, to say the least, cash-flow problems of significant proportions. The Cambodian operation—variously estimated to cost between $1.5 and $2.5 billion—may be the proverbial straw to break the UN treasury's back. At the same time, the governments most able to pay for an expansion of international operations, led by the United States, deliver self-righteous lectures on efficiency and demand cost reduction. President Bush, who proclaimed the phrase "new world order," told the Secretary-General in the spring of 1992 that he would not support any additional requests until after the November elections.

If the UN experience in Korea, the Congo, and Kuwait are relevant to other international undertakings with overtones of collective security, the end of coercion will sometimes bring with it vast management and decisional burdens. Modern fighting, or even economic sanctions, thrust heavy costs on local populations. Unless these populations are callously to be abandoned to death, vast humanitarian relief efforts will be needed. These require management that goes beyond policy decisions at the coalition level. The level of advance planning for such eventualities is not reassuring; while hastily recalled, past experience can be only a weak guide.

Political decisions also would be required to decide when enough coercion has been applied and when the goal has been attained. These decisions will obviously have a bearing on both the people injured and those displaced by coercion and the degree of international management to be applied to the coerced state. Once more, collective experience is too slender, episodic, and undigested to furnish a reliable guide. Hence, advance planning in international institutions would be highly rewarding but no doubt treated with skepticism by major military powers unless their policies undergo a good deal of adaptation.

The Uses of Collective Security

By digging deep into the foundations and practice, such as it has been, of collective security, the skepticism and cold water in much of this book may convince some that the idea can be written off. As one observer commented about the League of Nations, if the conditions for its successful functioning had been present, its collective security approach would not have been necessary.[1] But international politics and attempts to maintain peace and security nevertheless involve both unplanned and deliberate developments and striving by leaders and their allies for change.

The popularity of collective security, as Inis Claude also long ago pointed out, does signify a widespread rejection of international aggression as morally acceptable.[2] Also, the evidence that attempts to apply techniques akin to collective security suggests that it retains some theoretical *and* practical utility. That assertion has at least some empirical support in Ernst Haas's analysis of the use of the UN and regional organizations in maintaining peace and security.

Collective security was an idea born of need. In practical application, it has proved inadequate to achieve the high and rather inflated hopes that attended its institutionalization after two world wars. If we are now on the threshold of a new order resulting from sweeping changes in international relations, then the present exploration of collective security takes place at a time of opportunity without the background of a war among major powers.

The global community is taking a fresh look at the range of collaborative actions, which are suddenly not only desirable but also plausible, to deal with threats to international security. Throughout this book, and more particularly in the chapter by Lincoln Bloomfield, there is the dominant theme that the end of the Cold War demands that the United States rethink the bases of its national security policies. There is certainly no reason to believe that the defeat of Saddam Hussein presages a more peaceful Middle East or that there will be any greater stability there or in other parts of the so-called Third World than in the past. As the former Soviet Union undergoes internal changes, the interests of the United States may not be so intensely and obviously engaged in as many regions as in the darkest days of the Cold War. Yet, vital US interests are still at risk in a number of areas where regional strife prevails, and a collective response may be the most viable one. In Yugoslavia, for instance, both the need to restore stability in the Balkans as well as a more humanitarian perspective would seem to point toward a more vigorous, enforcement-like collective reaction to foster US interests, however defined.

Moreover, for all its purported success, Operation Desert Storm showed that the United States could not and should not undertake such missions without the active collaboration of other nations. In this light, serious consideration of collective security becomes imperative. Strengthening the system of collective security and, in the process, redrawing the line between sovereignty and domestic jurisdictions are tasks appropriate to the UN.

Unfortunately, however sanguine one is about the world organization, there will be no dramatic change in the UN constitution or in the behavior of states to transform the world organization into a full-blown collective security system, responsive consistently and professionally to all security crises. Significant incremental measures could promote more and better collaborative actions to counter threats to the peace at the dawn of the twenty-first century. At the same time, larger diplomatic and security roles for less-than-universal and regional organizations will no doubt emerge in tandem with greater efforts by the UN.

One central goal of this research has been to examine what the response of the United States should be to the opportunities and the obstacles that now present themselves to strengthen collective international security actions and to review the structures, particularly in the UN, that exist to deal with threats to the peace. Skepticism has been addressed as well. Doubts about the durability of the US commitment to a multilateralism in security affairs that excludes US hegemony, particularly in the Third World, remain. At the same time, there is also skepticism within the United States that US vital interests can be adequately protected, given the limitations to the nation's freedom of action that genuine multilateralism entails.

Most of the conflicts for which collective responses now are proposed are far less clear-cut than classical aggression. They certainly include violence, but of a sort occasioned by governmental breakdown, misgovernment, repression, resurgent nationalism, civil war, humanitarian disaster, and the need for tranquility to nurture reform. Nonetheless, they may directly threaten international peace and security, and thus they are candidates for collective action.

The breakdown of order in Yugoslavia and Somalia, and the specter of such in Cambodia, were preoccupations of all the authors here. Events have certainly deflated the balloon—largely filled with rhetorical hot air—of the so-called new world order. Yet, the international community is not standing still; its components—both governmental and unofficial—are groping for solutions. The UN Secretary-General has put forward an ambitious framework for the future,[3] which puts the ball squarely back in the court of governments whose leaders challenged him to do so at the Security Council Summit in January 1992. In this operational and conceptual flux, the theory and practice of collective security provides one helpful benchmark for policy analysts, opinion makers, and decisionmakers.

Collective security then endures as a symbol that enough organization exists or can be put together to coerce egregious offenders of the public order to halt their violations. It suggests that different levels of coercion, responding to something less than a catastrophic breakdown on a global scale, can be applied to reach goals that are acceptable to most governments. It does not overcome the difficulty of governance of international relations in the absence of an international government, but it still reminds us that a variety of instruments to attempt that task are conceivable and in part available to help maintain peace and security.

Notes

1. Walter Schiffer, *The Legal Community of Mankind* (New York: Columbia University Press, 1954), 199.

2. Inis L. Claude, Jr., *Power and International Relations* (New York: Random House, 1962), 204.

3. Boutros Boutros-Ghali, *An Agenda for Peace* (New York: United Nations, 1992).

About the Authors

MOHAMMED AYOOB is associate professor of international relations at James Madison College, Michigan State University. He has conducted research and taught at the Jawaharlal Nehru University, Australian National University, and the National University of Singapore and is the author of *India and Southeast Asia.* His articles have appeared in *World Politics, International Studies Quarterly, Foreign Policy, International Affairs, International Journal,* and *Asian Survey.*

LINCOLN P. BLOOMFIELD is professor of political science at the Massachusetts Institute of Technology. He is currently conducting research on international conflict and governance and is host of the *Christian Science Monitor* television program "Fifty Years Ago Today." He is the author of *The Foreign Policy Process: A Modern Primer.*

TOM J. FARER is professor of law and international relations and director of the Joint-Degree Program in Law and International Relations at American University. He has written extensively on human rights and international law and is recently the author of *U.S. Ends and Means in Central America,* with Ernest van den Haag.

LEON GORDENKER is research associate at Princeton University's Center of International Studies and visiting senior research scholar at the Ralph Bunche Institute on the United Nations. His research interests include general and regional international organization, especially diplomatic and operational aspects, and he is author of *The United Nations in the 1990s* and *Refugees in International Politics.*

ERNST B. HAAS is Robson Research Professor of Government at the University of California, Berkeley. He has conducted research on the concepts and process of international integration, and is author of *When*

Knowledge Is Power: Three Models of Change in International Organizations and *Learning and U.S. and Soviet Foreign Policy.*

JOHN MACKINLAY is visiting research fellow at the Watson Institute and director of a project entitled "Second Generation Multinational Forces." Recently retired as a lieutenant colonel in the British Army, his research has focused on the military aspects of peacekeeping and observation. He is author of *The Peacekeepers.*

OSCAR SCHACHTER is Hamilton Fish Professor Emeritus of International Law and Diplomacy at Columbia University. He has written extensively on law and practice concerning the use of force, peacekeeping, and conflict resolution, as well as international organization. He is author of *International Law in Theory and Practice.*

JAMES S. SUTTERLIN'S extensive US foreign service career has included positions in Germany, Israel, and Japan and as Inspector General of the Foreign Service. At the United Nations, he was director of the Executive Office of the Secretary-General. Currently he is director of research at Yale University's Institution for Social and Policy Studies.

THOMAS G. WEISS is associate director of the Watson Institute. He has held several positions within the United Nations system and is former executive director of the International Peace Academy. He is author and editor of numerous publications on international organization, including *Soldiers, Peacekeepers and Disasters, The Suffering Grass;* and *Third World Security in the Post–Cold War Era.*

Index

United Nations Observer Mission
(ONUSAL), 74, 87, 89, 114(n14)
United Nations Palestine Commission, 197
United Nations Participation Act (1945), 196
United Nations Protection Force
(UNPROFOR), 74
United Nations Security Council, 9, 11, 14,
30, 35, 53, 57, 74, 76, 82, 86, 94–96,
121–131, 132, 138(nn 13, 14), 161, 189,
196–197, 202, 212, 215; arms limits, 33,
34, 125–126; conflict assessment, 123,
124, 133, 137, 161; conflict
prevention/resolution, 122–130;
intervention, 26, 42(n21), 74, 75, 80, 87,
121, 124, 164; intrastate conflict, 122–123,
124, 125, 126; military enforcement, 122,
125, 127–129, 141, 142, 143, 146;
permanent members, 124, 141, 142, 147,
148, 215; regional security organizations,
84, 135–137, 161–166, 167, 170, 197, 218;
Resolution 598, 82; Resolution 669, 140;
Resolution 678, 81, 140, 143, 147;
Resolution 686, 81; Resolution 687, 75,
76, 81; Resolution 748 (1992), 43(n55);
Summit, 3, 34; veto, 11, 96, 130, 132, 196,
199. See also United Nations
United Nations Transitional Authority for
Cambodia (UNTAC), 74, 81–82, 87
United Nations Transition Assistance Group
(UNTAG), 74, 87, 89, 114(n13)
United Nations Truce Supervision
Organization (UNTSO), 81
United States, 11, 14–15, 29, 47, 73(table),
89, 91, 190–205, 208(n55), 218; Congress,
195; intervention, 30, 67, 94, 95, 155, 165,
193, 198; isolationism, 191, 192, 193, 194,
195, 206(n10); multilateral cooperation,
14, 15, 83, 97–98, 166, 191, 194, 195, 202,
203, 215, 219; regional security
organizations, 15, 70, 157, 163, 165, 166,
173–174, 177–178, 179, 180, 181, 203;
superpower, 180, 203–204; unilateral
action, 6, 35, 51–52, 53, 54, 56, 97, 140,
143, 147, 150, 165, 166, 180, 184(n47),
198, 199, 202, 203–204, 215, 218, 219;
and United Nations, 14, 15, 71, 81, 82,
128, 163–166, 190, 191, 194, 195,

196–197, 203, 204. See also Cold War;
Gulf War; Operation Desert Storm
Uniting for Peace Resolution, 198
Universal Declaration of Human Rights,
23
Universal Postal Union, 49
UNPROFOR. See United Nations Protection
Force
UNTAC. See United Nations Transitional
Authority for Cambodia
UNTAG. See United Nations Transition
Assistance Group
UNTSO. See United Nations Truce
Supervision Organization
Urquhart, Brian, 86, 95, 128

Vandenberg, Arthur H., 195, 196, 197
Venezuela, 77
Vietnam, 81, 82, 179, 199
Violence, 37, 40–41

War, 36–37
Warsaw Pact, 4, 13, 91
Water, 31, 32–33
Weiss, Thomas G., 48
West Bank, 28, 81
Western European Union (WEU), 178, 216
Western Sahara, 74, 87, 89, 98
WEU. See Western European Union
WHO. See World Health Organization
Willkie, Wendell, 194
Wilson, Woodrow, 21, 158, 191–193
Wolfers, Arnold, 205
World Bank, 90
World Court. See International Court of
Justice
World Health Organization (WHO), 76
World War II, 193

Yeltsin, Boris, 83, 202
Yemen, 28, 81, 140, 185(n73)
Yugoslavia, 29, 30, 48, 58, 74, 82, 90, 121,
124, 125, 135, 136, 177, 190, 198, 199,
200, 201, 202, 211, 213, 216, 218

Zaire, 93
Zimmern, Alfred, 192

About the Book

The end of the Cold War and the dissolution of the Soviet Union demand that the United States rethink its security policy. This volume examines what the U.S. response should be to the evolving opportunity to strengthen collective security, and also analyzes institutional mechanisms in the United Nations and in regional organizations that exist to deal with threats to the peace. The numerous theoretical and practical problems of guaranteeing international security in the 1990s provide the substance for analysis by leading scholars, many of whom also have had distinguished careers within international secretariats.

Emerging Global Issues
Thomas G. Weiss, Series Editor

———————————

Third World Security in the Post–Cold War Era
edited by Thomas G. Weiss and Meryl A. Kessler

The Suffering Grass:
Superpowers and Regional Conflict in Southern Africa and the Caribbean
edited by Thomas G. Weiss and James G. Blight

State and Market in Development: Synergy or Rivalry?
edited by Louis Putterman and Dietrich Rueschemeyer

Collective Security in a Changing World
edited by Thomas G. Weiss